# ARIEL
*The Complete Story*

## Other titles in the Crowood MotoClassic Series

| | |
|---|---|
| Aprilia | Mick Walker |
| BMW Motorcycles | Bruce Preston |
| BMW – The Racing Story | Mick Walker |
| BSA | Owen Wright |
| BSA Bantam | Owen Wright |
| Ducati 4-Valve V-Twins | Mick Walker |
| Ducati – The Racing Story | Mick Walker |
| Gilera | Mick Walker |
| Honda CB750 | Mark Haycock |
| Honda Gold Wing | Phil West |
| Honda GP Racers | Colin MacKellar |
| Laverda Twins and Triples | Mick Walker |
| MV Agusta Fours | Mick Walker |
| Norton – The Racing Story | Mick Walker |
| Royal Enfield | Mick Walker |
| Suzuki GSX R750 | Gary Pinchin |
| Triumph Bonneville | Paul Hazeldine |
| Vincent | David Wright |

# ARIEL
## *The Complete Story*

**Mick Walker**

The Crowood Press

First published in 2003 by
The Crowood Press Ltd
Ramsbury, Marlborough
Wiltshire SN8 2HR

www.crowood.com

© Mick Walker 2003

All rights reserved. No part of this publication may be reproduced or transmitted in any form or by any means, electronic or mechanical, including photocopy, recording, or any information storage and retrieval system, without permission in writing from the publishers.

**British Library Cataloguing-in-Publication Data**
A catalogue record for this book is available from the British Library.

ISBN 1 86126 645 6

**Dedication**
Dedicated to my American friend Bob McKeever Jnr, a lifelong Ariel fan.

Typeset by Florence Production Ltd, Stoodleigh, Devon

Printed and bound in Great Britain by CPI Bath

# Contents

| | | |
|---|---|---|
| Acknowledgements | | 6 |
| 1 | Pioneering Days | 7 |
| 2 | The Sloper | 18 |
| 3 | Side-Valves | 25 |
| 4 | Military Service | 34 |
| 5 | Square Four | 39 |
| 6 | Competition Models | 81 |
| 7 | Overhead-Valve Singles | 93 |
| 8 | Overhead-Valve Twins | 121 |
| 9 | The Arrow Racer | 141 |
| 10 | Colt | 148 |
| 11 | The Futuristic Leader | 155 |
| 12 | Prototypes | 173 |
| 13 | Arrow and Golden Arrow | 183 |
| 14 | End of an Era | 199 |
| Index | | 207 |

# Acknowledgements

Like Royal Enfield, I feel that the Ariel marque has never been given the recognition by the general public that its history, innovation and range of motorcycles deserved. Ariel was in fact one of the true pioneers of the British motorcycle industry: Triumph, BSA and Norton may be better remembered today, but for the first half of the twentieth century, Ariel often led the way in both design and marketing. For example, before they were sold by owner Jack Sangster to their 'bigger' rivals, Ariel was the first British company to have an American sales representative!

Ariel's post-war decline reflects everything that was wrong with the once-great British motorcycle industry. As part of the BSA empire its independence was ever more restricted, new and exciting designs were never allowed to reach production and eventually even its traditional home at Selly Oak fell under the BSA Group's axe. Study *Ariel – The Complete Story* and you will see just how and why the entire British industry failed. But the history of Ariel is also one of achievement, often against considerable odds. The Ariel factory, its men and machines are proof of just how great the marque really was – the bikes, the designers and the riders all played their parts.

Edward Turner's legendary Square Four was in many ways the forerunner of today's sophisticated, expensive four-cylinder superbikes. Then there was Sammy Miller and his Ariel HT5 GOV132, who are universally seen as the greatest-ever combination of man and machine in the trials world. Finally, Val Page's Leader, with its stillborn 700cc flat-four engine, pointed the way forward for the luxury touring motorcycles of the future.

Ariel enthusiasts from all round the globe made an input into this book. The marque has a strong following in North America, in both the USA and Canada, and I would like to thank my friends from across the Atlantic including: Bob McKeever Jnr, Bob Hansen, Terry Naughtin, Arvid Myhre and James Kowan. From Scotland Colin Dunbar, who has a nice collection of Ariels, helped provide information and photographs. His fellow countryman Peter McPherson, who I met while taking part in a classic rally from Dunrobin Castle in 2002, provided more inspiration by writing the Overhead-Valve Singles chapter. Likewise Mike Trail, who originally contacted me about spares for his Ducati, but then sent me information and photographs of his FH Huntmaster six-fifty twin. Chris Bayliss was another who helped, sending me original copies of the Arrow-Leader workshop manual and handbook.

Former Ariel man Roger Barlow provided an insight into the politics of the factory in its final years, and has been a friend for many years.

As in previous books I have found that old motorcycles generate enthusiasm and passion in their owners. These people are truly the most genuine of souls and are always willing to help and share experiences – this is much appreciated.

Many of the illustrations came from old Ariel works files, the balance coming from several of those mentioned above and from my own archives.

In compiling *Ariel The Complete Story* I was left appreciating all that was best – and worst – of the once-great British motorcycle industry. In my opinion, Ariel were the victims of mismanagement by the BSA group, rather than their own failings. The Ariel marque and its many fans world-wide can hold their heads high. The 'House of the Horse' deserves its classic status – on merit.

# 1  Pioneering Days

The Ariel marque is able to point to its name being used long before motorcycles were created. This first use of the name began in the spring of 1847, when the London-based Whitehurst & Company began marketing, unsuccessfully, the Ariel wheel, intended for horsedrawn vehicles and fitted with what today is widely considered to have been the world's first pneumatic tyre – the strangely named Thompson's Pneumatic Belt.

## James Starley and William Hillman

In 1871 the Ariel name appeared again. This time with somewhat more success, when James Starley and William Hillman (the latter to win fame later for his automobiles) began building and selling lightweight bicycles. Based in Coventry, these were of all-metal design and the work of Starley, who was later to be known as the 'Father of the British Cycle Industry', because of his many technical innovations that led to the advancement of the pedal cycle in Great Britain.

## The 'Ordinary'

Known as the 'Ordinary', today it would be called a Penny-Farthing on account of the large front and small rear wheels; weighing 51lb (23kg), it was a considerable advance over the existing Michaux type then in existence.

A particularly interesting innovation of the new Ariel bicycle was the construction of its wheels and the method Starley employed for spoke tensioning. Each spoke pair was formed by passing steel wire through an eye in the rim and securing the two ends at the hub. The entire wheel was tensioned by a crossbar attached to the hub, from the ends of which two short adjustable tie rods ran to the rim. Tensioning these rods rotated the hub relative to the rim, thus increasing the tension equally on all of the spoke pairs. At the hub the ends of the spokes were secured simply by their curved ends, without any other attachment.

During 1872, as a form of publicity for their new creation, James Starley and William Hillman each rode one of the Ariel cycles from London to Coventry. The distance was some 90 miles (145km), and of course, unlike today, there were no motorways, or for that matter anything other than dirt tracks! More publicity was generated when a specially prepared Ariel cycle, ridden by J T Johnson, gained a victory at the Molyneux Grounds, Wolverhampton, in one of the first races organized for such machines.

However, towards the end of 1872, Starley and Hillman parted company, both going their separate ways. James Starley, now with a fresh partner, Borthwick Smith, began a new business in Hales Street, Coventry. Here they built both cycles and sewing machines.

The next event, that occurred in the mid-1870s, was the move to the Ariel Works, situated in Spon Street, Coventry; the sewing-machine side was later transferred to a separate business address in Crow Lane, Coventry. At the same time, Smith and Starley disposed of the Ariel two-wheel business to Messrs Haynes & Jefferies. By early 1876 H & J were marketing the Tangent bicycle.

## The Ariel Name is Registered

There followed over the next few years a tortuous route, whereby the Ariel name was not used and in fact various people connected with the Ariel name, including Starley and Haynes & Jefferies, continued to play a role in the background, together with Dan Rudge (the founder of the Rudge Whitworth motorcycle marque). Then on 1 November 1893, cycle manufacturers Charles Henry Guest and Louis Barrow, who for a considerable time had been trading as Guest & Barrow in Aston, Birmingham, registered the Ariel brand name as their own. Guest & Barrow's new Ariel bicycles (with the front and rear wheels of the same diameter) were given their public launch at London's Crystal Palace, the event being the National Cycle Show. However, this business venture hit the financial rocks only months later in March 1894.

## The Dunlop Connection

Next, the Ariel name was taken up by Harvey du Cros. In 1890 he had formed in Dublin a company to exploit commercially John Boyd Dunlop's invention of the pneumatic bicycle tyre. However, it was not until late in the next decade that Ariel came into the picture. By now the Dunlop business was booming, with Harvey du Cros as its Chairman. In December 1896 the corporation acquired the Ariel trademark, and from January 1897 began marketing cycles for children under the Ariel name. At that time, neither Dunlop nor Ariel had production facilities of their own and so the manufacturing side was undertaken by the Birmingham-based Cycle Components Company.

Rival cycle manufacturers objected strongly to Dunlop selling anything other than tyres – and certainly not in direct competition as with Ariel products. In fact, at that time the Ariel and Dunlop badges were essentially similar renderings of two entwined serpents forming a tyre on a wheel.

## Cycle Components Ltd

Alongside Dunlop's own expansion over the 1890s had come an equal one by Cycle Components Ltd, which had first had links with the du Cros empire in 1894. Cycle Components' Selly Oak-Bournbrook premises had expanded rapidly, and in the following year, 1895, came the arrival of a man whose family was to play a pivotal role in the Ariel motorcycle – the Scotsman, Charles Sangster.

Sangster, and the Australian-born Selwyn F Edge, were both well-known racing cyclists of the day and close friends of the du Cros family; they became directors of Cycle Components, with Harvey du Cros, Jr as Managing Director. The latter replaced Robert Hall, who

*When the new Ariel Cycle Company was formed on 1 November 1897, it had a very similar trademark to the related Dunlop concern.*

was so annoyed by this that he subsequently resigned from the company in 1897 to form his own firm. Charles Sangster now became Cycle Components' General Manager, a position he held when it began manufacturing bicycles for the Ariel Cycle Co Ltd in 1897.

## Ariel Goes It Alone

At the end of 1897, following the uproar from the cycle trade, the Ariel name and products were sold to Cycle Components by the Dunlop Pneumatic Tyre Company. With the passing in Parliament of the *Locomotives on the Highway Act* on 14 November 1896, the maximum legally permitted speed for powered vehicles on the British highway was raised form 4mph to 12mph (6.4km/h to 19km/h). This acted as a spur to encourage companies (including some from the cycle trade) to begin developing internal combustion engines of their own. Previously, this new form of engineering had been passed over by British firms, thus giving continental European countries such as Germany and France a lead in this new field.

## A Three-Wheeler Arrives

In the early days, many of the fledgling vehicles had three, instlead of four or two wheels. One such device was Ariel's first stab at producing a powered vehicle. Charles Sangster and Selwyn Edge convinced their fellow directors and management that Cycle Components should produce a motor tricycle. So it was that on 18 November 1898, such a vehicle, powered by a licence-built, French-designed de Dion 1¾hp single-cylinder engine, made its debut at the National Cycle Show, Crystal Palace.

The actual displacement of the engine was 239cc (66 × 70mm) and it was equipped with aoiv (automatically operated inlet valve), this being located immediately above a mechanically operated side exhaust valve. This form of inlet valve was retained in place by a light spring and was 'sucked' open by the descending piston on the induction stroke.

The contemporary French de Dion-Bouton three-wheelers had their engines mounted behind the rear axle and this was found to cause the front wheel to 'lift' on uneven or bumpy road surfaces – particularly during acceleration or when approaching maximum speed. In an attempt to prevent this, in the Ariel the power unit was positioned just forward of the rear axle, this position being first employed by Paul Renouf, designer of the Birmingham-built Accles motorcycle of 1896.

*Patented Carburettor*
A feature of Ariel's tricycle was its surface evaporation carburettor. This operated on the basis of one of three compartments of the partitioned casing that fitted in the space between the top and front frame tubes and the saddle pillar support. This patented casing featured a front top compartment for the pair of ignition batteries, whilst the central compartment (the largest) was the fuel tank. A needle valve, which was seated in a taper hole (in the base of the fuel tank), had a threaded knob on the top of the casing, this allowing the rider to control the flow rate of the petrol from the tank into the vaporizer (surface carburettor reservoir). To the front of this was a vertical tube, passing right through the fuel tank and allowing air to pass directly into the vaporizer. This tube also housed an indicating wire with a float attached to its lower section, thus showing the height of petrol in the carburettor.

*Lubrication*
The lubricating oil for the engine was stored in a cylindrical tank at the rear of the saddle pillar. Lubrication was achieved by a hand pump positioned on the nearside (left) end panel of this tank. The single-geared differential drive to a pair of rear wheels, unlike that on the rival de Dion-Bouton design, was totally enclosed and ran in oil; the overall gear ratio was 4.8:1.

*Pioneering Days*

*A Choice of Ignition*

The Ariel tricycle offered a choice of ignition – either paraffin-heated tube or battery/coil. This was dependent on the purchase price, with the tube-equipped machine costing 80 guineas, and the battery/coil device 75 guineas. Other technical features of the design included: an exhaust valve lifter; pedalling gear; a handlebar-mounted ignition switch; a compression top on the cylinder head; two band brakes and a choice of Dunlop or Warwick tyres. The dry weight was 200lb (90kg).

## A New Engine

In early 1899, a new de Dion type engine of 289cc (70 × 75mm) was introduced into production. Nominally rated at $2\frac{1}{4}$hp, this produced just under 2.6bhp (compared with just over 1bhp for the old unit). As proof of the latest engine's abilities, it is recounted that on 2 August 1899 the Ariel Factory Manager, Jack Stocks, completed a journey of 488 miles (785 km) in a single day – a fantastic achievement considering the early stage in the development of the internal combustion engine and the poor quality of the highway system at that time.

In the same year, Charles Jarrot (a famous racing motorist of the day) took a brand new Ariel motor tricycle with him to New York, for the Madison Square Automobile Show. There followed a highly impressive speed test on the local banked cycle track at Morris Heights. This resulted in Ariels being imported into the USA from the following year, 1900.

## A Quadricycle

In 1900, the next move, by the Ariel Motor Co, another Cycle Components manufacturing subsidiary, was the marketing of a four-wheel vehicle – essentially similar to the tricycle, but with an extra wheel at the front and increased seating capacity. The story of the Ariel four-wheeler is covered in a separate boxed section on page 17.

On 17 January 1902, Cycle Components Manufacturing was re-registered as simply Components Ltd. This led to Jack Stock leaving the company (to work for de Dion-Bouton in London), whilst Harvey du Cros, Jr terminated his direct involvement with Components' affairs, thus surrendering his place on the board. Charles Sangster now assumed charge of the firm's future in the role of Managing Director, a position he was to hold for the next three decades or so. Frederick Warwick became Chairman, with Harvey du Cros Jr, Selwyn F Edge and Frank Moore as co-Directors; H Whitton was Company Secretary. At that time, Components Ltd had four separate trading companies:

- Ariel Motors Co Ltd – motorcycles, cars, motor-tricycles and motor quadricycles
- Ariel Cycle Co Ltd – bicycles
- Midland Tube & Forging Co Ltd – one of the largest drop forging operations in Great Britain
- Fleet Cycle Co Ltd – Fleet trademark bicycles.

## The First Ariel Motorcycle

The first Ariel motorcycle, powered by a 1½hp Minerva engine of 211cc (62 × 70mm) made its bow at the 1901 National Show for the 1902 season. Like Ariel's first tricycle, the motorcycle (at the time referred to as a 'motor bicycle') featured an air-cooled aoiv (automatically operated inlet valve). Running on a compression ratio of 4.5:1, Ariel claimed just over 16bhp at 1,800rpm – which meant a maximum speed of 20mph (32km/h) in perfect conditions. When displayed at London's Crystal Palace Show in February 1902, the 1½hp Ariel cost £45 – this was against the firm's quadricycle, which at the same venue cost £150. During 1902, the engine size of the Ariel-Minerva motorcycle was increased to 239cc (66 × 70mm), the rating now being 2hp.

## Ariel's Own Engine

The next step in the history of the Ariel motorcycle came in March 1903, with the introduction of a new machine possessing an engine of the company's own design. Charles Sangster had realized that the day of the automatic inlet valve was coming to an end. So the new power plant featured a 249cc (65 × 70mm) side-valve layout. This incorporated two parallel 'poppet' valves, one inlet, the other exhaust, located at the rear of the cylinder. These valves were operated by tappets from a transversely mounted camshaft. This

*The very first Ariel motorcycle was powered by a 211cc (62 × 70mm) Minerva single-cylinder engine; power was transmitted direct from the crankshaft to the rear wheel by belt.*

was located at the rear of the cylinder, driven at half-engine speed by courtesy of a vertical spiral worm gear off the crankshaft.

*A Rear-Mounted Cambox*
A pair of small holes connecting the rear-mounted cambox with the inside of the crankcase allowed centrifugal rotation of the crankshaft flywheels to gather up and throw outwards oil to lubricate the camshaft, valve-gear and so forth. This oil then ran out of the cambox and through another hole to the top of the spiral worm-shaft casing. The worm then fed the oil back to the crankcase by means of a reverse form of Archimedean-pump action.

*A Larger Side-Valve*
By September 1903 it was possible for the first time to specify a sidecar (then called a 'side-carriage'). However, fitting a sidecar (and carrying passengers) meant that the original 249cc engine size was inadequate. So for the 1904 season a new 373cc (65 × 79mm) side-valve (sv) was introduced. Known as the No 1 model (the original smaller-engined machine was continued), the 373cc sv featured solid forged-steel flywheels, larger phosphor bronze bearings, a revised contact breaker assembly and a Longuemare spray-type carburettor. The 249cc model retained the surface evaporation carb, the workings of which were explained earlier.

Another machine, the No 2, was essentially the same model, but with its overhead inlet valve converted to mechanical operation. This was opened by a cam operating a rocking lever, to which a rod was attached that pulled the valve down against the tension of its spring.

## A Redirection in Policy

During early 1904, the Ariel Cycle Co took over control of the motorcycle side of Components' operation, whilst at the same time the Ariel Motor Co (*see* boxed section) concentrated its effort purely on the four-wheel models. Then in March 1904 a 417cc (82 × 79mm) engine size replaced the previous year's 373cc – both being side-valves. All production Ariel motorcycles employed the Longuemare spray-type carb, because of its superior overall abilities compared to the surface evaporation instrument.

1905 was a bad year economically, and Ariel responded by pruning back its motorcycle range to two models: the No 1 3hp at £36 10s and the 2½hp No 2 that sold for £31. There were even worries, expressed by Charles Sangster, that if things did not improve the motorcycle division was seriously at risk of going under. But this did not happen – and as explained elsewhere the four-wheel side fared even worse.

Having successfully weathered the storm, 1906 saw something of a mini-boom, with no less than four models (one a tricar) being offered, of which the largest was a 6hp JAP-powered v-twin solo. All four featured single-geared belt transmission, spray carburettors – and all three motorcycles came with unsprung front forks.

For 1907 the Ariel motorcycle range continued unchanged, but for 1908 Ariel discontinued production of its tricar and introduced bottom-sprung leading-link front forks for its 2½ and 3hp bikes.

This range continued to be offered in 1909, but magneto ignition now became standard fitment on the 2½hp model. This machine was equipped with the new Brown & Barlow handlebar-lever-operated carburettor. There was also a form of variable gear/adjuster pulley for the engine driveshaft. This featured an external sliding flange that could be opened outwards – against the force of a spring – by means of a rotating cam ring operating against a fixed cam ring. The movable section rotated by way of a gear lever mounted on the nearside (left) handlebar, via a control cable. This lever could be locked in any required position by a twistgrip-operated locking device.

Ariel motorcycles have always been known for their excellent finish. The origins of this could be traced back to the pioneer period when special use was made of a rustproofing formula known as 'Coslettising'. Enamel was used for the frame, forks and tinware such as mudguards and toolboxes; the petrol tank had a metallic aluminium finish, with a hand-applied lining.

## A Radical New Approach

1909 was the final year in which the overhead inlet valve single-cylinder engine was offered. For 1910, a totally new engine was available. This meant that all existing motorcycles in the Ariel range were axed. The type that replaced them proved so popular that they were to remain largely unchanged for the next fifteen years. Power was provided by a White & Poppe 482cc (85 × 85mm) T-head side-valve power unit, in which the inlet and exhaust valve were placed apart by no less than 4½in (114mm). This feature led the series to be universally known as 'the Ariels with valves a-mile-apart'.

## White & Poppe

White & Poppe, an engineering company based in Coventry, had as its chief Alfred James White, whose father had formerly had been a director of the Swift Cycle Co (themselves closely related to Ariel through Components Ltd). With Arthur du Cros now Chairman of the Swift organization, it was perhaps unsurprising that Ariel and White & Poppe should co-operate together. And in a fair case of back-scratching, Charles Sangster soon acquired himself a seat on the board of Swift and thus of White & Poppe . . .

## A Stanley Cycle Show Debut

The new Ariel motorcycle range was given its public debut on Components Ltd's stand at the Stanley Cycle Show in November 1909. Two versions were displayed: one using the

*One of the vintage-type Ariel motorcycles with side-valve and vertical cylinder (the engine was manufactured by White & Poppe); again final drive was by belt. This photograph was taken during the early 1980s at a historic rally; the machine dates from just before World War I.*

## Pioneering Days

patented variable gear employed on the 1909 Ariel; the other with a simple adjustable belt pulley. The company claimed a power output of 3½bhp at 2,000rpm and featured fully adjustable tappets.

Thus Ariel continued to produce motorcycles powered by the 482cc (85 × 86.4mm) White & Poppe sv single engine successfully for a long period, although for the 1913 season a new 999cc (85 × 88mm) side-valve v-twin was offered, mainly for sidecar duties. In fact, Ariel offered it as a complete sidecar combination for £84.

### Another V-Twin

For 1914, a new 670cc (67 × 95mm) v-twin-engined model appeared – again virtually exclusively for sidecar work. This power unit was manufactured by Abingdon-Ecco of Tyseley, Birmingham (later known for its Abingdon King Dick tools). But within a short period the 670cc v-twin was also being sold by Ariel in solo guise, it being found equally suitable for both tasks.

### Corporate Revision – Ariel Works Ltd

In 1915 the Ariel motorcycle and automobile concerns underwent a corporate change of name, and became jointly registered as Ariel Works Ltd. By now, with the First World War in full swing, Ariel was supplying the British military authorities with various equipment, notably the v-twin motorcycles. These machines were also sold to Russia and Mesopotamia (Iraq). Components Ltd was a major manufacturer of armaments, including one of the first rack-retained bombs used by the RFC (Royal Flying Corps, the forerunner of the Royal Air Force).

Ariel Works Ltd was one of the very first manufacturers to re-commence civilian production at the war's end, this event being achieved in January 1919. At first, this was confined to building the 482cc White & Poppe single-cylinder-engined model. However, by April 1919 a new 795cc (73 × 95mm) side-valve v-twin Abingdon-powered model was in production.

November 1919 saw the first post-war Olympia Show, with Ariel displaying a quartet of models that made up the 1920 range. One of these was a new, larger single-cylinder machine. This followed the general lines of the White & Poppe-engined motorcycle, with the same bore size of 86.4mm, but the stroke having been increased significantly to 100mm,

*February 1914 advertisement describing Ariel's latest sporting success. The company was then based in Bournbrook, Birmingham.*

giving a capacity of 586cc. Besides providing more punch, lubrication had been uprated from splash to a mechanically operated pump. Engine power was transmitted to the rear wheel via a three-speed countershaft gearbox; both the primary and final drives were by chain.

An unfortunate feature of the immediate post-World War I period was that the cost of motorcycles shot up rapidly. The most expensive model in the Ariel range was the 998cc v-twin with three-speed countershaft gearbox, all-chain drive and sidecar, which retailed at £197 10s.

For 1922 the 586cc single was superceded by a 665cc (92 × 100mm) engined machine. The main reason was that the extra 'grunt' made the motorcycle more suitable for sidecar duties, which at that time this was a growing sector of the motorcycle market in Great Britain. However, apart from the newcomer having its chain-driven magneto mounted at the rear of the engine, the machine was very much as before.

Ariel also used another new engine at that time, the 993cc MAG v-twin (again mainly for sidecar use) supplied by the Swiss company, Motosacoche. It was priced at £125 in solo guise, or £160 with a sidecar attached.

In November 1922, Ariel Works Ltd introduced a new lightweight machine, powered by a 249cc Blackburne side-valve single-cylinder engine. Fitted with a two-speed hand-change gearbox it was priced at £57 10s; the remainder of the range remained virtually unchanged.

New features throughout the 1922 Ariel range were the use of the internally expanding brakes on both wheels and the adoption of handpump-cum-drip feed rather than mechanical pump lubrication.

## A Choice of Six Models in 1924

A choice of six different models was offered in the 1924 Ariel catalogue, released at the end of 1925. This included the 249cc sv Blackburne-engined model, now equipped with a three-speed gearbox. In addition, a more sporting three-speed two-fifty ohv model was offered, this too featuring a Blackburne-sourced power unit. There were three White & Poppe-engined models and the now well-established 993cc MAG-powered v-twin.

The 665cc machine had been axed and, with the exception of one version of the 498cc three-speed Sports model that was equipped with chain-cum-belt drive, all-chain drive transmission was standardized throughout the Ariel range.

## Inflation

Inflation was now becoming a serious problem in the British economy. This in turn was to

*An Ariel sv single from the early 1920s, by now far more like a modern motorcycle with its sturdy frame, chain primary and final drives. Note forward-mounted magneto.*

# Pioneering Days

cause several motorcycle firms to go to the wall. Charles Sangster and his management team saw this happening and reacted by cutting the size of the company's motorcycle range. For the 1925 season the MAG-engined v-twin was discontinued, Sangster believing that he would be better served by concentrating the firm's efforts into the cheaper 249cc and 498cc models. A new 497cc (81.8 × 95mm) sports model was introduced. This engine displacement, including bore and stroke dimensions, was to be a feature of Ariel half-litre singles for many years to come. The power unit differed little in external appearance from previous five-hundred and six-hundred class Ariel engines of the White & Poppe design, with the inlet valve at the rear and the exhaust valve at the front. However, it was advanced in other respects with a roller bearing big-end, and a roller bearing supporting the drive-side mainshaft; but, as with all previous Ariel motorcycles, a cast-iron piston was employed.

Other features were:

- a patented Ariel decompressor
- redesigned three-speed countershaft gearbox, with hand-change
- primary chain totally enclosed in an oil bath
- EIC magneto
- Bonniksen speedometer
- hand-operated oil pump
- crankshaft-mounted shock absorber
- redesigned kick starter to provide greater angle of movement.

## Cycle Part Details

The first forks that Ariel employed at this time were made under licence with Druid patents, incorporating friction dampers and screw-down grease caps. A rigid, diamond-type frame was used, there were combined petrol and oil tanks and, as in the past, the rear brake was fitted at the front. The tool kit was carried in a small container attached to the frame below the tanks. Ariel also offered no fewer than four individual types of sidecar, comprising coach-built and polished aluminium-bodied versions in semi- and full-touring guises.

But once again the economic climate was to play a decisive role in Ariel's future path. With the clouds of depression looming, Charles Sangster took action, which involved some inspired moves.

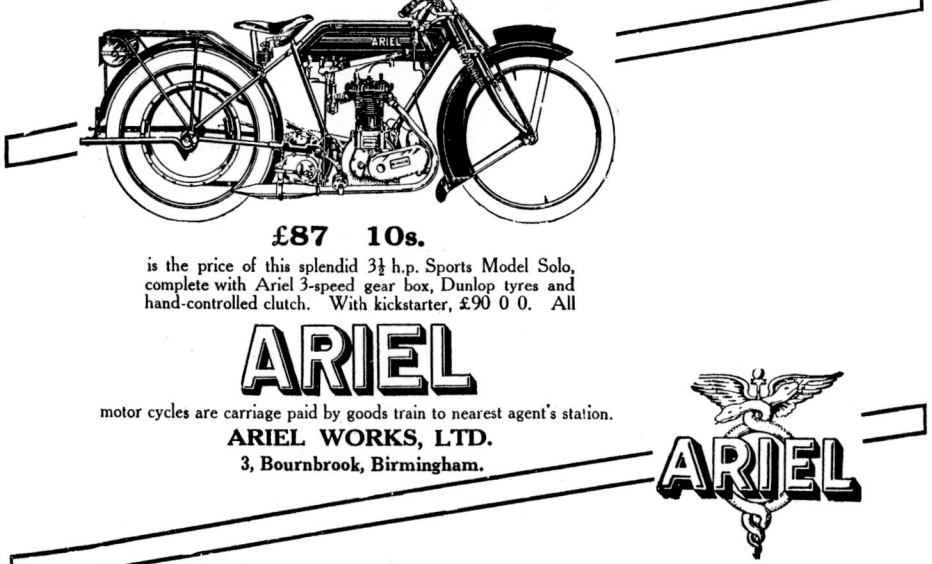

*July 1922; the 3½hp Sports Model, costing £90 with three-speed hand-change, Dunlop tyres and kick-starter. At that time, all Ariel motorcycles included delivery carriage paid by goods train to the nearest agent's station.*

## Val Page Arrives

First Sangster signed up JAP's brilliant young design chief, Val Page. JAP had decided to close its racing and development department at the end of 1925 and concentrate its efforts on the existing range of series production engines. Page had been the man behind Bert Le Vack's racing and record-breaking achievements. In addition, Jack Stocks, who had been in charge of Ariel's marketing, had decided to quit and set up his own business. And Vic Mole – whom Peter Hartley describes as a 'human dynamo' – was to leave his post in the West Country to search out a more challenging role at the hub of British industry in the Midlands. He was to become a vital element in the Ariel story.

All this is described in the following chapters – not only men like Sangster, Page and Mole, but Edward Turner, Charles Sangster's son Jack, Frank Anstey, Tom Davis, Laurence Hartley, Sammy Miller and Hermann Meier, to name but a few, all played important roles in making the Ariel name famous the world over.

---

**Four Wheels**

As recorded elsewhere, the first powered Ariel, a 1¾hp de Dion-powered three-wheeler built under licence, made its public bow at the London Crystal Palace Show in November 1898.

Ariel soon moved from tricycles to quadricycles, displaying a 3hp model at the 1900 National Show and, at the same time, unveiling a 9/10hp car powered by a parallel twin-cylinder engine and featuring a tonneau body. In August 1902 a 16hp four-cylinder Ariel, designed by Charles Sangster, was entered for the Automobile Club's Reliability Trial, but was destined to crash whilst on test and therefore was unable to start the event.

From 1904 the Ariel motorcycle division (Ariel Cycle Co) assumed a prominent position in the main company, Cycle Components, whilst the Ariel Motor Co was confined to car production.

In 1906, after flagging sales, the car company was reorganized as Ariel Motors Ltd and concentrated on a new range of large, conventional cars marketed as Ariel-Simplex. Financial problems, however, were never far from the surface, and the company was eventually bailed out thanks to a cash injection from the French Société Lorraine de Dietrich concern, which had been looking for a plant in Great Britain. It purchased Ariel's Selly Oak works from Cycle Components Ltd for £36,000 (around £5 million sterling at today's value).

By the spring of 1908 the Ariel car company was producing three chassis a week, with plans to manufacture Antoinette aircraft alongside its four-wheel products. However, the British Lorraine-Dietrich operation hit the rocks in 1910, resulting in an official receiver being appointed the following year.

Meanwhile, Ariel had made arrangements for its own cars to be produced in Coventry by the Coventry Ordnance Company, a branch of the famous Cammell Laird shipbuilding firm. Production continued with six models in 1913 and a pair of four-cylinder models in 1914, one of which continued until 1916 when war production took over completely, Ariel manufacturing motorcycles, bombs and other armaments.

In 1915 the car and motorcycle companies were registered jointly for the first time as Ariel Works Ltd, but following the end of the war in November 1918, no car production was attempted until 1922. With Ariel very much concentrating its efforts on the two-wheel front, a design by Jack Y Sangster (son of Charles) for an air-cooled, flat-twin 8hp car was taken up by Rover as the Rover 8, with Sangster Jr as Assistant Works Manager.

Jack Sangster soon rejoined Components Ltd as Assistant Managing Director to his father, and worked on the design of the Ariel Nine, with which the company made its post-war four-wheel return. The air-cooled, flat-twin engine of the Nine was manufactured by A Harper Sons & Bean Ltd, which had connections with Charles Sangster dating back to his cycle days.

However, the Nine's engine proved its downfall, not only being noisy, but also vibration-prone, which did not help either the occupants or its reliability record. The Nine's successor, the Ten, was not a success either and in 1925 Ariel car production finally ground to a halt. This time there was to be no relaunch and from thereon Ariel concentrated on two wheels instead of four.

As a point of interest, it should be said that the present-day Ariel, which produces the Atom, the specialist, limited-production British sports car, has no relationship with the old Ariel organization other than its name, the original brand name having passed into history in the morass of the BSA group's failure during the early 1970s.

# 2 The Sloper

Like the far more well-known Square Four series, the Ariel Sloper family of machines was introduced at the beginning of the 1930s. Featuring power units with the cylinders inclined at either 30 or 45 degrees from the vertical, these were in many ways just as innovative and exciting as Turner's four. The Slopers were produced in both ohv and sv guises and in a number of engine sizes including 248cc, 497cc, 498cc and 557cc.

Unfortunately, however, they came out at just the wrong time, as after the Wall Street stock market crash of October 1929, the world economy was in freefall. Even so, Ariel, to its credit, tried bucking the trend by coming up with a series of glamorous machines.

## Vertical and Inclined Cylinders

There were vertical engines and inclined (sloping) engines – including two-valve ohv, four-valve ohv and side-valves. Apart from Turner's four (*see* Chapter 5), there were eight models to choose from. Of the trio of 248cc (65 × 75mm) Colts, that now had cylinders inclined forward by 30 degrees from the vertical, the side-valve LB31 was priced at £37, the single-port ohv LF131 at £39, and the twin-port LF231 at £40. The larger models had their cylinder inclined more sharply at 45 degrees. The cheapest of these was the 557cc (86.4 × 95mm) SB31 side-valve at £52, then came the 498cc (86.4 × 85mm) single-port ohv SF31 at £55, but the most expensive Sloper was the technically advanced four-valve SG31 costing £60.

## Four Valves

Why four valves? Well, motorcyclists had been demanding ever-better performing machines. Marques such as Indian and Rudge-Whitworth had successfully proved the value of employing four valves. And in the early 1960s Honda would prove conclusively with its world-beating Grand Prix bikes that the individual reciprocating mass was less with four valves and therefore engine revolutions could be higher than a conventional two-valve design. In addition, the increased inlet valve area, when compared to a two-valve layout, enabled superior breathing and thus more power for a given engine size.

## Dry Sump Lubrication

By this time Ariel had switched from a wet sump to a dry sump lubrication system. In addition, the company had developed and patented a simple but highly effective oil-purifying device. This operated on the centrifugal force principle. In the conventional manner, this passed through the hollow main shaft, but instead of going direct to the crankpin it flowed from the centre via a hollow rod into a purifying container housed in the timing-side crank flywheel; centrifugal force generated by the rotating crankshaft thus threw any sludge or foreign bodies into the reservoir trap. Meanwhile, fresh clean oil was passed to the big-end bearing. This device was designed to be cleaned out every few thousand miles, access being gained by removal of the sump.

*Lovely Ariel publicity shot of the SF31 five-hundred 2-valve Sloper single, circa 1931.*

*Factory photograph of the 1931 498cc overhead-valve SF31 Sloper.*

## The Two-Fifties

Twin port was fashionable in many single-cylinder motorcycles in those days, including Ariels. However, the 248cc single, with its inclined cylinder, was only offered in single-port guise, as when fitted with a magdyno (and lighting equipment) it would have exceeded the upper weight limit of 224lb (102kg) that fell into a special tax bracket for lightweight machines.

Also Ariel had experienced frame problems on the two-fifties in 1930, so the 1931 models had an improved version. The engine, apart from having an inclined cylinder, was almost unchanged, the exception being that circlips were now used for the piston and a small-end bush was fitted to the connecting rod. Other features were larger-capacity oil tanks and a new design of timing cover for the engine.

## A Low Centre of Gravity

On the larger-engined models, with their steeper 60 degrees of incline for the cylinder, a major advantage was a lower centre of gravity. But why did Ariel not go the full hog and produce an entirely horizontal-cylinder-engined bike? One concern was that this would have given too long a wheelbase; as it was, the twin front downtubes were widely splayed to allow the cylinder to be mounted between them.

## Conventional Valve Operation

Both the two-and four-valve Sloper models employed conventional valve operation. The pushrods, being enclosed within oil-tight tubes, were sealed at their base with rubber oil seals, and operated by cam levers mounted on a common shaft. The rockers were fully enclosed (quite rare in those days) in a cast-alloy rocker box and lubricated by grease gun.

The four-valve SG31 employed a differently shaped rocker box from the two-valve engines and the rockers operated on roller bearings. As with the twin-port, two-valve Sloper, provision for separate tappet adjustment of each valve was available when the tappets made contact with the case-hardened end caps of each valve. As was normal practice on Ariels, the inlet valve guides were lubricated directly from the engine.

## A Double Roller Big-End

All the 498cc and 557cc Sloper engines featured double roller bearing big-ends and ball race main bearings, the latter being on either side of the crankcase. They also had die-cast aluminium alloy primary chain cases (with oil bath for the chain), 7in (178mm) front and rear brakes, a special four-speed Burman gearbox (that featured an operating spindle running on roller bearings) and the usual Ariel dry cork clutch (four-plate and from the primary chain case oil by way of sealing).

Oil to the engine was supplied by a gear-type pump driven by a spiral gear off the crankshaft at one-twelfth engine speed. This employed dry sump lubrication where the lubricating oil for the engine was stored in a separate tank on the offside (left) of the motorcycle. As already explained, a centrifugal filter system was located within the timing side crank flywheel.

## A Shared Frame

The frame used on the 498 and 557cc Sloper models was shared with the Square Four (*see* Chapter 5). This was of duplex construction and was a particularly sturdy (and heavy) device.

The Sloper models used a different fuel tank from that fitted to models equipped with a conventional vertical cylinder. As it was fitted lower, it had special raised knee grips moulded into the tank sides. Atop the tank was an instrument panel of standard Ariel layout for the period; an optional eight-day clock was an interesting feature. The Smiths-made speedometer was driven from the gearbox by a cable that passed through the rear section of the fuel tank.

## A Three-Fifty

Thanks to the very considerable success enjoyed by the 248cc Colt series of 1930, Ariel decided to offer a similar machine, but with an improved performance. This led the factory to launch, in March 1931, a 346cc (72 × 85mm) ohv version, coded MF31. This too featured an inclined cylinder, a twin-port detachable cylinder head (made, like the barrel, in cast iron), and retailing for a competitive £42. As with the two-fifty, magdyno lighting was available as a cost option.

The engine of the MF31 three-fifty featured pushrod tubes extending down to the top of the timing gear casing, the cast-in 'box-like' enclosure on the lower side of the cylinder barrel not being present as it was on the other Ariel ohv singles in the 1931 catalogue.

Lubrication was by courtesy of a twin-plunger oil pump operating on the same dry sump/centrifugal crank filter as on the larger Sloper engines. The gearbox was a hand-operated Burman-made three-speeder and the primary chain was encased in an aluminium oil bath.

The cycle parts were largely from the existing two-fifty series, which meant 5½in (140mm) brakes front and rear, girder forks and a rigid frame. However, the latter was redesigned for increased stiffness.

## A Side-Valve Addition – 1932

Early September 1931 saw Ariel announce its 1932 model range. This included the MB32, a new side-valve single of 346cc (72 × 85mm) and again featured an inclined cylinder; there was also a special export version of this machine. The model MF32 was an ohv Sloper using the same bore and stroke as the side-valve MB. This overhead-valve three-fifty was offered in both single- and twin-port versions – although only in two-valve form.

The 498cc four-valve single was offered in both sloping (SG32) and vertical (VG32)

LB32 248cc side-valve single three-speed gearbox.

MF32 347cc ohv single three-speed gearbox.

SB 557cc side-valve single four-speed gearbox.

SG 498cc ohv four-valve single four-speed gearbox.

guises. The two-valve SF had been discontinued, whilst the 557cc SB was still available.

At the London Olympia Show in November 1931, two further inclined cylinder machines were launched, both having a similar layout to the MB32 three-fifty side-valve single. These were the 4LB32 side-valve and LF32 ohv, the latter with twin-port cylinder head. Both displaced 248cc (65 × 75mm) and were clearly based around the outing LB31 and LF31 models.

*Common Features*

Features common to all the 1932 Ariel range were tool boxes manufactured entirely from pressed steel; redesigned front forks and a new 'fishtail' silencer. The front forks now featured a barrel-shaped central compression spring and a revised link action on the girders. Bronze bushes were specified, whilst all the bolts were case-hardened and ground. This resulted in considerably improved handling characteristics and greater comfort.

Considerable attention had also been paid to components such as wheel spokes, sprockets, handlebars, controls and steering damper, whilst the brakes had been considerably uprated, both in braking area and method of adjustment. The latter was of interest, being quite unusual; instead of being operated from the control rod at the rear, the fulcrum end of the brake shoe was now employed at this end. This not only had the advantage of being simple, but was also neat and had the effect of spreading wear over the entire brake shoe area.

*Larger Fuel Tanks*

The 498 and 557cc Sloper models had new, larger 3.125gal (14.4ltr) fuel tanks for the 1932 model year, with the instrument panel moulded flush with the top surface. These motorcycles were also equipped with a decompressor located, not on the camshaft, but instead on an auxiliary cam of the engine shaft. Another feature was that the dry sump lubrication was now variable. It could, however, not be turned fully off, thus there was no prospect of the engine being starved of lubricant by incorrect adjustment. As described by Peter Hartley, this system 'enabled extra oil to be given when the engine was new, or the pump could be set to deliver slightly more oil when a sidecar was fitted and the engine was required to work harder.'

All of the 1932 Ariel range had hand-operated gearboxes (except for the new four-valve VH32 sports model with vertical cylinder – *see* Chapter 7).

The fours and the 498/557cc Sloper had four-speed gearboxes, whereas the 248 and 346cc models had three speeds. Both the fours and the Sloper's also featured cast-aluminium-alloy primary chain cases and a quickly detachable plate was now specified to ease clutch adjustment.

## The 'Sevens' Test

As described elsewhere, in October 1931 Ariel Motors carried out a series of tests under ACU supervision in a successful attempt to win the coveted Maudes Trophy. For the endurance part of the tests, which were named 'Sevens' after the number of the ambitious series of feats attempted, an MB32 346cc inclined, side-valve model was built – from parts selected at random by an ACU official. Then, prior to the commencement of the test the engine was stripped for examination. Items such as the piston, small end and gudgeon pin received attention (the official bulletin described this as 'easing'). A magneto was exchanged for the existing magdyno and the motorcycle transported to the Brooklands track in Surrey so that the seven-hour endurance run could be carried out.

Piloted by Eddie Morris, Les Pearson and Sid Slater the bike covered 368 miles (592km) during the seven-hour period, averaging 52.58mph (84.6km/h), even though, midway through the proceedings, dirt in the carburettor caused problems. Riders were changed every seventy minutes, when refuelling also took place.

*Seven Minutes to Decarbonize*
To demonstrate how easy an Ariel motorcycle was to work on, another test was designed to attempt to decarbonize a VB32 557cc side-valve engine and to have the engine running again within seven minutes. Harry Perry and Ted Thacker carried out this task. Using only tools supplied with the motorcycle as standard equipment, the pair removed the cylinder head and scraped off the carbon from the combustion chamber and exhaust port, reassembled and had the engine going again in the amazingly low time of 4min 19sec.

*The Flexibility Test*
Another 557cc side-valve Sloper machine was used for the flexibility test. This was undertaken to prove that the machine would not overheat when ridden at a 'reasonable touring speed', the machine being sealed by an ACU official in each of the four gears, one at a time. Sid Slater was the rider chosen to do this, which he completed non-stop, except when the gear lever was sealed each time in the respective gear.

*Hill-Climbing*
Another of the seven tests was hill-climbing. For this, a 499cc four-valve SG32 Sloper, with sidecar fitted and with Harry Perry at the controls with one of the ACU observers in the chair, made seven ascents and descents of each of seven different, nationally famous hills. These were:

- Bwlch-y-Groes
- Dinas Mawddwy
- Alt-y-Bady
- Beggar's Roost
- Porlock
- Lynton
- Countisbury.

The machine ran faultlessly throughout, with only Bwlch-y-Groes proving a real challenge.

The 'Sevens' test was only one of many feats of endurance carried out by the Ariel works or by enthusiastic privateers during the late 1920s and early 1930s.

*A superbly restored example of the 1932 SG32 498cc (86.4 × 85mm) 4-valve, twin-port ohv single on display in the National Motorcycle Museum, Birmingham, 2002.*

## The World Tour

Probably the most publicized Ariel endurance feat was the fantastic 'World Tour' that ended in 1931. This feat of endurance was carried out by I S (Ivan) Kralichek-Soboleff, a former lieutenant in the White Russian Army. Riding a 499cc ohv model and sidecar, he set off for India. His subsequent journey, covering no fewer than 43,000 miles (69,187km), began in late 1929 and took him through Persia (now Iran), Lebanon, Egypt, continental Europe and Great Britain. He then travelled by ship across the Atlantic to Canada and thence down through the USA to South America, followed by another epic sea voyage, this time across the Pacific and Indian Oceans to Calcutta, his original starting point.

## Financial Woes

The collapse of the American stock market triggered by the Wall Street crash of October 1929 had a terrible effect on the economies of both the States and Europe in particular, leading to record numbers of bankruptcies and closures – and of course millions being put out of work. Sales of cars and motorcycles plummeted. By late 1930 the vast majority of British industry was on its knees, due in no small part to a combination of over-production brought on by the economic collapse. A number of car firms closed, including Coventry-based Swift, of which Charles Sangster was Chairman. The failure of Swift was a blow to Charles Sangster and he decided that it was time for Ariel, like several other motorcycle manufacturers, to diversify and manufacture three-wheelers as well.

Components Ltd, then the parent company of Ariel, had for several years marketed bicycles under the Fleet trade name. Fleet Motors Ltd had as joint Managing Directors Charles Sangster and his son Jack. This company then began producing light commercial three-wheelers as delivery trucks. November 1931 saw Fleet announce an Ariel 557cc side-valve-powered motorcycle-engined vehicle. However, soon all the Components Ltd companies, including Fleet, began to suffer, and by the late summer of 1932 crippling debts had been run up.

By September 1932, the whole group of Components Ltd companies, Ariel included, was in the hands of the Official Receiver. With Components Ltd and its subsidiaries in liquidation the fate of the marque hung in the balance. However, all was not lost, as Jack Sangster was able to buy up most of the production machinery from the remains of the Ariel Works Ltd, and he then set up in one of the old Components Ltd factories. So Ariel Motors (JS) Ltd came into being.

But as outlined in Chapter 6, this resulted not only in some of the key personnel, Chief Designer Val Page included, leaving, but also to a rationing of models. As the Sloper singles were expensive to manufacture, the decision – probably the correct one as it turned out – was to concentrate all future single-cylinder production on models using the vertical cylinder. And thus the distinctive Sloper series rode off into history.

*1932 Ariel MH32 Red Hunter with inclined cylinder; 346cc (72 × 85mm).*

# 3 Side-Valves

The last Ariel side-valve single, the VB 600, was finally taken out of production in January 1959. It was thus longer-lived than any other of the company's motorcycles if one includes its ancestors, the 557cc (86.4 × 95mm) models A and B that had been introduced for the 1926 season as part of design chief Val Page's facelift for Ariel. In fact, the VB's engine shared the same 86.4 × 102mm bore and stroke dimensions as the company's 1910 4bhp model.

## The 1926 Redesign

The 1926 redesign by Page (who had joined Ariel as Chief Designer from the London-based JAP concern where he had held a similar post), made a major impact on Ariel's fortunes, even though most of the cycle parts had remained unchanged and 'pioneer' in appearance. However, Page did deal with one vital aspect in this area – braking – by fitting powerful 7in (180 mm) brakes on both wheels.

## A New Frame

For 1927 there was a new frame, but this gave problems, plus a new gearbox and saddle tank. For 1928, the troublesome frame was redesigned – this being the year in which the famous horse trademark made its debut. The 1928 frame differed considerably in design from the previous year's device. Although it still provided the traditional low riding position, it was much stronger and less prone to whip because of its greater degree of triangulation and thus rigidity. It sported a one-piece steel head stock and, unlike the 1927 frame, had straight as opposed to curved front and rear downtubes. The 1927 frame, because of these curved tubes, had not only provided inferior handling, but in several cases had actually broken.

## Dry Sump Lubrication

The next innovation of importance concerned the lubrication, with a dry sump system being introduced for 1929, together with a twin plunger oil pump bolted to the inner timing case and driven by the camshaft.

With the arrival of the 1930s, Ariel had three side-valve models in its range: the 248cc (65 × 75mm) LB and the 557cc A and B. Both of these latter models had a vertical cylinder, three-speed gearbox, the B being the de Luxe version.

## The VB Arrives

1931 was the first year that the VB description was used, being catalogued as the VB31. Confusingly, the A model was coded SB31 and although it retained the 557cc engine side it had an inclined cylinder. In 1932 the VB32 again had the vertical cylinder, the SB32 an inclined one. As a point of interest, the 248cc (65 × 75mm) LB became the LB31 in 1931 with the cylinder inclined forward by 30 degrees; this was replaced by the LB32 the following year, before being discontinued. There was also the 346cc (72 × 85mm), but this was only offered for a few months in early 1932.

So when the 1933 model range was announced at the end of October 1932 only

# Side-Valves

*1927 Page-designed Ariel side-valve single, with rear magneto, cradle frame, improved forks and the first of the large brakes.*

the 557cc engine was offered in side-valve guise. However, there were three versions:

| | | | |
|---|---|---|---|
| VA3 | Standard | three-speed | £43 10s |
| VA4 | Standard | four-speed | £45 10s |
| VB | De luxe | four-speed | £49 10s. |

## Financial Problems

Unfortunately, at the same time as Ariel was announcing its 1933 programme, the marque was suffering severe financial problems. In fact, in September 1932 Components Ltd (the then owners of Ariel Works Ltd) had been placed in the hands of the Official Receiver. But behind the scenes Jack Y Sangster, who was Joint Managing Director with his father Charles, was fighting to save the business with which the Sangster family had so long been associated.

With Components Ltd and its subsidiaries in liquidation, Jack Sangster 'now a wealthy man in his own right', as Peter Hartley described him in his book, *The Ariel Story*, was able to purchase the vast majority of the machines, spare parts and tooling, and restart production in what, under the old regime, had been the works of the Endless Rim Co and which he had also purchased at the sale.

In addition, Jack Sangster was able to install some of the machinery in the four-storey service building of the old Ariel car business,

*1929 248cc side-valve engine with enclosed valve springs. Like the ohv unit this had a ribbed crankcase. A double plunger oil pump was incorporated in the timing case.*

which he also owned. With these premises as his production base, Sangster Jr was able to continue the manufacture of Ariel bikes as a private company, trading under the title Ariel Motors (JS) Ltd. Meanwhile, his father Charles Sangster passed away, his death no doubt hastened by the financial goings-on.

*Page Moves On*

The liquidation of Components Ltd saw Val Page take up a new post of Chief Designer at the Triumph company in Coventry (where he subsequently designed a brand new ohv six-fifty parallel twin). Meanwhile, Page's position at Ariel was taken by Edward Turner, who carried on Page's initial work on the new ohv Red Hunter single-cylinder range (*see* Chapter 8). The new Ariel board of directors had three men: Jack Sangster (Managing Director and Chairman); Herbert Hughes; and A S Lucas (the General Manager). Tom Davis was appointed Sales Director. And the new concern was able to capitalize in the coming years thanks to getting what was in effect a debt-free start to life.

## A New Era

So it was that the Ariel marque was able to enter a new era, that over the next few years was to be the firm's golden period.

One of the key reasons for the financial difficulties – besides the effect of the Great Depression brought on by events across the Atlantic which sparked the Wall Street crash in October 1929 – had been a combination of having too large a range of differing designs and too great production costs. To resolve this situation, the board of the new company, Ariel Motors (JS) Ltd, sensibly decided to rationalize the situation. This meant that when the 1933 Ariel range was announced in the autumn of 1932, it consisted of only twelve models and, as we already know, a quarter of these were centred around the 557cc vertical cylinder side-valve engine. As *The Motor Cycle* said in late 1932: 'Even the low-priced 550cc side-valve (model VA) has an astonishingly fine performance, and shows a timed speed in the neighbourhood of 70mph.'

## Sharing Components

A feature of the Ariel regime during the mid-1930s was the sharing of component parts between models. This benefited the side-valves, because they utilized the latest advances in cycle part design with their more glamorous brothers. For example, when the 1934 model range was announced in late 1933, many of the ohv model's items were included in the specifications. For example, the new front fork, the rubber-mounted handlebar mounting, the ribbed section mudguard, the frame – in fact, virtually everything that was not actually a part of the overhead valve gear itself! This compared favourably with rival manufacturers whose side-valve models were the poor relations due to using inferior components and design. The Ariel VA and VB models were the quality option – not the cheap and nasty poor relation!

An unusual feature of the 1934 side-valve Ariels was that they had no tappet guides. The construction at this point was, in fact, very much like that of an ohv engine. The rocker-type cam followers were just the same as those used on the ohv units, and the tappets very like short pushrods that connected with the bottom end of the valve stems instead of the overhead rockers.

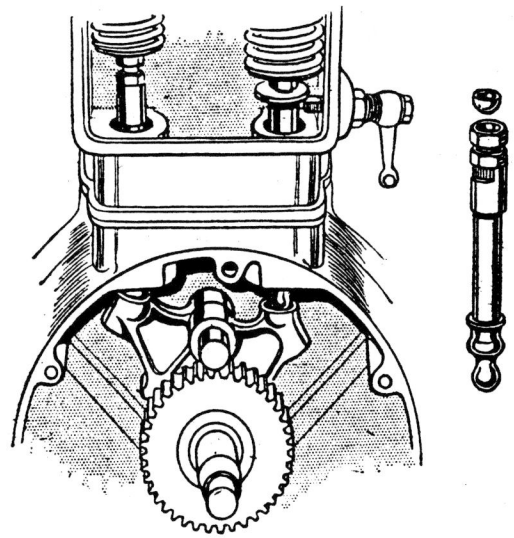

*The 1934 model year introduced this new form of tappet arrangement for the side-valve engine.*

## Considerable Change for 1935

Considerable change was made to the 557cc side-valve engine for the 1935 season. The detachable cylinder head had been modified internally to provide a different shape of combustion chamber. The exhaust valve was made of the same material as that used on the ohv singles, and it was cooled better than in previous years. This was achieved by providing a clear air passage around the exhaust port. In addition, the connecting rod and piston had been improved, the former being wider in section than before, though the weight had been reduced.

A whole host of changes had been introduced to the running gear of Ariel's range – including the side-valve machines. These included a cost option QD (quickly detachable) rear wheel, improved gearbox adjustment, clutch, riding position, steering damper, horn mounting and a new and more effective 'fishtail' on the silencer.

## A Bigger Engine Size for 1936

When details of the 1936 Ariel range were released in mid-September 1935, it was seen that, as a whole, it had been consolidated and simplified and the lower-priced 'Standard' models discontinued. Of the eight-model range, only the £57 10s VB remained in the side-valve ranks. However, the engine had been increased in displacement from 557 to 598cc, by increasing the stroke size to 102mm. A worthwhile improvement in power had resulted, coupled with an improved level of smoothness and silence, in particular top gear performance at low speeds.

*Other New Features*
All the single-cylinder engines, including the VB side-valve, had new crankcases, these having been stiffened up to ensure a higher level of rigidity in service. Another new feature was a patented dry clutch of increased size, housed in a compartment completely isolated from the oil bath provided for the primary chain; full technical details are contained in Chapter 5, as this clutch was shared with other 1936 Ariel models, including the Square Four. Other changes shared throughout the range that year were:

- new steering head races
- chrome-plated fuel tank
- polished gearbox castings
- a new enlarged toolbox
- improved toolkit
- four-speed foot-change gearbox (although hand-control was available to special order without extra charge)
- new silencer, still of fishtail design.

*In 1935 the 557cc side-valve model was available in three specifications: Standard three- or four-speed and de luxe (illustrated) four-speed.*

## Minor Modifications in 1937

For the 1937 model year, only minor modifications were made. This was partly due to the amazing success that the single-cylinder models (including the side-valve VB) had made the previous year, in both the showroom and in competition (see Chapter 7). These changes were very much refinements rather than redesign.

All Ariels were now fitted with automatic voltage control. Also, the metal tool box had been given rubber seals to exclude water, and was locked by a single, central fixing screw.

A slight alteration had been made to the crankshaft assembly, both to increase rigidity and to improve balance. The clutch had also come in for some modification. The fixing between the clutch body and its sprocket had been improved and strengthened so that the plain portion of the six connecting bolts was more robust, whilst the slotted edge of the clutch body had been provided with an outer ring that prevented the possibility of its opening out, which would lead to excess play and rattle in the outer splines.

## Modified Cam Gear in 1938

For the 1938 season the VB incorporated a modification to the cam gear (actually the fitment of VH Red Hunter cam profiles), which resulted in better performance. Other changes (shared by other models in the range) were to the front brake, outer gearbox shell, damper knob and a new headlamp with a bulbous front glass. The price had risen to £62 10s.

## 1939 Economy Model

A new 497cc (81.8 × 95mm) side-valve single, coded VA joined the Ariel ranks for 1939. Basically, it was an economy version of the six-hundred VB. Changes included a cylindrical silencer, unvalanced mudguard, a 2.5gal (11.4ltr) fuel tank with an instrument panel and narrower 3.25 × 19 tyres; the VA cost £57 compared to £60 10s for the larger side-valve model.

## The War Intervenes

Then came the Second World War and play stopped for six long years before peacetime production resumed in the summer of 1945, with a six-model range, including the VB six-hundred side-valve. By the time the 1947 model range was announced in late August 1946 the VB cost £139 14s – over twice what it had been in pre-war days – thanks to the devaluing of the pound sterling and the imposition of purchase tax.

## Post-War Developments

Post-war, the VB was built almost exclusively for the sidecar market. For 1947 the VB was given Ariel's new telescopic front fork, but the Anstey link plunger frame was only a cost option (as it was at that time on other Ariels, including the top-of-the-range Square Four). For 1951 a de luxe version was offered in a particularly dignified black and chrome finish.

## An Aluminium Cylinder Head

A significant change came for the 1952 season, with the fitment of an entirely new cylinder head in aluminium alloy. Like its ohv brothers, the VB had also been given deeper finning for both the head and cylinder barrel (the latter remaining in cast iron). Two additional cylinder head studs (making nine in total) were used. The improved cooling with these measures was said to have lowered, by 100°C, the running temperature of the engine under normal conditions. The new head and barrel was not interchangeable with the old, which had remained largely unchanged since the 598cc engine had been introduced for 1936. The price of the VB had by now risen to £181 8s 11d (including UK taxes). Power output was up from 15½bhp at 4,600rpm, to 17bhp (at the same engine revolutions).

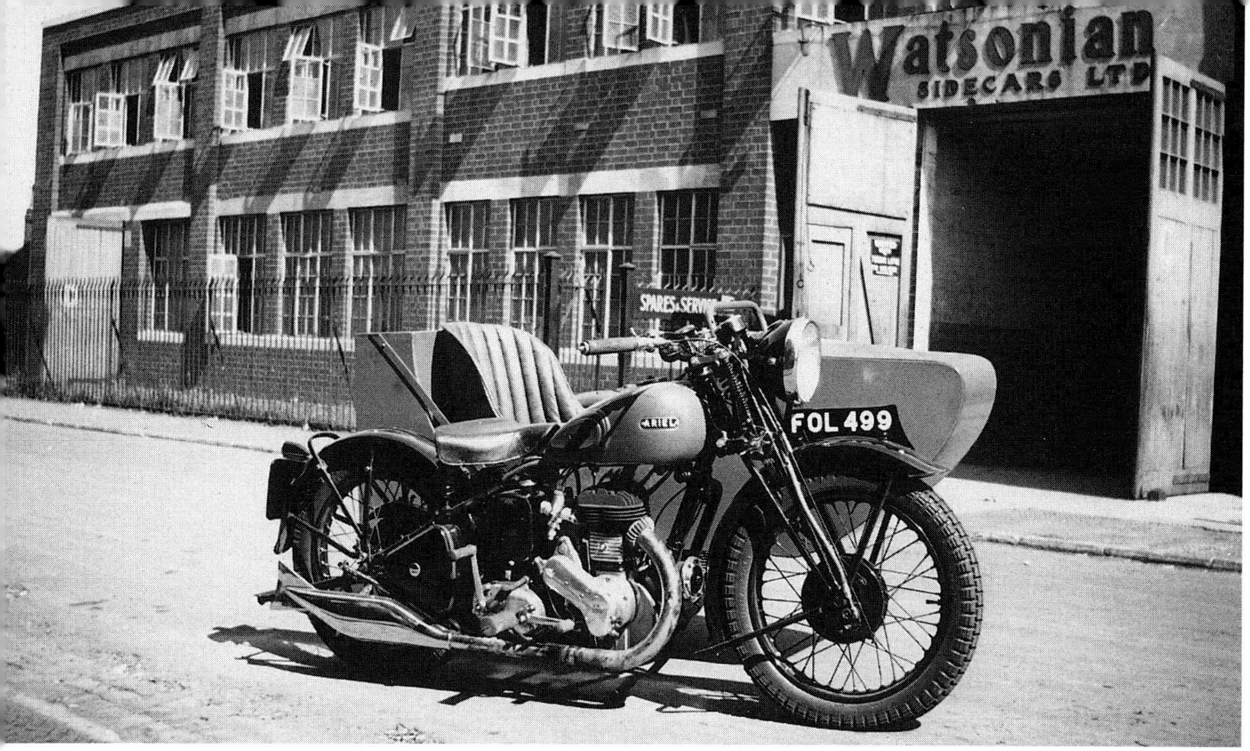

*One of the 598cc VB 600 side-valve singles outside the Watsonian sidecar factory, circa 1938. The larger engined side-valve had arrived for 1936.*

## A Swinging Arm Frame

When the 1955 range was announced in September 1954, several improvements were introduced for the VB. Most notable was the new Ariel duplex frame with swinging arm rear suspension (which had made its bow on the ohv singles and the twins a year earlier). Also new was the fitment of an Amal Monobloc 1in carburettor, replacing the previous Amal 276 instrument of the same choke diameter.

*Engine Modifications*
Engine modifications included the fitting of a Vacrom top piston ring, and a rise in compression ratio from 5:1 to 6:1. A cleaner finish had been obtained by die-casting the aluminium alloy cylinder head, whilst the exhaust header pipe had been reduced from 2in (50mm) to 1¾in (45mm) in diameter. A rigid-frame version of the VB continued to be offered, the price differences being £186 for the swinging arm model, £174 for the rigid framed bike.

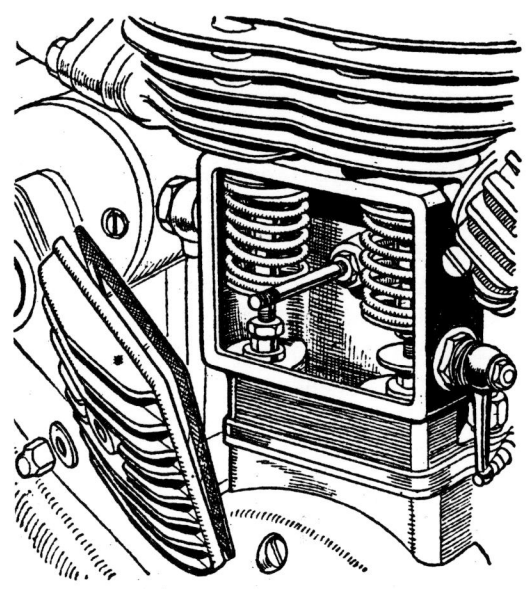

*How the valves were enclosed on the 1938 VB 600 engine.*

Brochure illustration showing the 497cc (81.8 × 95mm) Model VA, costing £57 10s in 1939.

| | VA 500 1939 | | |
|---|---|---|---|
| Engine | Air-cooled side-valve single with vertical cylinder, two-piece vertically split aluminium crankcases; cast-iron cylinder head and barrel; double collar bearing big-end; high tensile steel connecting rod | Frame | Cradle-type, brazed steel construction; single front downtube |
| | | Front suspension | Girder fork |
| | | Rear suspension | Unsprung, rigid frame |
| | | Front brake | 7in single-sided drum, SLS |
| Bore | 81.8mm | Rear brakes | 7in single-sided drum, SLS |
| Stroke | 95mm | Tyres | 3.25 × 19 front and rear |
| Displacement | 497cc | | |
| Compression ratio | 5:1 | **General Specifications** | |
| | | Wheelbase | 56in (1,422mm) |
| | | Ground clearance | 5in (127mm) |
| Lubrication | Dry sump, twin plunger pump | Seat height | 28in (711mm) |
| Ignition | Magneto, 6-volt | Fuel tank capacity | 2.5gal (11.4ltr) |
| Carburettor | Amal, downdraught | Dry weight | 355lb (161kg) |
| Primary drive | Chain | Maximum power | 13bhp @ 4,400rpm |
| Final drive | Chain | Top speed | 69mph (110 km/h) |
| Gearbox | Four-speed, Burman, foot-change | | |

*Side-Valves*

| VB 600 1945 | | | |
|---|---|---|---|
| Engine | Air-cooled side-valve single with vertical cylinder, two-piece vertically split aluminium crankcases; cast-iron cylinder head and barrel | Front suspension | Girder fork |
| | | Rear suspension | Unsprung, rigid frame |
| | | Front brake | 7in single-sided drum, SLS |
| | | Rear brakes | 7in single-sided drum, SLS |
| Bore | 86.4mm | Tyres | 3.25 × 19 front and rear |
| Stroke | 102mm | | |
| Displacement | 598cc | **General Specifications** | |
| Compression ratio | 5:1 | Wheelbase | 56in (1,422mm) |
| Lubrication | Dry sump, twin plunger pump | Ground clearance | 5in (127mm) |
| Ignition | Magneto | Seat height | 28in (711mm) |
| Carburettor | Amal 276 1in | Fuel tank capacity | 3.25gal (1.48ltr) |
| Primary drive | Chain | Dry weight | 365lb (166kg) |
| Final drive | Chain | Maximum power | 15bhp @ 4,400rpm |
| Gearbox | Four-speed, foot-change | Top speed | 72mph (116km/h) |
| Frame | Tubular, all-steel construction | | |

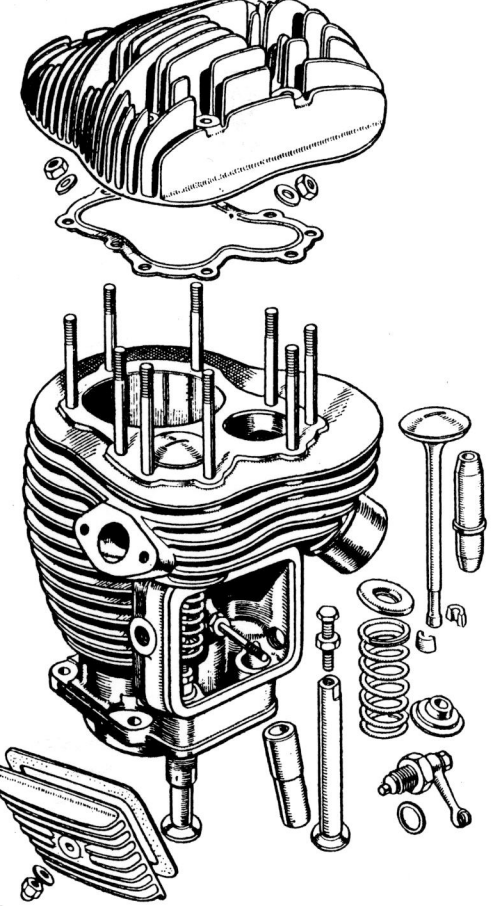

*Details of the top half of the 598cc (86.4 × 102mm) side-valve engine from 1952 with alloy cylinder head.*

## Style Changes for 1956

For 1956 the VB incorporated the style changes introduced that year across the Ariel range (except the 200 Colt). These included headlamp cowl (nacelle), full-width alloy brake hubs and enclosed rear chain (the latter a cost option), as well as a dual seat. In this guise, the VB was a particularly good-looking motorcycle and one which appeared capable of a far greater performance than it could actually achieve, although as a sidecar tug it was still an excellent choice.

From then on the VB was virtually unchanged until it went out of production in January 1959 – with all the other remaining four-strokes following a few short months later. Somehow, the BSA influence in later years largely passed by Ariel's remaining side-valve model, being as it was a relic of days gone by when Ariel was independent and better for it.

## VB 600 1958

| | | | |
|---|---|---|---|
| Engine | Air-cooled side-valve single with vertical cylinder, two-piece vertically split aluminium crankcases; aluminium cylinder head; cast-iron barrel | Frame | Duplex, all-steel steel construction |
| | | Front suspension | Telescopic fork |
| | | Rear suspension | Swinging arm, twin shock absorbers |
| | | Front brake | 7in full-width drum, SLS |
| Bore | 86.4mm | Rear brakes | 7in full-width drum, SLS |
| Stroke | 102mm | Tyres | 3.25 × 19 front and rear |
| Displacement | 598cc | | |
| Compression ratio | 6:1 | **General Specifications** | |
| Lubrication | Dry sump, twin plunger pump | Wheelbase | 56in (1,422mm) |
| Ignition | Magneto | Ground clearance | 5in (117mm) |
| Carburettor | Amal 376 Monobloc 1in | Seat height | 29in (737mm) |
| Primary drive | Chain | Fuel tank capacity | 4.5gal (20.5ltr) |
| Final drive | Chain | Dry weight | 365lb (166kg) |
| Gearbox | Four-speed, Burman, GB6, foot-change | Maximum power | 17bhp @ 4,400rpm |
| | | Top speed | 77mph (124km/h) |

*The 1954 VB 600. Producing 18bhp at 4,200rpm, its main purpose was to be a sidecar tug.*

*From 1955 the VB 600 used the swinging arm frame; this 1956 machine sports the changes introduced that year, including the full-width alloy brake hubs and headlamp nacelle.*

# 4 Military Service

Ariel was a major supplier of motorcycles to the British military services during both the World Wars of the twentieth century.

## The First World War

During the First World War of 1914–18, the Birmingham company not only manufactured a variety of armaments, but also a large number of the 3½hp (500cc) side-valve single. This model, in civilian guise, was first produced in 1910 and was powered by the White & Poppe 482cc (85 × 85mm) engine with vertical cylinder (*see* Chapter 1).

Other features of the 3½hp single's specification included a compression ratio of 5:1, 6-volt magneto ignition, a Brown & Barlow carburettor, three-speed hand-change gearbox, chain primary drive, belt final drive, rigid frame, friction-damped parallelogram front forks and 26in wheels, while braking was taken care of by a mechanical caliper on the front wheel rim, with a block on the belt wheel at the rear; the dry weight was 235lb (106.6kg).

Many of the 3½hp models were actually exported for war duties to other countries of the Allied cause, notably Russia. Others saw widespread use in Mesopotamia (Iraq). Of those supplied to the British forces (from the summer of 1914), only fifty-two examples were on strength when the Armistice came in November 1918.

## The VA3

After the conflict was over, there was a massive decrease in revenue for military equipment. It was not until the British War Office purchased an example of Ariel's VA3 model for evaluation in 1935 (along with six other examples from rival manufacturers) to fulfil a new military contract, that Ariel once more became involved in the supply of military motorcycles.

The example of the VA3, a side-valve 557cc (86.4 × 96mm) single was essentially a stock civilian machine, but with the addition of a military-requested crankcase shield, a Dunlop sports rear tyre and a specially made carrier mounted above the rear mudguard. During tests by the MEE (Mechanization Experimental Establishment), it was found that although general performance both on and off the road was reported as 'good', the machine was, however, difficult to ride over specific obstructions such as brickwork and tree stumps. Even so, at the completion of over 5,500 miles (8,850km) of hard testing the VA3 showed little sign of wear except for the top surface of the cylinder barrel and piston assemblies.

Although the Ariel came out of the tests well, it was not chosen for service use – mainly because it was then about to be replaced in 1936 by the VB model (*see* Chapter 3).

## Square Four Testing

Next, during October 1936, Ariel provided the War Office with an example of its 597cc (51 × 61mm) 4F (Square Four) overhead camshaft model for testing by the MEE. This was a totally standard civilian machine. It had been requested for testing because the military authorities felt that its performance and quietness would be an advantage in service. However, although it performed well in the tests (including off-road use), it was felt that its weight would have been a handicap for military use. An example of the larger displacement 997cc (65 × 75mm) ohv Square Four was also provided for testing – but with the same results.

## War Approaches Once More

As war approached in the spring and summer of 1939, so Ariel and other British mainstream motorcycle manufacturers were requested to provide various motorcycles for evaluation by the military authorities. In Ariel's case these included: 497cc VA side-valve single; 349cc W/NG ohv single, 497cc VH (Red Hunter) ohv single, 347cc NH (Red Hunter) ohv single, 497cc VG ohv single, 347cc NG ohv single and the 598cc VB side-valve single.

Although small batches of VH, NH and VG models were acquired in the period 1939–40 (the government effectively commandeering many civilian-produced models in the early months of the war), it was the specialized W/NG that became Ariel's principal military motorcycle of the Second World War.

## The W/NG

Production of the military W/NG began during 1940 and it was to remain in continuous production until 1945. The work of Val Page, the W/NG was based on the successful trials bike campaigned by works rider Fred Povey in the 1938 SSDT (Scottish Six Days Trial). A total of 47,599 W/NG models were built, making it the most numerous British military motorcycle with an overhead valve engine used during the 1939–45 war. There is no doubt that Ariel's W/NG was one of the best, if not *the* best, of all British-built military bikes of its era. This was due to a combination of its excellent overhead valve engine, four-speed foot-change gearbox and excellent ground clearance – which were thanks to its competition ancestry.

Strangely, the first order for this motorcycle had come not from the British, but the French government. However, with the fall of France in May 1940, none were actually taken on charge by the French. Although they were in fact dispatched early in 1940, the motorcycles spent the next five years largely forgotten in an Ostend warehouse. Unpacked, unnoticed and unused, after the war they were returned to Britain and auctioned off as war surplus!

*The famous Selly Oak, Birmingham, factory as it was in 1939, just before the outbreak of the Second World War.*

*Military Service*

## The Military Conversion

The military conversion of the design had included the removal of the instrument panel (located in the top of the fuel tank), the adoption of a substantial phosphor bronze bush in place of rollers for the gearbox selector mechanism, the removal of the adjustable oil valve, and the repositioning of the prop (side) stand. The original frame (but with a modified rear section) and girder front forks (specially extended) were retained, together with no form of rear suspension. Most bikes (but not all) were supplied with a pillion seat mounted on the rear mudguard, a pair of canvas pannier bags, provision for masked lighting, and an additional toolbox – and of course an overall coat of green drab (khaki) paint.

*Performance*
Besides being blooded in competition, the NG proved a particularly hard-wearing and reliable unit in military service. With its excellent performance – including a top speed of just over 70mph (113km/h) and an 'all-day' cruising speed of 55mph (88km/h) – the 347cc (72 × 85mm) W/NG was a popular bike amongst all those who rode her. This reputation was helped by the large Ariel brakes that could haul the machine down to a standstill far quicker than virtually any other military motorcycle of the era. All this, combined with a fuel consumption that usually exceeded 80mpg (3.52/100km) also provided it with a good range. As Roy Bacon once recalled, 'a nice machine to draw from the store.'

*W/NG Details*
The engine of the W/NG three-fifty ohv single was essentially the civilian NG (*see* Chapter 7) with its soft valve timing and modest 6.5:1 compression ratio. Power output was 17bhp at 5,800rpm. The top half (cylinder head and barrel) were both iron, with chain drive to the magneto/dynamo at the rear of the cylinder.

The primary drive retained the traditional Ariel dry clutch, which was housed in a separate compartment in the chain case under a

*No fewer than 47,599 346cc W/NG ohv singles were built for the British War Department during the conflict.*

detachable domed outer cover; there was an additional plate to improve performance and service life (both vital in the military role). It is worth noting that on early W/NG machines the case continued to be manufactured in aluminium, but as the war progressed, this material became more difficult to source (mainly due to the demands of the aviation industry), resulting in a change to a pressed steel chaincase cover (the same applying to the timing cover of the engine).

A four-speed Burman-made gearbox with foot-change was fitted, but in time, as with the primary chaincase and timing cover, this too surrendered its light-alloy shell for a cast-iron component.

At first, the handlebars continued to be rubber-mounted, but this proved a disadvantage when, under adverse conditions on rough terrain, riders experienced instances of them turning. So conventional clamps were soon adopted. As previously mentioned, the instruments were transferred from the petrol tank, so the speedometer was relocated to the top of the front forks on the offside (right) and driven from a gearbox attached to the front brake backplate. The ammeter was retained, but found a new home at the front of the lighting switch in a small panel set in the headlamp shell, this being standard Lucas practice.

The lighting switch featured four working positions: off; tail only; pilot-tail; and headlight. No dip switch was fitted, but there was a twin filament headlamp bulb, only wired to one side. Of course, due to blackout requirements, lighting was a real problem for servicemen. For example, on convoy work they were required to use the very small tail light only and when on other wartime duties the headlamp beam was largely of no use, due to the headlamp mask. In fact, many riders suffered quite serious accidents due to the vastly restricted use of the lights on motor vehicles during the war years, these often resulting in death – something similar to the problem of so-called 'friendly fire' in today's modern hi-tech war fighting.

## Other Models

Besides the mass-produced W/NG three-fifty, Ariel also built other military models for the British War Department during the Second

| W/NG 1940 | | | |
|---|---|---|---|
| Engine | Air-cooled overhead-valve single with vertical cylinder, two-piece vertically split aluminium crankcases; iron head and barrel; single exhaust port; roller bearing big-end; built-up crankshaft | Frame | Tubular, all-steel construction; single front downtube |
| | | Front suspension | Girder forks |
| | | Rear suspension | Unsprung, rigid frame |
| | | Front brake | 7in single-sided drum, SLS |
| | | Rear brakes | 7in single-sided drum, SLS |
| Bore | 72mm | Tyres | 3.25 × 19 front and rear |
| Stroke | 85mm | | |
| Displacement | 346cc | **General Specifications** | |
| Compression ratio | 6.55:1 | Wheelbase | 56in (1,422mm) |
| Lubrication | Dry sump, twin plunger pump | Ground clearance | 6in (152mm) |
| Ignition | Magneto | Seat height | 28in (711mm) |
| Carburettor | Either Amal 75 or 275 ⅞in/ Amal 76 1in | Fuel tank capacity | 2.62gal (12ltr) |
| | | Dry weight | 354lb (161kg) |
| Primary drive | Chain | Maximum power | 17bhp @ 5,800rpm |
| Final drive | Chain | Top speed | 71mph (114km/h) |
| Gearbox | Four-speed, foot-change | | |

Military Service

*Wartime advertisement from October 1940: 'In our small corner of the Empire – Ariel'. This was in response to the thousands of motorcycles built at the Selly Oak works for military service.*

World War. The most numerous of these came in 1943 when a batch of 6,466 248cc (61 × 85mm) ohv singles was delivered. These were virtually sleeved-down W/NG models – with few changes elsewhere to the engine or general specification.

The other notable machine was the 497cc W/VA side-valve single, but this was only built right at the beginning of the conflict as a stopgap machine, and was very much in the mould of the Norton 16H and BSA M20, but whereas these latter two machines were constructed in vast numbers, their Ariel counterpart was not. Instead, it served principally with the British Army in a variety of second-line roles; some were equipped with sidecars. Small quantities were also supplied to the Air Ministry (Royal Air Force) and the Ministry of Agriculture, the latter for use on the Home Front, notably by the Women's Land Army.

## At War's End

Relatively few of the WD Ariels from the Second World War survive in Great Britain today. The reason for this is that, after the end of the war in 1945, many war surplus W/NGs (which of course comprised the bulk of Ariel's military motorcycle production) were shipped overseas. This was due to the excellence of their performance and their relatively light weight and good handling characteristics compared to other manufacturers' WD bikes.

One has to remember that virtually all new British bikes were sold abroad for the first few years of peace and the Ariel was one of the most popular. During the Second World War, Ariel Motors delivered some 60,000 motorcycles, making it the fourth biggest supplier of powered two-wheelers during the conflict, behind BSA, Norton and AMC.

# 5 Square Four

The legendary Square Four series was a feature of the Ariel company's range from 1931 until the models' demise in 1959 – almost three decades later. Although never truly mass-produced, it was nonetheless the marque's flagship product.

## The Four-Cylinder Motorcycle

Of course, there had been earlier fours, not only British ones, but examples from the United States of America, Belgium, Denmark and Germany. What set Ariel's model apart was its cylinder layout: the Square Four had a remarkably neat and compact appearance (particularly the first prototypes that were tested in 1929 and 1930); a relatively low weight; and an almost complete lack of engine vibration. Another factor was its car-type horizontally split crankcases, which in those days were virtually unknown in the motorcycle world (although much later these were a distinctive design feature of modern Japanese machines).

The original prototype design, as described in Chapter 12, was not the same as the production Square Four. Instead, the prototypes produced and tested during 1929 and 1930 employed a much lighter, more compact

*The first Square Four was a five-hundred, this was followed in 1932, by a 601cc (56 × 61mm) version, the Model 4F/6.32.*

engine assembly using full unit construction of the three-speed gearbox, fitted into the standard frame and cycle parts from Ariel's existing 250cc model. But, as finalized, the production version, when it went on sale for the 1931 season, employed a separate four-speed hand-change Burman gearbox and was fitted into the much heavier 500cc Ariel Sloper, whose conveniently splayed front downtubes of the frame accommodated the revised Four Square engine with its single forward-facing carburettor with ease.

## Edward Turner

Quite how the Square Four was created and subsequently evolved could, as my late friend Brian Woolley once described, 'perhaps have been brought into being only in England'. Because, in what other country would a large and successful commercial company have recruited an unqualified amateur to execute the design of a machine that was intended as their flagship model? The following is what happened.

Edward Turner, recruited by Ariel in 1927, was not yet thirty years old, and with no formal training whatever was running his own retail motorcycle business in Dulwich, East London. During the 1920s he had designed the first in a series of prototype single-cylinder engines featuring ohc (overhead camshaft) valve operation. Then in January 1927, Turner started producing and marketing a development of this design featuring a 350cc face cam engine. Called the Turner

---

### Early Fours

Unlike elsewhere in Europe, Victorian England was still very much a society dominated by horse-drawn transport. In fact, there was a vast array of draconian regulations impeding development of self-propelled vehicles, including a speed limit of only 4mph (6.4km/h). It was only in 1896 with the passing of the Emancipation Act, that these restrictions were lifted and the new transport industry began to flourish. Despite this, it was an Englishman, Major (later Colonel) Henry Capel Lofft Holden, who built the world's first four-cylinder motorcycle in 1897.

Variable gears were still well over a decade in the future, so Holden relied instead on sheer power to overcome the inherent inflexibility of direct drive. Like the German pioneers, Hildebrand & Wolfmüller, he employed long, exposed connecting rods and cranks linked directly to the rear wheel spindle. However, his engine differed greatly from the Munich product.

The four cylinders were positioned in pairs, each like a straight unpinned pipe, closed at both ends. In each pipe was a long piston with a crown at each end, and explosions took place at alternate ends of the cylinders, giving an impulse on each stroke. With a total displacement of 1,049cc (54 × 114mm), substantial gudgeon pins, or 'crosshead' pins as employed on a steam railway engine, projected through slots in the cylinder walls to engage with the connecting rods.

Automatic inlet valves were employed, but the mechanically operated exhaust valves, lacking any convenient rotary motion in the engine to drive them, were actuated via a camshaft, chain-driven from the machine's rear wheel.

The four-cylinder Holden engine operated at a mere 420rpm, at which it produced 3.6bhp giving maximum speed of 24mph (39km/h). Limited production was undertaken by the London-based Kennington concern, but a change to water cooling was needed as early prototypes suffered overheating problems.

Originally, production had been planned to commence in 1898, but it was still not until the following year, 1899, that it actually got under way. Unfortunately, water cooling added to the already considerable weight of the Holden four, so it fared badly against the smaller cars that offered superior comfort, reliability and price. However, three examples were exhibited at the 1901 Stanley Show, and one was ridden from London to Petersfield, Hampshire, and back, some 106 miles (170km), without trouble. But that marked the swansong of the world's first 'Superbike'. An 1897 prototype of the Holden survives today in London's Science Museum.

Other notable early four-cylinder motorcycles included the Belgian FN, Austro-Hungarian Laurin & Klement, and the German Dürkopp.

Special, this sold for £75 and attracted considerable publicity in the motorcycle press. One such article in March 1927 had seen Vic Mole, head of Ariel's Sales and Publicity since 1925, visiting Edward Turner at his south-east London headquarters. Mole then returned to Ariel's factory in Selly Oak, Birmingham, and reported the findings of his meeting to company boss Charles Sangster.

Turner was subsequently invited up to Birmingham to meet Sangster. During this interview, Edward Turner outlined, amongst other things, his concept for an innovative four-cylinder engine. However, unlike other four-cylinder power units this was not an in-line or a vee type, but instead was an unusual 'four dot' or 'square four' configuration. Essentially, Turner's plan was to use in effect a pair of vertical twins, one behind the other. Mounted in a common horizontally split crankcase, the front and rear crankshafts were to be geared together – this was intended to overcome the effects of primary out-of-balance forces that had plagued the valveless twin-cylinder Lucas car engine of 1907.

The result of the Turner/Sangster meeting was that the latter offered the former a post in the Ariel design office under the company's Chief Designer, Val Page. However, Sangster made sure that Turner not only had a separate office where he was free to develop his four, but additional staff to help create the required engineering drawings. As recounted in Chapter 12, Turner was basically a free agent, able to design what he wanted – and regardless of cost considerations. The result was a masterpiece, but quite simply too expensive to produce on a commercial basis.

For the story behind the design and development of the Turner prototype machines, go to Chapter 12, but suffice to say that the Ariel board decided to instruct Val Page to carry out a redesign: 'Cut its costs by suitable alterations to the basic design as is deemed necessary' were the actual words.

When questioned shortly before his death in 1972, Edward Turner said of his relationship with Val Page: 'Excellent. At that time I was no production engineer, scarcely any sort of engineer in fact, and when it came to putting Square Four into production, I knew next to nothing about such things as material specifications. Val Page helped me enormously, and sorted me out in every direction.'

## A Show Debut

The production version of the Square Four, as modified by Val Page, made its public debut at the London Olympia Show in November 1930. As already mentioned, it was a heavier machine with separate hand-change gearbox and mounted in a frame and cycle parts from the company's existing 500cc Sloper single-cylinder model. Even so, it still created a sensation, as not only was it a four, with the unusual square configuration, but also sported an overhead camshaft and, of course, the general public could not compare it 'in-the-flesh' so to speak, with Turner's original version.

## Square Four Details

### The Engine

Page's redesign saw the original Turner engine's bore and stroke measurements of 51 × 61mm retained, giving a displacement of 498cc. A particular feature of the production engine was its overhung crank, the crankpins being disposed at 180 degrees to each other, for three of the cylinders. It had been all four on the Turner prototype, but for series production the nearside (left) rear crank was provided with an outer web so that it could drive back to the clutch and gearbox. The overhung crank arrangement had first been seen on Alfred Scott's two cylinder twin-stroke motorcycle in 1908.

### The Two Crankshafts

The two crankshaft assemblies were similar in concept, with a large helical gear cut on the centre of the flywheel. This expensive method

| 4F 500 ohc 1931 | | | |
|---|---|---|---|
| Engine | Air-cooled square four with chain-driven camshaft; iron cylinder head and barrel assemblies; two separate crankshafts connected by gears | Frame | Duplex cradle, all-steel construction |
| | | Front suspension | Girder forks |
| | | Rear suspension | Unsprung, rigid frame |
| | | Front brake | 7in drum, SLS |
| Bore | 51mm | Rear brakes | 7in drum, SLS |
| Stroke | 61mm | Tyres | 3.25 × 26 front and rear |
| Displacement | 498cc | | |
| Compression ratio | 5.8:1 | **General Specifications** | |
| Lubrication | Wet sump, gear pump | Wheelbase | 55in (1,397mm) |
| Ignition | Magneto, 6-volt | Ground clearance | 4.5in (114mm) |
| Carburettor | Single front-mounted Amal Type 74 | Seat height | 26.5in (672mm) |
| | | Fuel tank capacity | 2.5gal (11.4ltr)[1] |
| Primary drive | Chain | Dry weight | 398lb (180kg) |
| Final drive | Chain | Maximum power | 22bhp @ 6,000rpm |
| Gearbox | Three-speed, hand-change | Top speed | 74mph (119km/h) |

[1] A few machines had a larger tank, 3.12gal (14ltr)

of gear cutting was replaced by the spur type from engine number 200. In both types, they were enclosed by an inner case, and outboard of them sat a main bearing on each side, making a total of four (two per crankshaft). As already mentioned, the crankcase was split horizontally, with the bearings secured to the top section. Outboard of each bearing a flywheel was located and this carried the crankpin and roller big-end. The fourth crankpin was extended and joined its outer web in conventional fashion, whilst the inner webs were secured by nuts to the central flywheels.

The front crankshaft drove a half-time shaft by gears and was placed between the cranks near the top of the case and ran from its centre out to the offside. It carried a skew gear near its middle, which drove to a gear oil pump set low down in the wet sump.

At the offside end of the half-time shaft were a pair of sprockets, the inner of these driving the two-spark Lucas magneto at engine speed located at the rear of the cylinder block assembly. This magneto carried a dynamo on its back, whilst the outer sprocket was connected by chain to the camshaft and featured a patented Weller blade-end-spring tensioner to the camshaft. This ran in ball races in an aluminium cambox bolted to the cylinder head and carried eight rockers to operate the vertically placed valves. The upper sprocket incorporated a Vernier coupling, whilst the cambox was sealed by a top cover and lubricated by a separate feed from the oil pump. On the nearside end of the camshaft was placed a distributor for the ignition system and each drive chain was enclosed within a two-piece aluminium case.

*The Cylinder Head*

The cylinder head was manufactured in cast iron, whilst the separate one-piece cylinder block was of the same material. When used for high-speed road or racing use, all cast-iron Square Four models were to suffer problems from head warping. However, it should be stressed that this was not so when used at more moderate engine speeds.

The head supported a single Amal Type 74 $^{21}/_{32}$in carburettor, this being mounted at the front between the two forward-facing exhaust pipes, with its induction passage running backward to the centre of the casting, where a cruciform porting system connected each of the cylinders. The ports joined together with an outer passage to feed into the exhaust header pipes and thence into Brooklands 'Fishtail' silencers that ran along either side of the motorcycle.

*The Lubrication System*
The lubrication system of the original production Square Four engine relied on the lower area of the connecting rods actually dipping into the oil at the base of the crankcase to feed the big-end bearings. Actually, at the time this was quite common practice – and removed the need to drill small holes through the crankshaft. As Roy Bacon described them, these: 'dippers were narrow section fingers that reached down from the steel rods and scooped oil up and into drillways to the rollers'. The oil for the wet sump lubrication was carried in the crankcase itself – not in a separate external tank (dry sump) as on later series Square Fours.

In an engine blessed by a wealth of ball and roller bearings the designers felt that the lubrication system did not call for a great degree of sophistication; instead it depended largely upon old-fashioned 'splash'. The oil pump itself comprised a pair of gears, one of which supplied lubricant to the valve gear and camshaft, whilst the other maintained a predetermined level in the wet sump, returning surplus oil to a container cast at the rear of the crankcase.

*Aluminium Pistons*
The three-ring pistons were of aluminium alloy, and as explained earlier the cylinder block was of cast iron. This material was also used for the cylinder head. This meant that not only was the top end of the Square Four heavy, but iron neither conducts nor radiates heat as well as aluminium alloy, although it is cheap and easy to cast – and at the time those considerations were important, bearing in mind the worsening British economic climate. The parallel valves were disposed transversely in truncated pent-roof combustion chambers that undoubtedly resulted in both inlet and exhaust valves being shrouded quite badly and lowering the volumetric efficiency of the engine. The valves were operated by rockers from the single transverse camshaft, the valve gear being housed in an aluminium casting box bolted to the cylinder head.

The iron did indeed get extremely hot, and could warp under extreme conditions (racing or flat-out road use), or due to careless assembly. This was to prove a major problem for those wishing to use the Square Four in competition.

The running gear, which in effect was that of the 1931 model 500 Sloper ohv single, employed a widely spaced twin-front downtube, cradle frame, without any form of rear suspension; girder front forks (with a larger central spring); and 7in single-sided drum brakes front and rear. The fuel tank, which sported an instrument console on its top face, was chromium-plated and was of a teardrop shape, much admired at the time. Another feature was the front number plate, which was to be a characteristic of the Ariel marque for some considerable time. Essentially, the mudguard, which was deeply valanced, had this special number plate that was straight and not curved as was the conventional practice; instead, it featured a slight upwards tilt at the front end, vertical rear edge and curved front one that gave it a flair and a style that was instantly recognized.

The balance of the machine was the 500 Sloper, except for a relocation of the battery to the position occupied by the oil tank on the Sloper.

## *The Motor Cycle* Test

The first test of a production Square Four was carried out by *The Motor Cycle* in early April 1931. The tester was generally full of praise and besides complimenting the 'exceptionally good' handling, steering and brakes, was also mightily impressed by the flexibility and smoothness of the engine, saying: 'It was outstanding and made the gearbox appear unnecessary, except for the sidecar work.' The engine was called upon to accelerate strongly from as low as 10mph (16km/h) in top gear. In fact, from 10–30mph (16–48km/h) the Ariel five-hundred Square Four did only 0.4 seconds less than an eight-litre overhead cam Bentley sports saloon. Even when one considers that the British motorcycle press often seemed to be in the pockets of the industry in those days, the newcomer still created genuine enthusiasm. Weighing in at 408lb (185kg), the Ariel Four cost £75 10s.

## A Six-Hundred

In November 1931, a new six-hundred version of the overhead cam Square Four was launched at the Olympia Show. It had the advantage of being reduced in price to £71. Apart from having the wheelbase increased by 15in (380mm) and the cylinder bore size increased to 56mm (giving a displacement of 601cc), the bike was virtually identical to its predecessor (which was still available), but remarkably Ariel claimed it was slightly lighter. Another claim was that oil leaks, which the factory now admitted had been a problem on the earlier bikes, had been 'eliminated'. Ariel said that the prime reason for the larger engine size was to 'satisfy a demand for more power for sidecar work'.

Finally, both the five-hundred and six-hundred versions had additional cylinder finning for the 1932 model year – this obviously being in response to potentially damaging overheating problems when ridden hard.

*Central spring girder front forks from the 1932 six-hundred Square Four.*

*Six-hundred ohc Square Four with iron head and barrel assemblies; rear-mounted magneto, single front-facing carburettor; twin exhaust pipes and hand-operated three-speed gearbox.*

## 4F 600 ohc 1932

| | | | |
|---|---|---|---|
| Engine | Air-cooled square four with chain-driven camshaft; iron cylinder head and barrel assemblies; two separate crankshafts connected by gears | Frame | Duplex cradle, all steel construction |
| | | Front suspension | Girder forks |
| | | Rear suspension | Unsprung, rigid frame |
| | | Front brake | 7in drum, SLS |
| Bore | 56mm | Rear brakes | 7in drum, SLS |
| Stroke | 61mm | Tyres | 3.25 × 26 front and rear |
| Displacement | 601cc | | |
| Compression ratio | 5.8:1 | **General Specifications** | |
| Lubrication | Wet sump, gear pump[1] | Wheelbase | 55in (1,397mm) |
| Ignition | Magneto, 6-volt | Ground clearance | 4.5in (114mm) |
| Carburettor | Single front-mounted Amal Type 74 | Seat height | 26.5in (673mm) |
| | | Fuel tank capacity | 3.12gal (14ltr) |
| Primary drive | Chain | Dry weight | 400lb (181kg) |
| Final drive | Chain | Maximum power | 24bhp @ 6,000rpm |
| Gearbox | Three-speed, hand-change | Top speed | 76mph (122km/h) |

[1] From 1933 onwards, plunger pump.

*Nearside view of 1932 six-hundred ohc Square Four power plant, with camshaft-operated distributor and horizontally split crankcases.*

*Tank top instruments, switches and filler cap; circa 1932.*

## The Maudes Test

During October 1931, the new 601cc overhead cam Ariel Square Four Model 4F/6.32 (its official coding) was involved in the famous Ariel Sevens Test. Essentially this involved seven tests, the last being with the four-cylinder model – its objective was to cover 700 miles (1,126km) in 700 minutes at the Brooklands track in Surrey. A trio of riders were involved – Sid Slater, Ernie Smith and Ted Thacker.

However, the first attempt met with failure, when the engine seized after completing 301 miles (484km) – during which it had averaged 66mph (106km/h). Subsequently, another engine was constructed from component parts selected at random by ACU officials and the test restarted. As described in Peter Hartley's *The Ariel Story*, these included: 'slight grinding and filing of the engine parts; reduction of the pistons by 0.003in; lapping of the valve stems into their guides with grinding paste; increasing the play in the half-time shaft bearing by filing; removal of all sharp edges on the pistons and piston rings; and the easing of the gudgeon pins and connecting rods' little-end bearings'.

Ariel's engineering staff then ran the engine for some three hours on the bench, after which it was partially dismantled under ACU supervision. High spots were removed from the pistons by means of file and emery cloth, whilst the gudgeon pins were again slightly eased. The engine was then reassembled, mounted in the frame and the motorcycle ridden to Brooklands to repeat the reliability test. The next day, the rear sections of the mudguard and number plate were removed, wheel spindle nuts and the like were tightened, whilst the engine's contact breaker points and tappets were reset; again all under the watchful eye of the ACU observation team.

Finally, half-a-dozen practice circuits of the Brooklands track were completed; then at 8.17am on 20 October, the test restarted with the same three riders operating riding stints of seventy minutes each. After a period of 2hr 20min, the Square Four came in, its throttle and choke controls tightened and its rear wheel bearing slackened off. A new set of harder grade sparking plugs was fitted after 5hr 14min, and an engine oil change was carried out. The test was suspended after a total of 207 laps (570 miles) had been completed – owing to the onset of darkness – and the bike put under lock and key with an ACU seal until the next day, no adjustment being allowed during the interim. The next day, 21 October, the test was restarted and went on to complete 700 miles in a total of 668min 14sec, an average speed of 62.82mph (101.08km/h).

At the completion of the 700 miles, the tappets were again adjusted and the machine speed-tested over the flying start Brooklands Outer Circuit lap, during which it achieved an officially timed average speed of 87.4mph (140.6km/h).

## The Advertising Campaign

In the advertising campaign that followed Ariel's completion of the Sevens Test, the company organized a starting test for the 601cc four in which seven children were given the task of starting the engine with the kick-start lever – only the smallest had to have a second go to get it fired up! There is no doubt that during the early days of motorcycling, the British motorcycle industry was particularly adept at such feats to attract the public's attention to its models. In the dark days of the Great Depression during the early 1930s the competition for sales had never been fiercer.

When the 1933 Ariel range was announced in October 1932, a new frame common in design to the entire 8-model range was adopted. Unlike the old Sloper type with its widely splayed front downtube, the latest type employed a large diameter front downtube with a cradle base underneath the power unit.

## Modifications

In order to accommodate the four-cylinder engine, some modification had been necessary to the base casting; This, Ariel claimed, also had the advantage of 'simplifying ad cleaning up the design' to a very considerable extent. This meant that now the engine's lubricant was carried in the base of the crankcase, rather than a separate 'tank' within it as before. A new single plunger pump, driven from an eccentric on the camshaft, was sufficient to maintain oil circulation. As before, oil was delivered to the chamber that enclosed the geared flywheels and overflowed to troughs into which the big-ends dipped.

A separate lead was provided for the camshaft, whilst surplus oil drained by gravity to the sump. There was a suction filter in the base and a special Tecalemit filter on the delivery side that was quickly detachable for cleaning purposes. The ball valve of the pump was equally accessible, and it was claimed that the new system maintained the oil at a lower temperature. An oil dipstick was provided.

The four-speed Burman-made gearbox was provided with an improved and more accessible mounting, which was common to all the larger Ariel models. This gearbox was normally supplied with hand operation; however, a new foot-change mechanism was available as a cost option.

The exhaust of the Square Four, which incorporated tubular silencers with spiral baffles, had a new feature for the 1933 model year in the shape of a balance pipe (cross tube), which was located to join the two exhaust pipes just forward of the rear wheel. Ariel claimed that this had the effect of reducing noise and back pressure, and evening up the exhaust note as a whole.

The combined effect of these modifications was to reduce the weight of the machine by 25lb (11.3kg), the wheelbase by 1½in (38mm) and to improve the roadholding and steering. In addition, the six-hundred engine size had been standardized, with the five-hundred version now only available to special order. The 1933 600/4F (with hand gear-change) retailed at £72 10s, but the foot-change gearbox operation, Lucas Magdyno lighting set with panel light, and speedometer were all at additional cost.

## No Change in Price

When the 1934 Ariel range was announced in the autumn of 1933, the by-now famous four cylinder remained unchanged in price – and specification – except for improvements made to the whole range.

The range changes were:

- a revised spring fork with taper-tube blades and very rigid bridge pieces, in addition to which much larger friction discs were fitted to the shock absorbers on the front forks
- to the gearbox; the usual dog clutches had given way to the type of a dog in which an extension of the gears meshed with an internally toothed ring. This was claimed to give an improvement in the ease of changing, besides lessening wear on the dogs. Further, on all models on which foot operation was employed, a neutral indicator was provided
- an enamel elongated Ariel badge for both sides of the fuel tank was recessed into the tank so that the surfaces were almost flush, and was held in place by screws
- the headlamp shell now carried a built-in ammeter and switch
- rubber-mounted handlebars.

## The Depression Lifts

The effects of the economic depression lifted as the 1930s unfolded, so the fortunes of Ariel (and the rest of the industry) improved. In September 1934, when the 1935 models were announced, the number had increased to fourteen, and the price of the six-hundred Square Four had risen to £80, including electric lighting and horn.

# Square Four

The only alteration to the engine was that the crankcase had been stiffened up internally. On all Ariel models, excluding the 248cc single, the brake drums had been entirely redesigned. In place of the former pressings, the drums were now cast in chromidium, factory sources saying that these were unusually stiff and heavily ribbed on the outside. A further feature lay in the fact that the spoke flange was an extension of the brake plate, and not formed on the rim of the drum as it had been in the past.

An optional extra was a new QD (Quickly Detachable) rear wheel. This was fitted in conjunction with a hinged rear mudguard (also a new feature), with only a single spanner being needed when rear wheel removal was required. Actually, apart from the mudguard stay nuts, the only items that had to be touched were the wheel spindle and a distance piece. The brake drum and sprocket were carried on a separate axle, this having a bearing of its own, with the wheel having two self-contained journal bearings that needed no adjustment. A flange on the hub was provided with twelve holes that fitted over twelve ⅜in (10mm) pegs by means of which the drive was conveyed. When the central spindle was removed, the wheel could be drawn off the pegs and lifted clear of the machine, the entire operation taking merely a matter of seconds.

The gearbox adjustment had been revised, not only to make the operation simpler, but also so that it could not be accidentally altered. A drawback was now fitted instead of the previous link and eccentric-cam arrangement.

Wear on the clutch operating rod had also proved a problem and this was eliminated by arranging that the points where friction took place were liberally supplied with oil, and were away from the ingress of dirt. The outer clutch plate, too, had been stiffened, this now being of cast aluminium, capable of taking the spring pressure evenly, without distortion.

## A Change in Distributor Drive in 1936

The only change of note to the 601cc overhead cam Square Four for the 1936 model year (introduced in September 1935) concerned the ignition distributor. This was no longer driven from the nearside end of the camshaft. Instead, it was relocated to the offside of the machine – mounted vertically on the Lucas Magdyno and driven by worm and skew gears. Here it was effectively protected from the risk of oil leakage from the valve gear in the cylinder head area.

## OHV Rather Than OHC

Back in 1935 Edward Turner had redesigned the engine of the Square Four, but although prototypes of 600cc and 1000cc were running in 1936, and a detailed report of the new

*1935 six-hundred Square Four, with stiffened crankcase.*

1000cc engine appeared in the press, actual sales did not begin until early 1937. The official reason, at least, was that Ariel was so overwhelmed with business that it had no time to effect the necessary tooling for the new machines. In fact, by the time the new machines appeared, Turner himself had left to join Triumph, his place at Ariel being taken by Frank Anstey.

The new 1000cc (the 600cc was virtually identical except for bore size) featured vertically split crankcases, as opposed to the horizontal assemblies of the outgoing overhead cam model. The two halves were dowelled together to ensure correct alignment and, if you ever have to split the crankcases, don't forget the two bolts holding the 'bridge' between the cylinders.

Another change was from roller to plain big-ends. When interviewed during 1939, Edward Turner was asked why. His answer: 'Because they are quieter and if properly lubricated they last longer, being less sensitive to water due to condensation, and to scrubbing. Also, because I have always liked plain bearing big-ends.'

## More Differences

Gone, too, were the geared central flywheels, the overhung cranks – and of course the overhead camshaft. Instead, there were now two conventional crankshafts forged in steel and connected by keyed-on gears outside the crankcases on the nearside (left). Central flywheels were still employed, but they were bolted on, one to the left of centre, the other to the right, so that they overlapped. The crankshaft ran in roller races on the drive-side, plain white-metal-lined bronze on the right.

*1936 six-hundred 4F/6, showing primary drive cover and rear brake pedal arrangement.*

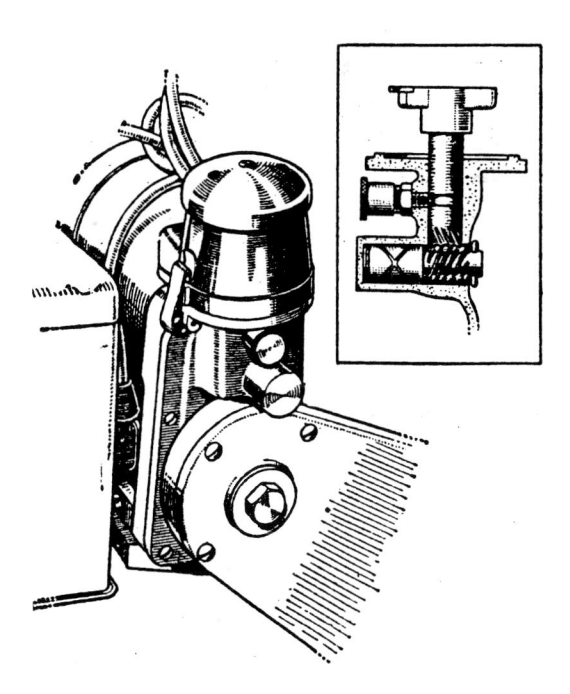

*New for 1936, the mounting of the Square Four distributor – relocated to the rear of cylinders. Inset: the skew-gear which drove the rotor.*

## Square Four

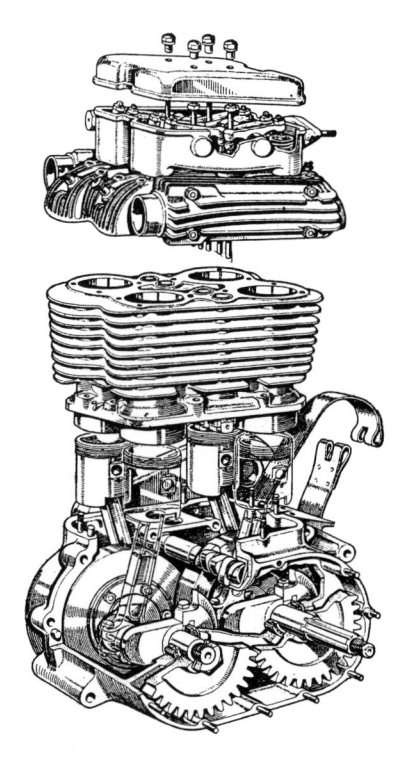

*The new-for-1937 4G 1000 Square Four. Its ohv valve gear was operated by pushrods, which were situated between the front and rear cylinders.*

### Light-Alloy Connecting Rods

Connecting rods were manufactured of Hiduminium RR56 light alloy; these forgings were heat-treated to 30-ton tensile strength, with the split white metal big ends and phosphor bronze small-end bushes. The new design had called for a total rethink on the lubrication front, so there was now a more modern high pressure system, with a double plunger pump. This circulated a pint of oil per minute at 2,500rpm and was driven from the camshaft. It was capable of maintaining a pressure of 60lb per square inch after feeding two main and four big-end bearings. Oil was pumped first to the main timing side bearings, then to the main oilway in the crankshaft, from where drilled ducts led to the inner side of the crankpins and big-end bearings. There was a bypass to the rocker shafts through which there was a pressure feed to each rocker bearing, and also to the pressure gauge.

### A Spring-Loaded Ball Relief Valve

A spring-loaded ball relief valve was located between the two plain bearings. In the body of the valve was a screw that was not intended

### 4G 1000 ohv 1937

| | | | |
|---|---|---|---|
| Engine | Air-cooled square four overhead valve, plain bearing big-ends; two crankshafts; connecting rods in RR56 alloy; iron cylinder head and barrel assemblies | Rear suspension | Unsprung, rigid frame[2] |
| | | Front brake | 7in drum, SLS |
| | | Rear brakes | 7in drum, SLS |
| | | Tyres | Front 3.25 × 19; rear 4.00 × 18 |
| Bore | 65mm | **General Specifications** | |
| Stroke | 75mm | Wheelbase | 54.5in (1,384mm) |
| Displacement | 997cc | Ground clearance | 4.75in (121mm)[3] |
| Compression ratio | 5.8:1 | Seat height | 26.5in (673mm)[4] |
| Lubrication | Dry sump, plunger pump | Fuel tank capacity | 3.9gal (18ltr) |
| Ignition | Magneto, 6-volt | Dry weight | 420lb (191kg) |
| Carburettor | Single rear-mounted Solex 26 FHDT | Maximum power | 36bhp @ 6,000rpm |
| | | Top speed | 95mph (153km/h) |
| Primary drive | Chain | | |
| Final drive | Chain | [1] Telescopic forks from 1946. | |
| Gearbox | Four-speed, Burman, foot-change | [2] Available from 1939 with plunger rear suspension option. | |
| Frame | Single front downtube; all steel construction | [3] 5in (127mm). | |
| Front suspension | Girder forks[1] | [4] 28in (711mm). | |

for adjustment, and should always be kept screwed home. Its purpose? To provide a method of removing the ball and spring for cleaning purposes. A breather pipe was located at the rear of the timing case. The oil pressure should register around 45psi under normal riding conditions.

Oil returned to the sump via the pushrod cover tubes, and was pumped back to the tank. This was yet another feature of Turner's redesign – dry sump instead of wet sump – the oil tank being located where the battery had been on the ohc Square Four, on the offside of the motorcycle above the gearbox. There was a gauze filter in the sump, within the crankcase, on the extractor side, and another filter in the oil tank on the suction side.

*A Transversely Set Camshaft*
Replacing the half-time shaft of the earlier engine there was a camshaft set transversely, this operating the overhead valves by pushrods (manufactured in dural with steel ends) in vertical tunnels cast into the cylinder block. An iron cylinder block was still used, and the head was also of cast iron with separate iron exhaust manifolds and retaining the internal x-shaped inlet manifold. However, the carburettor was now a Solex instrument, and was mounted on the rear of the aluminium rocker box casting that embodied an inlet passage interlined with the passages in the cylinder head. As before, the valves were set vertically and used dual coil springs (an inner and an outer). Commenting upon his use of pent-roof combustion chambers, Edward Turner said: 'This provides a compact and easily operable arrangement for the vertical valves.'

As to why he ditched the original overhead camshaft, Turner stated: 'With this large engine [the 1000 Square Four], the disadvantage of increased reciprocating weight is more than compensated by the high power output at moderate speeds. Also, with the camshaft in the crankcase it is possible to drive both camshaft and Magdyno with a single Weller-tensioned chain.' It is worth noting that the oil pump was driven by a peg engaging with a hole in the camshaft drive sprocket.

*The Geared Cranks*
Another interesting aspect of the 'new' Square Four concerned the gears that connected the two crankshafts. When questioned by an interviewer shortly before the outbreak of war in 1939 as to why he had used special gears, Turner's answer was: 'Yes, in conjunction with the gear manufacturers we decided on a 20-degree pressure angle, and a long addendum tooth (a tooth form having the greatest height above the pitch centre). This form compensates for variations between centres due to expansion, with the least possible amount of backlash.'

When asked if helical teeth would not have been an advantage, he replied: 'Only if the teeth were ground, and it is not so easy to grind helical teeth as straight teeth.' Finally, Turner revealed that the material used was: 'A 0.2 per cent carbon steel, because it can be treated so as to produce a very hard surface. The profiles of the teeth, of course, are ground.'

*Fibre Discs*
Fibre discs were pressed into the inside of the gears and riveted in position to prevent ring, and the gears were pressed onto their shafts and located by woodruff keys. Extractor threads were provided on these gears and, indeed, on all parts that might have to be withdrawn for overhaul.

## A 100mph Potential

The new one-litre engine – actually 997cc (65 × 75mm) – produced 38bhp at 5,500rpm and had a top gear performance that spanned 10–100mph (16–160km/h). With this redesign, the Square Four adopted Ariel's innovative clutch of the Burman gearbox being 'dry' outside the oil bath primary chain casing and instantly accessible by the removal of a bolt-on cover. The six-hundred version

## Square Four

*A feature of the pushrod Square Four model was the use of a rear-mounted carburettor (a Solex 26 FHDT) on his 1938 4G 1000; compare the ohc model's frontal location.*

was essentially a one-thousand model with the bore size reduced to 50.4mm, giving a displacement of 599cc. The 600/4F cost £84 when it went on sale, compared to £90 for its bigger brother, the 1000/4G. The smaller Four weighed in at 399lb (181kg) against 421lb (191kg) for the one-thousand. This demonstrates the falsity of the often perceived belief that, with the advent of the pushrod engine, the Square Four became overweight.

### Foot-Change as Standard

A four-speed, foot-controlled Burman gearbox was now standard fitment and this, together with the engine and clutch, was

52

# Square Four

*The ohv six-hundred 4F Square Four. Offered between 1938 and 1940, it was practically identical to the 1000 4G, but for its 599cc smaller 50.4mm bore size; the stroke remained unchanged at 75mm. Note unvalanced mudguards.*

carried in a frame similar, but not identical to the outgoing ohc six-hundred model; both shared a single front downtube that became a cradle underneath the crankcases. There was also a new design of Lucas Magdyno, with the oil for the dry sump lubrication system in the triangle area of the rigid frame on the offside, the battery having been relocated to a matching position on the nearside. The toolbox in the final section of the rear triangle had been modified to exclude the ingress of mud and water and also featured an improved method of fixing.

A 4gal (18ltr) tank was provided for the 600 and 1000 Square Fours, whilst the rear tyre of the larger model was 4.00 × 18 against 3¼ × 19 of the six-hundred. Both models shared the distinctive Ariel 'Red Hunter' claret finish (including chromed/painted fuel tank), although black and chrome were available as an option.

## The Brooklands Test

Ariel advertised the new 1000/4G as being 'capable of 10–100mph in top gear'. To prove this claim, an official test took place at Brooklands in 1937. In very wet and windy conditions, and watched by Edward Turner himself, F W S (Freddie) Clarke reeled off lap after lap of the Surrey speed bowl at between 99 and 100mph. This performance went a long way to silence the doubters. Also, one has to realize that Turner's design was not intended as a sports bike. As he put it: 'The main idea was to provide a four-cylinder engine small enough for use in a solo motorcycle, yet producing ample power for really high performance without unduly high compression, racing cams, or a big-choke carburettor. In fact, I was aiming at the ultimate reliability with the minimum of attention.'

In a road test published by *The Motor Cycle* in August 1938, the performance, smoothness and fuel economy were all strongly praised. In fact, the tester 'tried hard to find some point to criticize, but if I am honest I cannot'. He ended by saying: 'This 1,000 miles will live long in my memory. I have never enjoyed motorcycling more.'

## Torrens' Marathon Journey

Another article, again published in *The Motor Cycle* by Torrens (Arthur Bourne) was about a 3,000-mile (4,827km) journey, that included a long trip across Europe to Bavaria, carried out over a two-week period with one of the first 1000/4Gs built in the autumn of 1936. Much of the purpose was to cover the ISDT (International Six Days' Trial). Torrens was full of enthusiasm for the new 1000 Square Four.

*One of the new 997cc (65 × 75mm) 1000 4G models in the United States of America circa 1940, with pillion passenger and leather side bags.*

The following extracts give a view of how he saw the newcomer:

> The machine is a top-gear mount. Up hill, down dale, through villages, you can stay in top gear. I have trickled the machine up a 1-in-7 hill in top gear without even a suspicion of snatch. The other end of the scale I cannot speak about. At 86mph on an upgrade on the Munich autobahn the machine was still accelerating, although I was sitting bolt upright. At 80mph the engine was running without effort – just a dynamo-like smoothness.

He continued by saying:

> Where one scores so decisively is in the fact that the engine is always working well within its capabilities, in the thrilling, flashing acceleration, and in the way the machine gobbles up hills. Not only are there these assets, but there is real silence and, therefore, one has performance which can be used.

However, one very definite point of criticism (although as this was one of the very first of the new models produced and, as such was virtually a pre-production bike) centred around the foot-change Burman gearbox:

> Were the machine not so much a top-gear mount, one might criticize the gear-change. Care and time are required if one is to make a completely silent upward change. The clutch, which frees perfectly under all conditions, seems to keep on spinning and, therefore, one is liable just to crash the change slightly. No harm can, of course, result, but care is needed if on upward changes the gears are to slide into mesh noiselessly.

Other tests of the era mentioned 'efficient mudguarding', 'an oil-tight engine' and the 'excellent' forward-mounted prop (side) stand – this latter item being located on the offside of the machine.

Slow sales saw Ariel drop the 600 model for the 1938 season, whilst the 4G 1000 carried on unchanged. But when the 1939 range was announced at the beginning of September 1938, there were seen to be no fewer than three Square Four machines. The existing 1000 was retained, and supplemented by another machine of the same displacement with a rather less luxurious specification. In addition to these two, the '600' was reintroduced, in, said Ariel, 'greatly improved form'. The prices were: 4G 1000 de Luxe £89 10s; 4H 1000 Standard £83 10s; 4F 600 £79 10s.

## A Spring Frame

Undoubtedly, the introduction of the Frank Anstey-designed spring frame was the outstanding news. This was to be made available on all the 1939 models in the Ariel range with the exception of the two-fifties, at an additional charge of £10. Although Anstey said that his keynote was 'simplicity', its action was unusual. The seat and chain stays terminated in a massive lug that formed the housing for the main and rebound springs. Running down the central axis of this housing was a substantial rod, enclosed by a tube. The nuts that secured the rod at the top and bottom clamped this hardened guide tube and a collar near its lower end formed the abutment for the upper and lower springs. Anchored to the chain stays by means of short links were stirrups – there being one stirrup and one spring housing on each side of the frame – which carried the spring abutment and the rear wheel spindle. A road shock caused the rear wheel to rise and carry with it the stirrups and spring abutments, thus compressing the upper springs. As the wheel returned to the normal position the stirrup fell, and the smaller or lower springs checked the rebound.

Because the spring abutments and their vertical sleeves moved in a vertical plane, were the wheel spindle to move in a like manner, the chain tension would have been continually

*1938 997cc Model 4G, nearside view of engine.*

varying. Thus, the short links by which the stirrups were attached to the chain stays were designed to obviate this. So, as the sleeves and springs moved upwards in a straight line, the links moved rearwards. The wheel spindle, since it was mounted at the rear of the stirrups, which were pivoted, could not move in a straight line, but was compelled to follow an arc – and because the pivotal point of the stirrups was continually altering, owing to the straight-line movement of the springs, the wheel spindle followed a wide arc instead of a narrow one. This arc corresponded with that described between the gearbox sprocket centre and the rear wheel centre; consequently, the chain tension did not vary.

## Auxiliary Front Fork Springs

Another change common to all 1939 model Ariels, except the two-fifties, was the fitting of auxiliary damping springs to the front forks. Another innovation was a tapered handlebar. In the middle, where the bar was held in the Ariel rubber mounting, the diameter was 1in (25mm) and from this point it tapered to ⅞in (23mm) at the ends. All models now sported

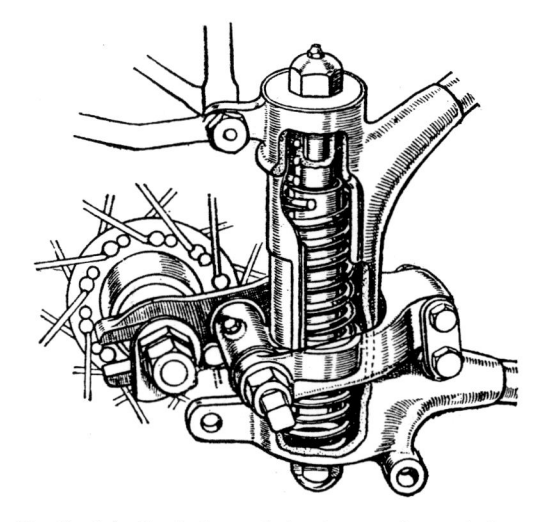

*Details of the Frank Anstey-designed sprung frame, which made its debut for the 1939 model year. However, it remained a cost option for many years.*

a new pattern rear number plate, smaller than before, with a streamlined rear lamp on a rubber mounting let into the top. All the four-cylinder models (plus the 500cc singles) also had modified saddle positions, the seats having been mounted an inch further back than previously.

| 4F 600 ohv 1939 | | | |
|---|---|---|---|
| Engine | Air-cooled square four overhead valve, plain bearing big-ends; two crankshafts; connecting rods in RR56 alloy; iron cylinder head and barrel assemblies | Frame | Single front downtube; all steel construction |
| | | Front suspension | Girder forks |
| | | Rear suspension | Unsprung, rigid frame |
| | | Front brake | 7in drum, SLS |
| Bore | 50.4mm | Rear brakes | 7in drum, SLS |
| Stroke | 75mm | Tyres | Front 3.00 × 19; rear 3.25 × 19 |
| Displacement | 599cc | | |
| Compression ratio | 6.9:1 | **General Specifications** | |
| Lubrication | Dry sump, plunger pump | Wheelbase | 54.5in (1,384mm) |
| Ignition | Magneto, 6-volt | Ground clearance | 4.75in (121mm) |
| Carburettor | Single rear-mounted Solex 26 FHDT | Seat height | 26.5in (673mm) |
| | | Fuel tank capacity | 3.25gal (14.7l) |
| Primary drive | Chain | Dry weight | 420lb (189kg) |
| Final drive | Chain | Maximum power | 23bhp @ 5,600rpm |
| Gearbox | Four-speed, Burman, foot-change | Top speed | 73mph (118km/h) |

## Square Four

The differences between the existing 1000 4G de luxe and the 1000 4H Standard/4F 600 were:

- unvalanced mudguards
- 3.25gal (14.8l) fuel tank
- saddle with no backrest
- black-enamelled rims fitted to non-detachable wheels
- cylindrical silencers
- no prop stand.

After the outbreak of the Second World War at the beginning of September 1939, Ariel, like many other major British motorcycle manufacturers, continued to sell motorcycles to the civilian population for the first few months. Ariel's 1940 range was announced in the press at the beginning of November 1939. All three Square Fours were continued to be listed, although the prices had increased as follows: 4G 1000 de luxe £96 10s (from £89 10s); 4H 1000 Standard £90 10s (from £83 10s); 4F 600 £86 10s (from £79 10s). The spring frame was still a £10 option on all three versions.

### Early Post-War Days

As mentioned in Chapter 4, the Square Four was not produced for the military forces, although some were used by other government services during the war, so it was not until the summer of 1945 that Ariel resumed peacetime production.

As *Motor Cycling* reported in its 26 July 1945 issue:

> The fact that the concern is still engaged in the manufacture of WD [War Department] machines limits the amount of plant available for civilian production; for this reason the successful 'constant chain tension' Ariel patent spring heel [the Anstey-designed plunger rear suspension already described] is not immediately available, although at a later date it will be fitted to any model in the range as an optional extra at time of ordering. For the same reason, a new hydraulically damped telescopic spring fork, although fully developed, must be held in abeyance until later in the season, when it will be optional on all models at slightly increased price.

*Brochure illustration showing the immediate pre-war Square Four models, the 1000 4G costing £90, the 600 4F £84.*

*Square Four*

## The New Telescopic Front Fork

The new telescopic front fork *(see* separate boxed section within this chapter for a full technical description) was to be fitted first to Ariel's range-topper, the 1000 4G de luxe (the other two Square Fours were not offered post-war). Briefly, these new forks were fitted with low-rate springs and featured hydraulic absorption. There was a progressive cut-off in both directions, shock and rebound, with at extreme deflections a cushion of trapped oil. The total travel was 6in (153mm), which could be divided, in the case of a solo machine, into roughly 3in (76mm) movement in each direction. The same springs were used for both solo and sidecar work. These new forks, together with the patented Anstey link plunger rear suspension, put Ariel right at the forefront of motorcycle development to compete on both home and world markets as the long years of conflict gave way to the open fields and sunshine of peace.

*January 1947 advertisement for the 1000 4G, little changed from its pre-war days except for the fitting of the new Page-designed telescopic front forks.*

## Telescopic Forks

During the Second World War, Val Page had spent a considerable part of his time working on two projects – the new ohv vertical twin-cylinder motorcycle and an equally new set of hydraulically operated telescopic front forks. Full details of these were released by the press in mid-1946, but in reality they had been under design, development and testing for a considerable time before. In fact, *The Motor Cycle*'s 'Torrens' (Arthur Bourne) had himself tested them some two years earlier, in 1944.

Compared to Ariel's existing girder-type forks, which gave a total deflection, up and down, of approximately $3^{3}/_{4}$in (95mm) there was a full $6^{1}/_{4}$in (159mm) of movement.

Manganese-carbon steel of 40–45 tons/sq in tensile strength was employed for the main fork tubes (stanchions). These were $1^{3}/_{8}$in (86mm) diameter at the lower clip and tapered in both directions, up and down to $1^{1}/_{4}$in (32mm), with a parallel lower portion.

White-metal-coated steel bushes, each with three circumferential oil grooves, formed the bearing for the sliders (bottom legs). To prevent oil leakage, oil seals with the main body of synthetic rubber, lipped and spring-loaded, acted on the main tube in each leg.

General construction of the forks was as follows: the steering column was pressed into the bottom yoke and secured by a taper pin, which, incidentally, locked the steering damper – the latter mainly provided for sidecar work. The main tubes (stanchions) were clamped in the yoke by socket screws after being pulled up to the top yoke by means of the conventional hexagon plugs. Thus the top shoulder on the steering column, which carried the upper yoke, positioned the whole fork.

An interesting feature was the arrangement of the steering head adjustment. Immediately above the top head race was a flanged cover washer (dust excluder) and then came a spring washer of domed formation. This latter component provided pre-loading of the bearing and, Page discovered during his test programme, was found to obviate the need for adjusting the steering head bearings in the conventional manner.

The instructions for steering head adjustment were simple in the extreme – simply rotate the adjusting nut until it was in contact with the spring washer and then give it one turn only. This, Page stated, placed a load of some 100lb on the bearing, instead of the 10 tons which an amateur mechanic could apply when adjusting their steering head bearings! The adjustment, in view of the aforementioned shoulder, was of course independent of the forks.

Oil provided the damping medium and the Ariel fork provided a progressive cut-off, giving a comfortable, but fully controllable, performance.

The new forks were fitted to the 4G 1000 Square Four and the VH 500 and NH Red Hunter singles from June 1946 onwards. Later, they became a standard fitment across the range, including the VB 600 side-valve singles and in due course the 500 and 650 ohv twins.

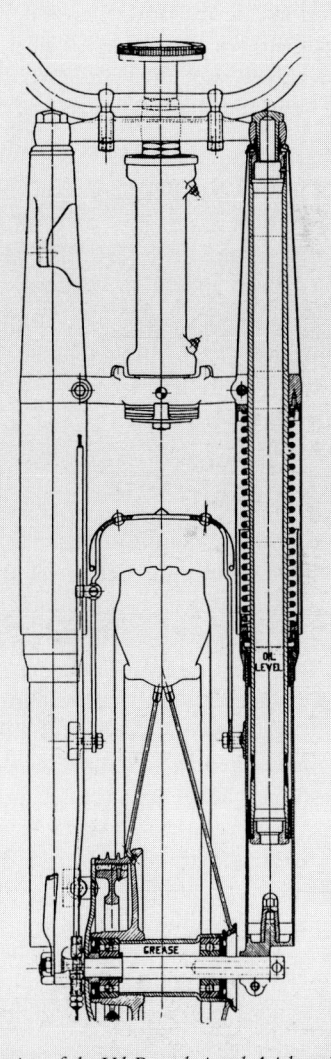

*Factory drawing of the Val Page-designed Ariel-made front fork assembly. These had a movement of $6^{1}/_{4}$ (159 mm) and were widely acclaimed by press and public alike when they became available in 1946.*

## The 1947 Programme

When *The Motor Cycle* carried news of the 1947 Ariel programme in its 29 August 1946 issue, it said:

> In order to maintain output as high as possible, and thus enable the maximum number of potential owners to get on the road, Ariels are unlikely to include any new models in their 1947 programme. However, telescopic forks, described in *The Motor Cycle* of 27 June, are now fitted as standard on all models, and the famous Ariel spring frame is shortly to be available in limited numbers.

Six models were now listed in the Ariel range, of which the 4G 1000 Square Four was the largest. Next there was a pair of Red Hunter sporting ohv singles (the VH 500 and NH 350); the VG (500) and NG (350) ohv de luxe singles and the VB 600 side-valve single – the latter mainly intended for sidecar work. The spring frame option cost £15 4s 9d (including UK purchase tax).

## Detail Changes in 1948

The 1948 range (announced in early September 1947) brought details of the new 500 Twin (*see* Chapter 8), otherwise the existing range was continued. For 1948 all models were to be fitted with a Smith's chronometric-type speedometer in place of the grip-governor type – but otherwise the Square Four remained unchanged from the previous year.

In July 1948 *The Motor Cycle* tested the latest 4G Square Four equipped with telescopic forks and the optional plunger rear suspension. The tester made much of the model's low-speed abilities saying:

> It is frequently suggested that for town work small low-powered machines have advantages over larger machines. As a generalization that statement may be true, but there is no denying that the Ariel Square Four has many characteristics that make it a most attractive mount in traffic and under all low-speed conditions.

He went on to list these advantages:

> In the first place, the manoeuvrability and general handling at walking speeds are first rate, and the rider is unaware of the machine's bulk. Secondly, the engine responds to the opening of the throttle in a most zestful manner, so that full advantage can be taken of the opportunities for accelerating past slower traffic. Thirdly, the performance in the indirect gears, or in top, can be used to the full, with a minimum of noise from engine, transmission and exhaust. Fourthly, the excellent telescopic fork, in conjunction with the spring frame, 4in section rear tyre and large saddle, give luxurious comfort over the worst of town roads. Finally, the brakes require a minimum of physical effort to stop the machine quickly enough for any reasonable emergency.

With its big reserve of power, the tester also found that: 'the Square Four is an attractive proposition for two-up riding'. In fact, a pillion seat and footrests were fitted to the test bike. He continued: 'The addition of a 10-stone passenger in no way impairs the excellent handling of the machine and makes a hardly perceptible difference to the performance.' The riding position, starting (hot or cold), speedometer accuracy and engine that 'remained free from oil leaks' all came in for praise.

However, criticism was levelled at the nearside exhaust pipe, which 'limits the downward movement of the rear brake pedal, and to operate the pedal it was necessary to remove the foot from the rest'. Another shortcoming was 'with the standard sparking plugs fitted, consistent riding at 75mph or above caused pre-ignition'. The tester also noted: 'A certain amount of piston slap was noticeable with the engine cold, one piston in particular being more noisy than the remaining three; the crankshaft gears and overhead valve rockers were also audible.' In fact, he went as far as commenting: 'The engine was not so quiet mechanically as expected and was thought to be below the general production standard in this respect.'

Another comment concerned the gear-change quality: 'During the first few hundred miles of the test all upward gear changes were harsh and accompanied by clashing, but towards the end of the test the change improved markedly till smooth, quiet changes were readily achieved.'

As a pointer to the situation regarding the British market at the time, the test ended with the following statement: 'In all-round performance the Ariel Square Four is an outstanding machine. A high proportion of the output goes overseas [in fact, no spring-frame models were actually available on the home market] and in world markets it is a worthy representative of advanced British motorcycle design.' The UK price (including purchase tax) was £228 – if, of course, you could have actually bought an example. Even then this did not include the spring frame or speedometer, which were additional charges.

## Another Redesign

For the 1949 model year Ariel introduced what was officially known as the 4G Mark I.

The main changes concerned an alloy top end to replace the old cast-iron components and a switch from magneto to coil ignition. Much of the bottom half of the engine remained the same as before. The differences are explained here, but the majority of the cycle parts were unchanged.

One journalist of the day called the new aluminium alloy cylinder head: 'a masterpiece of foundry work'. This featured rocker boxes and inlet and exhaust passages in a single clean casting. The exhaust ports were finned both horizontally and vertically, and the cylinder head was narrower than the outgoing cast-iron assembly. Nickel-chrome steel was employed for the valve seats – these having the same expansion rate of the alloy head itself; they were a press fit. The spark plug inserts were of bronze, screwed and pegged into position. The rocker boxes were now integral with the head so that a superior transfer of heat from the head to the box could be achieved.

The cylinder block was now also of aluminium alloy, but remained a one-piece

### 4G Mark I 1000 ohv 1949

| | | | |
|---|---|---|---|
| Engine | Air-cooled Square Four overhead valve, plain bearing big-ends; two crankshafts; connecting rods in RR56 alloy; aluminium cylinder head and barrel assemblies connected by gears | Front suspension | Telescopic fork |
| | | Rear suspension | Rigid or plunger at extra cost[1] |
| | | Front brake | 7in drum, SLS |
| | | Rear brakes | 7in drum, SLS[2] |
| | | Tyres | Front 3.25 × 26; rear 4.00 × 18 |
| Bore | 65mm | **General Specifications** | |
| Stroke | 75mm | Wheelbase | 56in (1,422mm) |
| Displacement | 997cc | Ground clearance | 5in (127mm) |
| Compression ratio | 6:1 | Seat height | 28in (711mm)[3] |
| Lubrication | Dry sump, plunger pump | Fuel tank capacity | 3.5gal (16ltr)[4] |
| Ignition | Coil, with car-type four-cyl contact breaker and distributor | Dry weight | 412lb (187kg) |
| | | Maximum power | 34.5 |
| Carburettor | Single rear-mounted Solex 26 AHD | Top speed | 97mph (156km/h) |
| Primary drive | Chain | [1] 434lb (197kg) with suspension. | |
| Final drive | Chain | [2] 8in (203mm) 1951 onwards. | |
| Gearbox | Four-speed, Burman, foot-change | [3] 1950 onwards 29in (737mm). | |
| Frame | Single front downtube; all steel construction | [4] 1951 3.75gal (17ltr); 1952 4gal (18ltr). | |

assembly. Into this, four cast-iron liners were press-fitted. Unlike the old cast-iron block, the pushrod tunnels were cast in as two slots and the head gaskets no longer had special inserts for the pushrod tubes, just a row of four holes for the rods themselves.

The tappet blocks were a push-fit into the cylinder block and the tappets were manufactured in two sections with a spring between them to keep all the valve gear in contact at all times. As soon as the cam came off the base circle the two parts touched and worked as one.

*A Cleaner Appearance*
The new all-alloy engine was now much cleaner, with the cylinder head and barrel helping greatly in this regard. Unlike the old iron-engined bike, there were now no kinks present in the exhaust system. Aluminium alloy is, of course, a good conductor of heat, but beyond this fact, cooling had been particularly studied. There was a scoop that directed air upward amongst the fins of the barrel block and head, and improved air passages had been provided to lead air to the rear cylinders. Unobstructed finning was used, so that air could reach the roots of the fins. Since the rocker boxes were now integral with the head there was a superior transfer of heat from the head to the box, and the entire area was kept cooler.

*A Modified Crankcase*
The crankcase was changed so that the oil filter was centrally located in the base of the sump, whilst the timing chain tensioner was uprated to prevent it stretching out flat under stress reversal. From its position in the timing cover, the pressure relief valve had been transferred to the end of the front crankshaft, and was accessible from the outside of the engine. An advantage was that the valve acted at a predetermined pressure inside the crankshaft itself and not in the general lubrication system. And, for the first time, the pressure shown on the oil gauge was now the actual pressure at the big-ends.

A two-cam engine shaft shock absorber was now employed operating on a splined sleeve, which was in turn splined to the crankshaft, thus providing not only an efficient operation but a larger angle of movement compared with the three-cam type previously fitted.

The components such as the big-end shells, connecting rods, little-ends, pistons and

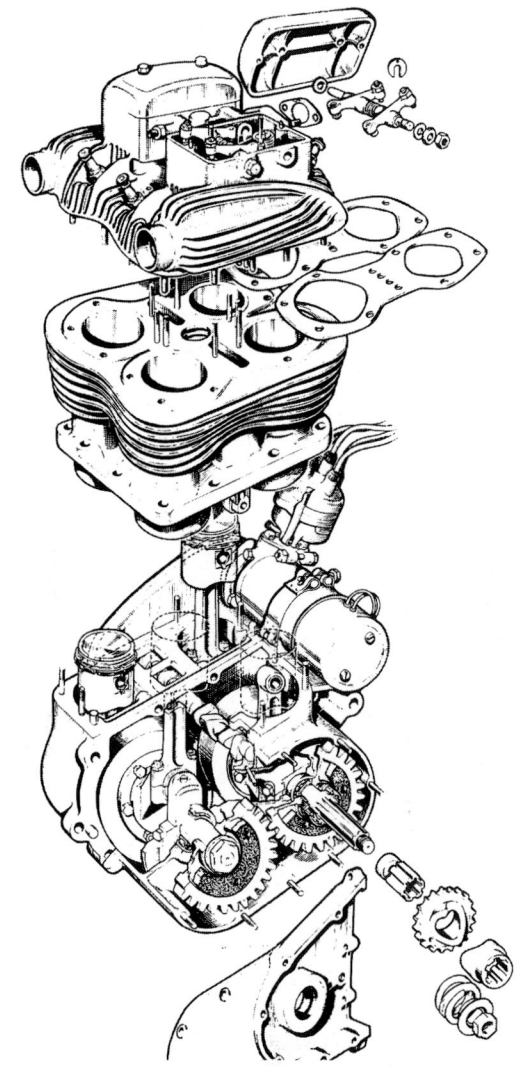

*For the 1949 model year Ariel introduced the 4G Mark I. The main changes concerned an alloy top end to replace the old cast-iron components and a switch from magneto to coil ignition.*

gudgeon pins were as before. The same applied to the main bearings – the front crankshaft having a single roller bearing on the drive-side and a white-metal lined bronze bush on the timing side. Two roller bearings, one of which was an outrigger, were used on the driving side of the rear crankshaft, that also had a white-metal lined bush on its timing side, and both crankshafts were operated by gears.

The lubrication of these coupling gears was improved, by providing a trough on inside of the crankcase that caught oil flung off the big-ends and one of the pushrod tunnels. From this trough, a pipe took the oil directly to the teeth of the coupling gears at their point of engagement. A self-adjusting synthetic rubber oil seal between the rear crankshaft's outrigger roller race prevented oil from passing through into the primary chaincase.

*Fixing Points*
No fewer than twenty fixing points were used for the attachment of the cylinder head to the cylinder block. In no case was a bolt screwed directly in the aluminium; instead, studs and nuts were used. Twelve head studs were employed with their nuts bearing against the cylinder block; the remaining eight were block studs and had nuts bearing against the cylinder head. In plain view, the twelve formed a circle outside that was formed by the eight others. For accessibility, one of the nuts was of the sleeve type. There was a copper asbestos sealing gasket between the head and barrel assemblies.

*Rocker Box Covers*
Each secured by two sleeve nuts, the two separate rocker box covers were small, but were well-ribbed for increased strength. A separate spindle was used for each rocker, and positive lubrication was provided as part of the overall lubrication system. Rocker box wells now sloped towards the centre so that there was no tendency for oil to pass down the bronze valve guides (instead of down the pushrod tunnel and thence, possibly, find the way into the region of the sparking plugs).

*Valve Details*
In place of the former loose hardened caps fitted to the ends of all valves in the outgoing 'iron' engine, the ends of the inlet valves were now case-hardened and the exhaust valves were Stellite-tipped in the interest of preventing wear.

*Ignition by Coil*
In place of the previous model's magneto, the 1949 4G Mark I Square Four's ignition was by coil through a car-type distributor driven at half engine speed by a substantial skew-gear from the dynamo shaft. The distributor incorporated automatic advance and retard, whilst the coil was mounted on the rear mudguard under the sprung saddle. Warning light, ammeter and ignition switch were all located in the headlamp shell. Dynamo output was 72 watts. This provided ample current for the 36-watt headlamp bulb, the coil, accessories and battery charging for the 6-volt system.

*4G Mark I distributor for the coil ignition system.*

## Square Four

*Flange-Mounted Dynamo*

A three-point fixing was employed for the flange-mounted dynamo, which featured a steady-cradle and metal strap towards its rear section. Any slight alteration in timing that might be required was carried out by loosening a pinch-bolt and rotating the body of the distributor. In order to prevent the ingress of water a rubber sleeve totally covered the top of the distributor and, until they were protected by the rear of the fuel tank, the spark plug (HT) cables as well. Moving the dynamo from its former position, when used with the magneto, allowed for freer circulation of cooling air and there was more space to dismantle, if required, the float chamber of the Solex carburettor.

*A More Upright Front Tank*

In line with other 1949 Ariel models, the use of a more upright front fork had increased the steering lock by a total of 15 degrees, whilst there were now slightly larger clearances between the fork legs and front mudguard. With all these significant changes the other good news was that the price of £228 including UK purchase tax remained unchanged. However, the spring frame was still a cost option.

## The 100-Hour Test

With the arrival of the Mark I, with its aluminium cylinder head and barrel, Ariel conducted a 100-hour test in its Research and Development department in early March 1949. The official factory press release read: 'To ascertain the effect of sustained high speed at power upon all parts, especially bearing surfaces, and to test the ability of the engine to maintain its power for long periods without overheating, we have devised a unique 100-hour test.'

In the 10 March 1949 issue *The Motor Cycle* reported the event:

> Last Friday one of the new 997cc Ariel Square Four engines began a 100-hour bench test. It is planned to run the engine about 10 hours each day. Friday's period of the test was carried out at a running-in speed, after which there are to be 80 hours at 4,000rpm with three-quarters of the maximum torque load. Then there will be a final 10-hour spurt at 5,000rpm and full torque load.

A couple of weeks later Ariel Motors issued a detailed report on the completion of the 100-hour bench test. The resultant figures were unofficial, because the test was carried out by the works rather than the ACU. For the first 10 hours, engine speeds varied between 1,000 and 3,000rpm. This, Ariel stated, would have given an average speed of 36mph and a distance of 360 miles, assuming the engine had been in a frame and the high solo (4.3:1) top gear had been employed. After this initial bedding-in period, the valve clearances were checked, also the tightness of the nuts. Then followed 80 hours, in 10-hour sessions of three-quarter throttle and 4,000rpm equal to 5,730 miles at 71.6mph. Finally, there were ten hours at full throttle and 5,000rpm resulting in, it was stated, the equivalent of 90mph.

All-in-all, this was something of a coup for Ariel, with *The Motor Cycle* commenting: 'Possibly this test will spur other manufacturers to undertake similar projects'.

## Testing the Alloy-Engined Model

In its 26 May 1949 issue, *Motor Cycling* carried out an exhaustive test of the new alloy-engined Square Four. Its headline read: 'Britain's only Production Four-cylinder Motorcycle is Put through its Paces; Acceleration which gives 0 to 92mph in under half-a-minute!' The test began: 'Lighter by no fewer than 32lb than its predecessor with cast-iron cylinder block and head and perhaps just a little more of a "good looker", the new "Squariel" combines the docility of a side-valve with the out-and-out performance that can be equalled by very few vehicles, whether two-or four-wheeled.'

Comfort, handling, performance and engine torque were highly praised. Braking also received favourable comment: 'For normal purposes the rear brake could be ignored and all braking done was that at the front. This was probably the most effective single-drum brake that the tester has so far encountered and really firm application would lock the front wheel.' Starting was, especially when hot, 'almost ridiculously easy'. Whilst performance in top between 20–80mph (32–129km/h) 'was literally breathtaking', the tester went on to say, 'In no part was any hesitation apparent and the hand of the speedometer appeared to be directly connected to the twist-grip.'

However, it was found that fuel consumption was 'more than usually sensitive to throttle openings, and too much use of the vivid acceleration available was naturally detrimental to economy'. Overall, *Motor Cycle* recorded averages of 39mpg (7.3/100km) in town and 52mpg (5.4/100km) in the country.

At the conclusion of the test, the tester noted: 'Several small points cropped up which perhaps could be borne in mind for future consideration.' These included: 'The riding position was not as fully adjustable as one could wish, the saddle was on the low side and this, in conjunction with the wide tank, made the tester's legs ache after 50 or 60 miles on the road', and, 'at continued high speed the near-upright position tends to induce fatigue'.

Once again, engine noise was commented on: 'Although at normal speeds the valve gear was difficult to hear above the wind and the swish of the tyres, the sound of its operation

*This beautiful 4G Mark I and single seat sidecar was photographed by the author at the VMCC Founders Day, Stanford Hall, 27 July 2002. Note security lock on front wheel!*

was present as a continual subdued chatter', whilst 'Vibration was mainly confined between 45 and 50mph and could be felt on the over-run down through the engine rev range.' Another complaint was that 'when pulling the Ariel from the prop stand, the weight was very apparent, and a stand that keeps the machine in a more vertical position would help'.

However, the *Motor Cycling* test ended by saying: 'These are small points and do not detract in any way from the excellence of the machine as a whole; it is, indeed, the outstanding specification and performance that makes them apparent. The 'Square Four' always has had, and always will have, a character entirely of its own, and modifications and improvements are rather in the nature of 'gilding the lily'.

## 1950 Changes

A number of detail changes arrived for the 1950 model year. These are listed below:

- the speedometer was transferred from the top of the fuel tank to a steel pressing bridging the top of the fork legs. In turn, switches, ammeter and so on were transferred from the headlamp shell to the tank top
- ease of tank removal had not been forgotten, hence the leads to the light switch were fitted with snap connections, where they were accessible near the seat lug
- the rear wheel was now quickly detachable
- the edges of the cooling fins for the engine were polished
- the seat height was raised by 1in (25mm) to 29in (737mm)
- a new type of prop stand was fitted to the base of the frame cradle tube, replacing the original stand that hinged from a point at the bottom of the front downtube. The new stand was of the spring-up type and was now on the offside (left) of the motorcycle
- a modified rear brake pedal which had been moved from the inside of the exhaust pipe to the outside, and the position of its pivot raised so that the pedal could no longer foul the exhaust pipe
- tubular mudguard stays
- new Lucas 7½in (190mm) pre-focused headlamp with domed glass.

The price had risen to £246 7s 8d including UK taxes.

## More Modifications in 1951

When the 1951 range was announced in September 1950, a certain number of modifications common to all Ariel models had been introduced 'to improve appearance and ease maintenance tasks.'

Several of these concerned the fuel tank. A new die-cast alloy top fork bracket was not only the home for the speedometer, but also formed an attractive fork-top facia and, as the ammeter had been transferred to the headlamp, the tank was now devoid of an instrument panel. This enabled the filter cap to be moved to the centre and gave an additional 0.25gal (0.1ltr) capacity. To ensure that a petrol pump nozzle did not foul the centre tunnel of the fork, two cutaways permitted easy entrance and non-splash filling. The oil pressure switch was now mounted in a small circular tank inset.

Another 1951 model change was to the rear mudguard stay arrangements, which were far neater than the ones they replaced. A single tube, bent at 90 degrees with an integral plug at the apex of the bend, replaced the three separate stays used previously. A lifting handle, also of tubular construction, was attached to the stay at one end and bolted to the mudguard at the other.

### Rear Wheel Removal

Rear wheel removal was facilitated by the manner in which the mudguard pivoted forward from a bridge, attached to the seat stays beneath the saddle, and by the way in which the stays were slotted to receive the set screws at their point of attachment.

A wide, chrome-plated metal strap secured by a couple of punch bolts replaced the narrow, hinged fitting that previously located the battery, whilst the front number plate was now of aluminium and held in a light-alloy casting with concealed fittings. Increased saddle comfort had been achieved by the use of chrome-plated barrel springs that replaced the original parallel coil assemblies. To reduce engine noise, an improved design of piston was fitted which was claimed to reduce slap. A shorter foot-change pedal improved the gear change.

*A Larger Rear Brake*
A notable change saw the 7in (178mm) rear brake replaced by an 8in (203mm) assembly with a die-cast alloy back plate, a change that did not affect the quickly detachable operation, which remained standard equipment on this model.

With the disappearance of the tank instrument panel and its involved wiring, the ignition switch was relocated adjacent to the Solex starting control, under the saddle. Also new was the larger 20amp hour battery fitted to a carrier on the nearside (left) of the machine, beneath and slightly to the rear of the saddle. The price remained unchanged – and the spring frame continued to be a cost option at an additional £19 1s.

## The 4G Mark II

'New 100mph Square Four', shouted the headline in the 6 November 1952 edition of *The Motor Cycle*. The model, designated 4G Mark II, was a new addition to the Ariel range, costing £287 10s – compared to the 4G Mark I, which continued (to remove existing stocks!) at £281 2s 3d. Ariel claimed that the new model benefited from cooler running thanks to the redesigning of the cylinder head, improved performance and fuel economy.

*Four-Pipe Exhaust*
On the Mark II, there were four, instead of two, exhaust header pipes. Previously, the

*A 1952 4G Mark I two-pipe alloy engine showing details such as exhaust header pipe, spark plug location, extended primary cover, battery, single seat and ignition coil.*

exhaust manifold and the complete induction tract were cast integrally with the light-alloy cylinder head. The new cylinder head casting had two separate, bolted-on exhaust manifolds, each of which embodied two exhaust ports. The distributory section of the induction system was cast integrally with the head and was of cruciform design. That is to say, in plain view it was x-shaped; a short, vertical tunnel leading to the middle of the x. A straight induction manifold was bolted on to the summit of the head casting. Therefore, the incoming charge flowed horizontally at first, then vertically, whereafter it encountered the middle of the x and was distributed into each of the four tracts leading to the combustion chambers.

The advantage of this system was that, since the inlet temperature was lowered, a greater weight of charge was provided. Bore diameter

*Square Four*

*A 1952 Ariel advertisement showing an 1898 Ariel tricycle and the latest alloy-engined 4G Mark I Square Four – billed as 'The world's most powerful motorcycle'.*

*October 1953 advertisement proclaiming the arrival of the new four-pipe Mk II.*

# Square Four

of the induction choke had been increased from ⅞in (22mm) to 1in (25mm), and that of the distributory inlet tract from ¾in (19mm) to ⅞in (22mm).

## A Separate Exhaust Pipe for Each Port

A separate 1¼in (32mm) diameter exhaust pipe was provided for each port, with the pipes running in pairs to merge into a single 1½in (38mm) diameter at each side of the motorcycle. Ariel claimed that exhaust interference of one cylinder with another was eliminated by this method.

The valve rocker spindles were carried on four separate steel blocks bolted to the cylinder head; these were pressure-fed with oil. Two cast aluminium rocker box covers were fitted.

## A Gear-Type Oil Pump

The Ariel design team had modified the crankcase to accept a gear-type oil pump. This was of the same capacity as the original plunger-type, but provided a steady flow of lubricating oil as distinct from a pulsating flow. A pressure release valve was incorporated in the gear pump. No change had been made to the crankshaft assembly or the connecting rods.

## Split-Skirt Pistons

Split-skirt pistons were now fitted. These were available in either 6.7:1 or 7.2:1, depending upon available fuel. The concave-crown pistons previously employed gave a compression ratio of 6:1. Cast in Lo-Ex silicon alloy, the cylinder barrel had been provided with increased finning area.

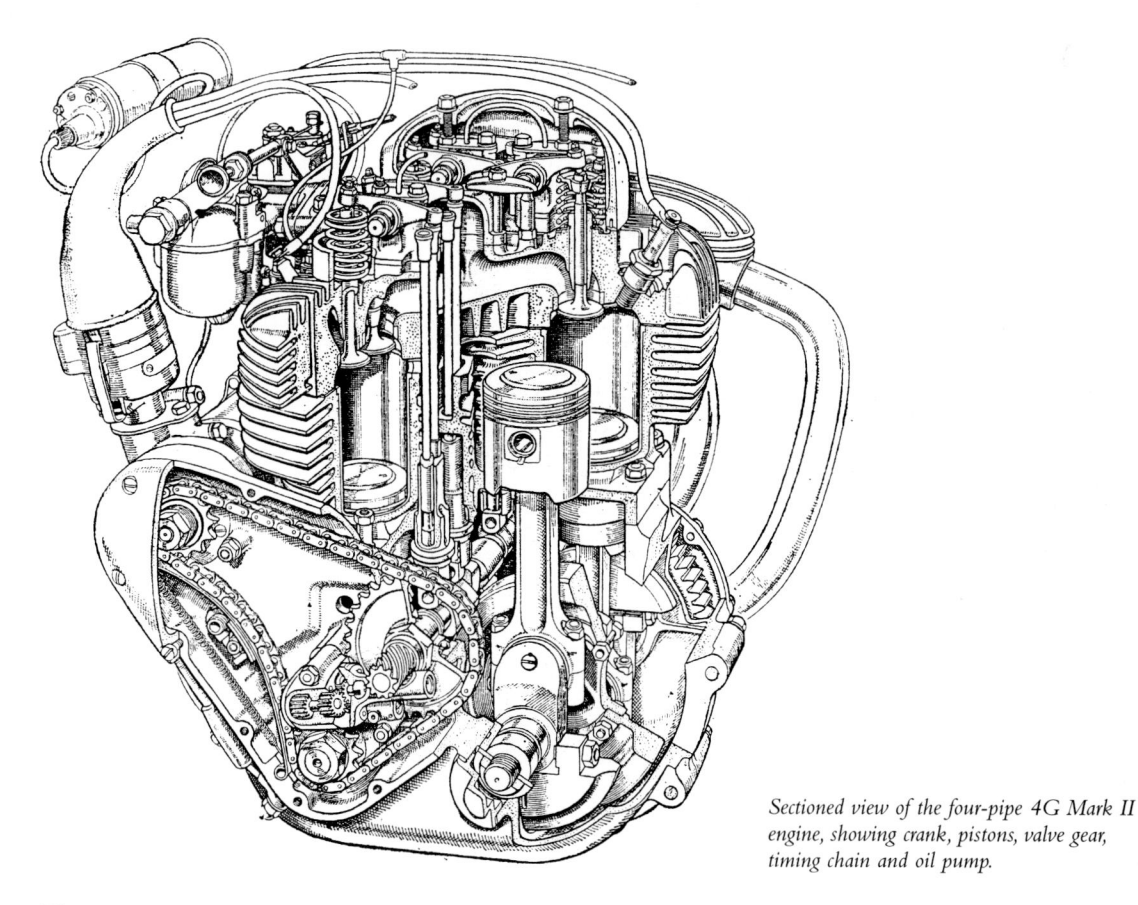

*Sectioned view of the four-pipe 4G Mark II engine, showing crank, pistons, valve gear, timing chain and oil pump.*

## Square Four

### Neoprene Clutch Inserts

So that the transmission would be able to cope with the additional power output of 40bhp at 5,600rpm (6.7:1 compression ratio) or 42bhp at 5,800rpm (7.2:1), the cork inserts of the three-plate dry clutch had been replaced by Neoprene components. Gear ratios on the 4G Mark II were: 4.07, 5.32, 6.92 and 10.8:1. At 100mph (160km/h) in fourth (top) gear, the engine speed was around 5,300rpm – some 300rpm below maximum.

### A Five-Gallon Tank

A new, much larger, 5gal (22.7ltr) capacity fuel tank took pride of place on the new 4G Mark II. This sported a centrally located filler cap, while the sides of the tank were extended downward well below the actual tank base – this, said Ariel, 'was to improve appearance'. There was a new dual seat that purchasers could specify in place of the single sprung saddle. A new Lucas stop/tail lamp was also fitted.

The four-cylinder models (which at that time still included the Mark I as well as the Mark II) were finished in a distinctive new Wedgwood Blue, with white-lined fuel tanks and blue wheel rims. When *The Motor Cycle* tested an example of the new 4G Mark II in its 23 April 1953 issue, it found many of the previous faults gone and recorded a maximum speed of 97mph (156km/h).

*New for the 1953 season, the 4G Mark II four-pipe model. This was offered in a distinctive Wedgwood blue (including the frame). Note last of larger metal Ariel tank badges.*

## 4G Mark II 1000 ohv 1953

| | | | |
|---|---|---|---|
| Engine | Air-cooled Square Four, overhead valve, plain bearing big-ends; two crankshafts; connecting rods in RR56 alloy; aluminium cylinder head and barrel assemblies connected by gears | Final drive | Chain |
| | | Gearbox | Four-speed, Burman, foot-change |
| | | Frame | Single front downtube |
| | | Front suspension | Telescopic fork |
| | | Rear suspension | Plunger |
| | | Front brake | 7in drum, SLS |
| Bore | 65mm | Rear brakes | 8in drum, SLS |
| Stroke | 75mm | Tyres | Front 3.25 × 26; rear 4.00 × 18 |
| Displacement | 997cc | | |
| Compression ratio | 6.7:1 | **General Specifications** | |
| Lubrication | Dry sump, plunger pump | Wheelbase | 56in (1,422mm) |
| Ignition | Coil, with car-type four-cyl contact breaker and distributor | Ground clearance | 5.5in (140mm) |
| | | Seat heigt | 30in (762mm) |
| Carburettor | Single rear-mounted Solex 26 AHD; from engine number Pl 10 1954 SU Type MC2 | Fuel tank capacity | 5gal (22ltr) |
| | | Dry weight | 425lb (193kg) |
| | | Maximum power | 40bhp @ 5,600rpm |
| Primary drive | Chain | Top speed | 100mph (160km/h) |

## 1954 – An SU Carburettor

A year later when the 1954 Ariel model range was announced, the Square Four in its latest 4G Mark II guise was unaltered except for the fitting of an SU-type MC2 carburettor. This had come in after tests had shown that it gave superior performance when compared to the previously fitted Solex instrument. The use of the SU had necessitated slight modifications to the frame. The Square Four was now the only model in the Ariel range to retain the patented Anstey-designed plunger-cum-short trailing-link rear suspension.

A more traditional finish of black with gold linings, chrome-plated tank flutes and a band along the base of the fuel tank sides partway to the rear – and chrome-plated wheel rims with black centres – replaced the Wedgwood Blue, white and chrome finish of the 1943 4G models. Also new were round plastic tank badges (finished in red and gold), replacing Ariel's 'winged' metal type previously fitted. The dual seat was now standard equipment. The price of the 1954 4G Mark II had risen to £294 including UK purchase tax.

*Close-up of Anstey plunger rear suspension from a 4G Mark I.*

*Square Four*

*A 1954 4G Mark II – first year of the smaller, circular tank badges.*

**MODEL 4G**

**1000 c.c. SQUARE FOUR**

**ENGINE:** Four cylinder O.H.V. 65×75 mm. 997 c.c. (2.56×2.95=60.8 cubic inches). Aluminium alloy cylinder with wear resisting detachable sleeves. Aluminium alloy cylinder head with valve seat inserts. Twin counterbalanced alloy steel crankshafts coupled by hardened and ground gears. Light alloy connecting rods with white metal liners. S.U. variable choke carburetter with air cleaner. Double gear oil pump. Lucas coil ignition incorporating 70 watt voltage controlled dynamo with built-in distributor and automatic ignition control. 6 volt 20 amp. hour battery.

**FRAME:** Full cradle type with lugs for sidecar attachment either side. Ariel patented plunger rear suspension. Forged steel girder spring-up rear and strong tubular front stands, also prop stand.

**MUDGUARDS:** Wide D section with tubular stays. Rear guard can be lifted for easy wheel removal.

**BRAKES:** Ariel design of great power, ensuring positive and progressive action. 8 inch diameter rear, 7 inch diameter front. Car type fulcrum adjustment.

**LIGHTING EQUIPMENT:** 7½ inch headlamp incorporating lighting switch and ammeter. 6 volt battery. Stop and tail lamp. Electric horn.

**FINISH:** Superbly finished throughout in best quality black enamel.

*Page from the 1954 Ariel brochure, showing the four-pipe 4G Mk II.*

73

*Square Four*

## Little Change for 1955

There was little change to the Square Four when the 1955 Ariel range was announced in early September 1954 – the introduction of a steering lock with keys and an integral type of horn push were the only innovations. The price of £294 remained unchanged.

## 1956 Innovations

All Ariel's models (with the exception of the 200 Colt) received a distinctive headlamp cowl when the 1956 range was announced to the public on the first day of September 1955. There were also new full-width hubs (again excluding the Colt lightweight), but whereas

*October 1955 advertisement showing Ariel line-up of single-, twin- and four-cylinder power units.*

the other models received these front and rear, only the front assembly was fitted to the four-cylinder model.

## Headlamp Cowl

A one-piece steel pressing in 20-gauge material, the headlamp cowl was to become a distinctive feature of the Ariel motorcycles of the last half of the 1950s. Besides streamlining the front section of the motorcycle in the area of the headlamp, it also replaced the fork shrouds and lamp brackets formerly fitted. The upper and forward section of the cowl, which bore a decorative chrome-plated strip, also served as a headlamp peak. Flush-fitting screws in the side of the cowl secured the headlamp shell and provided vertical adjustment to the headlamp beam. The 7in (178mm) pre-focus light unit was a new Lucas model featuring an arrangement whereby the dipped beam was offset to the left (not found on export models intended for use when riding on the right-hand side of the road). The pilot light was located in the reflector.

Mounted in the top of the cowl-cum-fork top assembly, the instrument console housed a lighting switch, speedometer and ammeter. The speedometer light bulb also illuminated the ammeter. All the electrical leads to the instrument panel were equipped with snap connection.

The handlebar was secured by a cast aluminium clamp with concealed retaining nuts. A new combined horn button/dip switch assembly was fitted to the left side of the handlebar.

## Cast Aluminium Full-Width Brake Hub

The new cast aluminium full-width front brake hub incorporated a 7in (178mm) centralized brake, equipped with 1½in (38mm) wide linings. Internally, the hub featured integral stiffening webs; externally it was finned for cooling. The brake drum was a cast-iron liner and two wheel bearings were of the deep groove, journal variety and were housed in a 2½in (64mm) diameter steel sleeve, the liner and sleeve being cast in.

The brake shoes and shoe plate were aluminium-alloy die castings. In addition to the normal pull-off springs fitted to the shoes, a supplementary return spring was arranged

*The full-width alloy front hub arrived for 1956, together with the headlamp nacelle. However, the original single-sided rear hub and plunger rear suspension remained.*

internally at right-angles to the cam spindle axis. Of coil pattern and employed 'in tension', the supplementary spring had one end attached to the shoe plate and the other end to the cam spindle; application of the brake slightly extended the spring.

*A New Oil Tank*
A new oil tank was fitted, that increased the oil capacity from 5pt (2.8ltr) to 1gal (4.6ltr). This was, Ariel claimed, an effective way of further reducing the operating temperature of the engine – the larger capacity reducing the running temperature of the lubricant. To permit the fitting of this larger tank, the toolbox was relocated to the nearside (left) of the bike.

*The Dynamo Drive Ratio is Increased*
During early 1956, the gearing of the dynamo drive was increased. Formerly, this was at engine speed. However, now the gearing was 1.2:1 and the benefit was that the dynamo cut in at 25mph (40km/h) in top gear instead of 30mph (48km/h). In consequence of this speed-up, it was necessary to slow down the distributor – driven off the dynamo – to keep its operation in phase with the engine.

## 1957 Clutch Changes

When the 1957 range was announced in early September 1956 there were changes to the clutch. Essentially, these brought about an increase in torque-transmitting ability and a quieter operation. Previously, the innermost plate in the clutch drum – a plain steel plate – had been located against a shoulder on the clutch centre, causing some chatter in use between the aforementioned plate and the shoulder. For 1957 the inside face of the drum had four friction-material segments riveted to it, with the first plate bearing against them.

A minor change was made concerning the cowling around the headlamp that had been introduced a year earlier – with the frontal appearance improved by the adoption of a chromium-plated grille that bridged the gap below the headlamp.

## A Price Rise in 1958

September 1957 saw the arrival of the 1958 Ariel range. The models remained unchanged, including the Square Four. However, this did not apply to the price, which had now risen to a hefty £336 16s 6d (including UK taxes).

By now, one could almost feel that the Square Four had come to a crossroads – either it needed updating yet again for the new decade of the 1960s, or it would simply fade away. Sales had never been spectacular; 'steady' would have been a more suitable description, but as the end of the 1950s came into sight they were at their lowest ebb since the early 1930s.

## The End in Sight

The Ariel development team obviously appreciated this and, in fact, had designed and constructed a swinging arm prototype (*see* Chapter 12). Unfortunately, by this rime Ariel was firmly under BSA control and the swinging-arm framed Square Four never reached production.

When the new Leader two-fifty twin cylinder two-stroke made its bow in July 1958 (*see* Chapter 11) the case for continuing *any* of Ariel's by now aging four-stroke range was thrown into question, and the writing was clearly on the wall when *The Motor Cycle* dated 30 October 1958 said: 'Following the precedent set last year, the entire range (excepting the VB side-valve, which was discontinued, and the brand-new Leader) is to be carried forward into 1959.' So it was that, together with the range of ohv singles and the twin-cylinder FH Huntmaster 650, the 4G Square Four Mark II was discontinued in August 1959.

As Roy Bacon was to recall later: 'With the scrapping of the four-stroke line the Squariel went, mourned by those who accepted the handling for the sheer pleasure of riding such a smooth machine with such acceleration. It was an expensive machine, but for those that could afford it the charm of wafting up hills and not having to flog the engine was worth it.'

*Final full year of production of the Square Four was 1958, as this Ariel publicity material recalls; the axe fell the following August, bringing down the curtain on a unique model series which had a lifespan of almost three decades.*

## The Healey Four

The Redditch-based Healey brothers, George and Tom, were to play the last hand in the Square Four saga. In 1964, a full five years after production had finally come to an end, they had purchased a Square-Four-engined sprint bike, but finding spares something of a problem, they began to make their own – after all, they did own a first-class engineering company. Making their own spares soon led to manufacturing batches for sale to the general public. The official Ariel spares business was set up in 1967.

The next stage in the story came when they met up with Roger Slater (before his Laverda import days). At that time Roger was involved with the Vincent marque, or at least selling Egli-framed machines. So soon the Egli frame and Ariel 4G 1000 Square Four engine became what in modern terms would be described as an 'item'. The resulting motorcycle used, as the Healey catalogue said: 'The spine frame, race developed. No curved tubes, amazingly good road-holding, and an oil reservoir in its backbone.'

The Egli frame was chrome-plated (as was the swinging arm, with Metal Profile front forks and an Italian Grimeca 4LS front drum brake. As mentioned, the engine had the lubrication system improved and an oil cooler added, but the standard model's four-speed Burman gearbox remained. The result – with four chrome megaphone silencers – was an attractive motorcycle. Again, according to the Healey catalogue: 'A bike for riding. For the long distance men, whether basking in the bliss of coastal roads in high summer, or needing the security and faith of a trustworthy machine in mountain blizzards.' That was all true, except for, as one commentator described it: 'the seat was short and had the appeal of a plank!'

The first production Healey 1000/4 arrived as the 1970s dawned and a small number were built exclusively to order for several years.

In 1973 an improved specification, and a new seat, arrived. By the mid-1970s more changes had occurred, including the fitting of an hydraulically operated front disc brake (some bikes had double disc and cast-alloy wheels) and an alternator had been grafted onto the rear crankshaft.

By 1976 the definitive Healey arrived with disc brakes on both wheels and a matt black exhaust system (still with separate silencers), but like its series production brother (or should that be father?), the Healey 1000/4 became uneconomic to produce and the type did not survive into the 1980s. Today, Healey-built machines are highly prized and one pristine example resides at the National Motorcycle Museum, Birmingham, to prove what could be achieved by a small British engineering company.

*G C and T Healey of Redditch built and sold a version of the Square Four with 1000 4G four-pipe engine housed in an Egli-type chassis with modern running gear during the late 1960s and most of the 1970s. Engine improvements saw changes to the lubrication system and the fitting of an oil cooler.*

# Square Four

From the instant, electric response necessary for fast line chopping where constant direction and throttle changes are the order of riding, to long sweeping highway curves demanding not just precise steering, but an unwavering line during the accelerating keel into speed, the 1000/4, while cornering faster than most, corners safer than most as well.

No vibration, only the rythmic thrum of four cylinders and their immense torque. Lighter than the current mass produced "Superbikes", the Healey 4 will outperform the best of them throughout its performance range, top gear running easily from 19—110+ mph. All accomplished in a manner available only to riders on mildly tuned, litre engined machines. Whether for relaxed commuting, luxury touring or fast sports riding, the Healey 1000/4 covers the entire motorcycling spectrum as only a thoroughbred can.

Each motorcycle is hand built by craftsmen with a complete understanding of the machine they designed and the men who ride them, yet all are supported by a full scale spares and servicing system.

The Healey 1000/4 freedom wheeling in the classic style.

**Specification:**

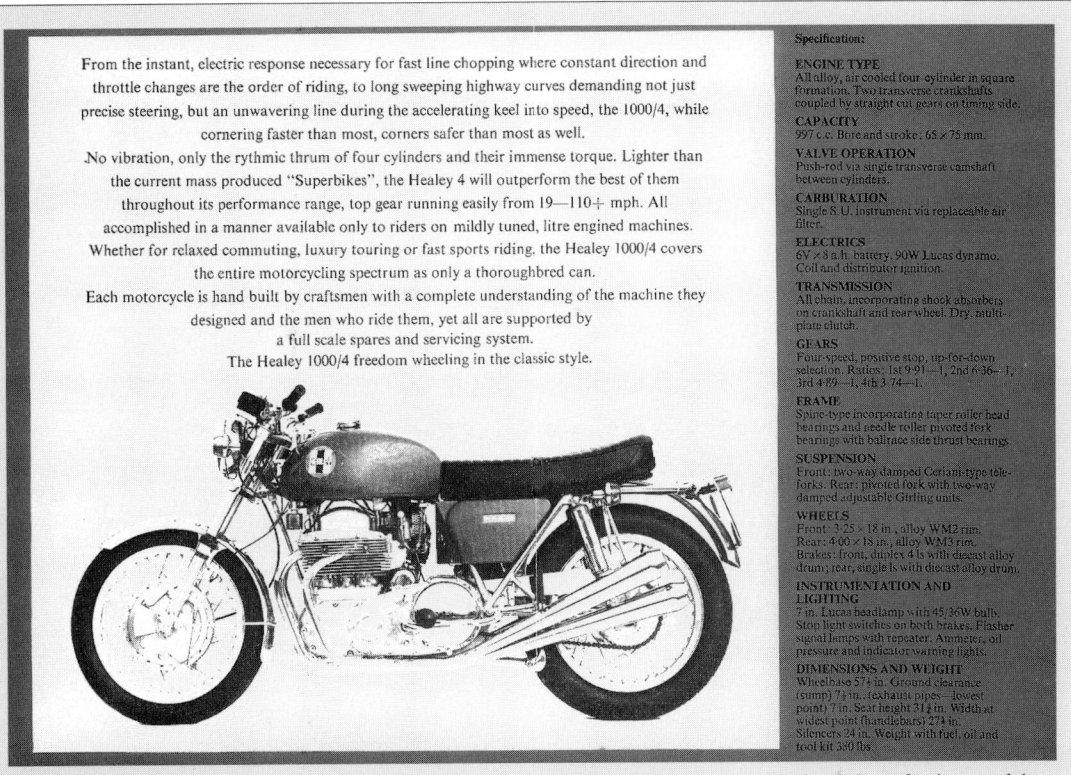

**ENGINE TYPE**
All alloy, air cooled four-cylinder in square formation. Two transverse crankshafts coupled by straight cut gears on timing side.

**CAPACITY**
997 c.c. Bore and stroke: 65 x 75 mm.

**VALVE OPERATION**
Push-rod via single transverse camshaft between cylinders.

**CARBURATION**
Single S.U. instrument via replaceable air filter.

**ELECTRICS**
6V x 8 a.h. battery. 90W Lucas dynamo. Coil and distributor ignition.

**TRANSMISSION**
All chain, incorporating shock absorbers on crankshaft and rear wheel. Dry, multi-plate clutch.

**GEARS**
Four-speed, positive stop, up-for-down selection. Ratios: 1st 9.91—1, 2nd 6.36—1, 3rd 4.89—1, 4th 3.74—1.

**FRAME**
Spine-type incorporating taper roller head bearings and needle roller pivoted fork bearings with ballrace side thrust bearings.

**SUSPENSION**
Front: two-way damped Ceriani-type tele-forks. Rear: pivoted fork with two-way damped adjustable Girling units.

**WHEELS**
Front: 3.25 x 18 in., alloy WM2 rim. Rear: 4.00 x 18 in., alloy WM3 rim. Brakes: front, duplex 4 ls with diecast alloy drum; rear, single ls with diecast alloy drum.

**INSTRUMENTATION AND LIGHTING**
7 in. Lucas headlamp with 45/36W bulb. Stop light switches on both brakes. Flasher signal lamps with repeater. Ammeter, oil pressure and indicator warning lights.

**DIMENSIONS AND WEIGHT**
Wheelbase 57½ in. Ground clearance (sump) 7¼ in. (exhaust pipes—lowest point) 7 in. Seat height 31¼ in. Width at widest point (handlebars) 27¼ in. Silencers 24 in. Weight with fuel, oil and tool kit 380 lbs.

*The Healey recreated the aura of the four-cylinder Ariel, but in a modern package. It was an updated classic for the age of the Superbike. But it remained a rare sight as production was strictly limited.*

*Healey logo — worn with pride.*

*Neat fitting oil cooler installation for the Healey 1000/4.*

*The Ariel Square Four four-pipe 4G Mark II and double adult sidecar were a familiar sight on British roads during the 1950s. This was, of course, before the arrival of the Mini and the subsequent boom in small cars.*

## Attempts at a Reprieve

Once the news that the axe had fallen on the Square Four was made public, there were three attempts at a reprieve. The first came from Ariel itself after the news caused a mini-boom in demand for the four-cylinder model, but the BSA board was not to be swayed from its decision. In any case, it was a mini-boom, not a maxi one.

The others were private ventures. One was from the British Healey concern (*see* separate boxed section on pages 78 and 79). The other effort came from across the Atlantic, from Canada.

The Canadian venture envisaged an increase in displacement to 1150cc, overhead camshaft, fuel injection, electric starting and shaft drive. But this plan, which surfaced in the mid-1960s, long after production in England had ceased, ultimately came to nothing.

The Healey enterprise was, in its own way, quite successful and saw a series of developments which spanned the 1960s and 1970s, but it was not a factory effort and so, of course, could never hope to be anything more than an expression – albeit an excellent one – of the special builder's art.

And so one of the British motorcycle industry's greatest and most enduring models finally faded into history.

# 6 Competition Models

The Red Hunter name first appeared in 1932. As the Ariel catalogue put it: 'The Red Hunter is introduced to answer the demands of the sporting rider who wishes to combine fast road work or trials with occasional racing.'

## Four Valves

For 1932 the five-hundred VH32 had a four-valve vertical engine and stroke dimensions of 86.4 × 85mm, giving a displacement of 499cc. The detachable head had four valves, actuated by enclosed rockers mounted on roller bearings (lubricated by grease gun). Compression ratio was 6:1 with a 7.5:1 high compression piston supplied loose with the bike. Transmission was by a Burman three-speed foot-change gearbox via a Burman multi-plate cork clutch.

Unfortunately, the four-valve head was to give trouble, particularly in competition, with cracks developing between the valve seats, and so the factory switched to a conventional two-valve, twin-port cylinder head from 1933 onwards.

*International Six Days Trial; circa early 1930s. Riders are left to right: H Nelson, G Patterson, R MacGregor, H Steel, W MacQueen – the machinery Sunbeam, Brough Superior, Ariel and Rudge, respectively.*

*Competition Models*

## 250, 350 and 500cc

It was in this guise that the 250, 350 and 500cc Red Hunters (together with their de Luxe versions) were to enjoy a production run covering the next twenty-six years, although the 250 Red Hunter was not reintroduced when production resumed at the end of the Second World War.

Over the years, much design revision took place, with various modifications to the valve enclosure made in an attempt to keep lubricant in and dirt out, until in September 1937 it was announced that the 1938 model would have all-enclosed rocker boxes. Oil was then fed to the rocker spindles from a point off the engine's timing cover. This arrangement was designed by Frank Anstey, who took over when Val Page transferred to Triumph, and who had previously been with Rudge. Anstey was also the designer of the famous plunger frame with swinging links that was introduced for the 1939 season.

Unlike the majority of the rivals which made more specialized competition machinery, the Ariel Red Hunter series was intended as a Jack-of-all-trades, being equally suitable for trials, hill climbs, sprinting, scrambles, grass track or even racing at Brooklands. The most successful racing examples were those prepared by the legendary Laurence Hartley and ridden by the likes of riders such as Jock West and Peter Ferbrache (pre-war and post-war respectively). Thus the Red Hunter became a mainstay of British motorcycle sport throughout the 1930s, 1940s and 1950s.

*The purpose-built 499cc VH Competition 1938 model; based on the series production Red Hunter ohv single.*

*American Bob Hansen at a half-mile dirt track event with his Ariel five-hundred Competition model, 1950. Later, in the 1970s, Bob was team manager for the American Kawasaki squad at Daytona.*

*The Watsonian International Sports sidecar was widely used in trials with, usually, an Ariel single (or the new twin) attached.*

# The ARIEL *Competition* HUNTER
## 500 c.c. MODEL V.C.H.

This model has been specially designed for trials and competition work in which light weight and ease of handling over the most arduous courses are the prime considerations.

Although light in weight, this machine retains the robust construction characteristic of all Ariel products, while the engine has ample power with positive control at all speeds.

### SPECIFICATION

**Engine:** 81.8 × 95 mm. (497 c.c.) O.H.V. single cylinder. Aluminium alloy cylinder barrel with nickel iron liner. Aluminium alloy cylinder head with stainless steel valve inserts, highly polished ports, forged steel flywheels, large diameter mainshafts mounted on two heavy-duty roller bearings and one ball bearing. Large double roller caged big end bearing. The engine is specially bench tested and tuned.

**Lubrication:** Dry sump, employing dual plunger pumps—large capacity supply pump—half gallon capacity separate oil tank.

**Ignition:** Magneto B.T.H. racing type.

**Gearbox:** Four speed wide ratio, foot control, two-plate neoprene clutch, built-in speedometer drive. (Close ratio gears and three-plate neoprene clutch for scramble machines.)

**Speedometer:** 120 m.p.h. trip mounted on front forks.

**Frame:** Short wheelbase, fully brazed steel tube construction. Polished duralumin mudguards, flat and tubular stays. Tool box.

**Transmission:** Polished aluminium oilbath primary chaincase, rear chain fully protected.

**Exhaust System:** Single-port low-level exhaust pipe with upswept silencer.

**Wheels:** Dunlop Trials Universal tyres 4.00 × 19" rear, 3.00 × 21" front. (Sports tyres to special order). Chromium rims, red centres, lined gold.

**Fuel Tank:** 2¼ gallon capacity, finished chromium and red, lined gold.

SPRING FRAME CANNOT BE FITTED TO THIS MODEL

### TECHNICAL DATA

| | | |
|---|---|---|
| Wheelbase | | 54" |
| Overall length | | 84" |
| Handlebar width | | 27" |
| Saddle height | | 30" |
| Ground clearance | | 5½" |
| Weight, dry | | 300 lb. |
| Fuel consumption | | 50/60 m.p.g. |
| Oil consumption | | 2,000 m.p.g. |
| Engine b.h.p. at | | 25 |
| engine r.p.m. | | 6,000 |

| | Wide | Close |
|---|---|---|
| Solo gear ratio, top | 6.05 | 5.75 |
| Solo gear ratio, third | 9.16 | 7.2 |
| Solo gear ratio, second | 12.6 | 9.7 |
| Solo gear ratio, low | 19.1 | 15.3 |
| Engine sprocket solo | 19 teeth | |
| Compression ratio | 6.8 | |
| Links in front chain | 80 × ⅜" pitch | |
| Links in rear chain | 91 × ⅜" pitch | |

**PRICE**
including Speedometer
£180 . 0 . 0
plus Purchase Tax
£48 . 12 . 0

ARIEL MOTORS LIMITED · BIRMINGHAM · ENGLAND

*Period advertisement showing the VCH 500 Competition model during the early 1950s. Alloy cylinder barrel and head, telescopic front forks, but still a rigid frame.*

## Competition Models

A feature of the Red Hunter was its overall package. The engine was tough, simple and easy to work on, and spares were relatively cheap and plentiful thanks to Ariel's policy of interchangeability across its range.

If one had to pick one branch of the sport at which the Red Hunter was particularly successful it would have to be trials. In pre-war days this had mainly meant one-day events, especially for clubmen and the SSDT (Scottish Six Days Trial). Then in the post-war era Ariel embraced the ISDT (International Six Days Trial). Great Britain was dominant in those early days of peace, winning the event from 1948 through to 1951 and again in 1953. C M (Bob) Ray rode in the Vase team in the first and last years, and in the Trophy team in the others. In 1950 he and the other Ariel riders took the manufacturer team award using the new Page-designed 498cc ohv twin (*see* Chapter 8). These bikes, although they appeared stock, were actually quite special.

## Special Features

Special features abounded – both to speed up maintenance work and also to make the bikes as suitable for a particular event as possible.

Besides alloy tanks and aluminium front brake hubs (measures intended to decrease weight), there were several technical features of note. For example, Burman made special gearboxes with wide ratios, but the most interesting innovation concerned the Anstey link plunger rear suspension. This was equipped inside the main pillar on which the slider operated and, despite the small oil capacity, did allow the employment of much softer rote springs that improved handling over rough ground. The riders carried small oil guns, topping up the system as and when needed.

*The victorious British Trophy teamsters from the 1950 ISDT. Left to right: R H M Viney (AJS), P H Alves (Triumph), C M Ray (Ariel), W J Stocker (Royal Enfield) and F M Rist (BSA).*

## Over-the-Counter

The demand for an over-the-counter competition bike during the early 1950s was filled by the special VCH Red Hunter. Introduced in 1949, it featured the latest version of the venerable 499cc (81.8 × 95mm) ohv single-cylinder engine with single port head, these longer-stroke dimensions having outlived the shorter-stroke ones. Again, one had the option of 6.8 or 7.5:1 compression pistons. The remainder of the VCH version of Ariel's big single included:

- telescopic forks
- rigid frame
- 3.00 × 21 front and 4.00 × 19 rear knobbly tyres (racing tyres to order)
- competition magneto (BTH)
- four-speed wide ratio gearbox (a close ratio for scrambles and road racing)
- two-plate clutch (three-plate for scrambles and road racing)
- single low-level exhaust with upswept silencer
- aluminium cylinder head and barrel
- engine specially bench-tested.

## Sidecars

The biggest successes during the early to mid-1950s were without doubt when a third wheel was attached – the Ariel and sidecar (both single and twin) proving a formidable combination. Frank Wilkins and Kay (later to become Mr and Mrs Wilkins) were to become the big names in sidecar trials. Frank Wilkins had ridden Ariels pre-war; in 1947 he was riding Nortons but soon moved on to Selly Oak-built machines. The post-war Wilkins-Ariel saga began properly in 1948 when Frank built

*Number 236 is the Ariel 500 twin ridden by the late Phil Mellors at the start of the 1952 ISDT at Bad Aussee, Austria, 18 September 1952. Phil is tickling the float chamber of his machine's carb!*

*Ariel advertisement celebrating Bob Ray's Gold Medal success in the 1952 ISDT on his KHA five-hundred twin. He was a member of the British Trophy team.*

*Even more Ariel ISDT success came in the 1953 event – four entries, four gold medals. Ariels also won the manufacturers team award with riders Bob Ray, N S Holmes and W S G Parsons, all riding 500 twins.*

| VCH Competition Hunter 1949 | | | |
|---|---|---|---|
| Engine | Air-cooled overhead valve single with alloy cylinder head; alloy barrel with nickel iron liner; double roller caged big-end | Front suspension | Telescopic forks |
| | | Rear suspension | Unsprung, rigid frame |
| | | Front brake | 7in single-sided drum, SLS |
| | | Rear brakes | 7in single-sided drum, SLS |
| Bore | 81.8mm | Tyres | Dunlop Trials Universal: 3.00 × 21 front; 4.00 × 19 rear |
| Stroke | 95mm | | |
| Displacement | 497cc | | |
| Compression ratio | 6.8:1[1] | **General Specifications** | |
| Lubrication | Dry sump, twin plunger pump | Wheelbase | 54in (1,372mm) |
| Ignition | BTH racing magneto | Ground clearance | 5.5in (140mm) |
| Carburettor | N/A | Seat height | 30in (762mm) |
| Primary drive | Chain | Fuel tank capacity | 2.5gal (11.4ltr) |
| Final drive | Chain | Dry weight | 300lb (136kg) |
| Gearbox | Four-speed, foot-change | Maximum power | 25bhp @ 6,000rpm |
| Frame | Fully brazed steel tubular construction; single front downtube | Top speed | 75mph (121km/h) |
| | | [1] 7.5:1 for scrambling. | |

a 1936 five-hundred Red Hunter engine into an ex-WD 350NG chassis. When he teamed up with Kay, they were immediately successful, soon receiving works support for their efforts.

They went on to win the British Experts title four times, the ACU Trials Star and several gold medals in the ISDT. The author caught up with the pair one day at a VMCC race meeting at Snetterton in Norfolk during the early 1980s – they had ridden their final outfit (a twin-cylinder model) from their Midlands home to the event.

Peter Wraith was another famous name in the sidecar trials world to pilot an Ariel outfit.

## A New Pair of Models

For solo use Ariel had struggled and by 1953 the dual-purpose, rigid-framed VCH was essentially obsolete, superseded by more advanced machinery, notably the BSA Gold Star and the AMC (AJS and Matchless) singles. So Ariel set to and came up with a pair of models (both five-hundreds): the HS (Scrambler) and HT (Trials). Both used the all-alloy engine with the Hunter-type bottom end. The HS ran a high compression ratio of 9.1:1 and pumped out a healthy 33bhp at 6,250rpm. Other features of the HS model included a Burman GB gearbox (using conventional road ratios). For 1954 only, an Ariel TT9 was fitted, thereafter one of the new Monobloc instruments; in both cases the size was $1^3/_{16}$in (30mm). A wide range of alternative sprockets, jetting and the like were available to enable competitors to set up their bikes for the course or prevailing weather conditions.

## American Needs

American needs were catered for by the inclusion in the HS's specification of a dual seat and the option of a magdynamo and QD lighting kit, in place of the Lucas racing magneto, the former for green lanes/desert riding.

## Drive-Side Oil Seal

Unlike the series production roadster motor, the engine of HS had an oil seal fitted into the drive-side crankcase half – this running on the driveshaft to prevent oil loss into the primary chaincase. This was needed, as the issue of oil escape from the crankcase into the chaincase only arose thanks to the higher engine revolutions and sustained full throttle used in actual competition.

The HS scrambler shared features such as tyre sizes (3.00 × 21 front and 4.00 × 19 rear), petrol tank and abbreviated mudguards with its trials brother, HT. However, the latter bike had wider ratio gears for its Burman 'box (still a GB type) and a much lower 5.6:1 compression ratio. Additionally, HT shared the same

*The legendary Ariel pairing of husband and wife team Frank and Kay Wilkins, photographed by the author in 1984 – still with the same faithful twin cylinder model – over two decades from their competition days.*

## Competition Models

*Ariel HS 500cc Scrambler, with swinging arm frame; 1954.*

*Finnish brothers Matti ? (51) and Raimo Rein ( racing Ariel HS Scramb sponsored by impo? Helkama; circa late 19?.*

cam timings as the roadsters, unlike the much fiercer figures for the HS scrambler. A Lucas Wader magneto was employed – whilst the option of a magdynamo and lighting equipment remained an option.

### Swinging Arm or Rigid Frames?

Although the HS scrambler made use of the new duplex swinging arm frame, the HT retained at first the rigid type, at least as far as paying customers were concerned. However, the Ariel works riders soon ditched the rigid rear end in favour of first the duplex swinging arm frame similar to the HS scrambler and the roadsters, but from the spring of 1955 it came with a modified lightweight frame especially for trials use.

### Entry at the Scottish

After proving the design in one-day events, in May 1955 the Ariel riders took in the Scottish Six Days. Effectively this was to be the beginning of what was to emerge as the HT5, to many the finest big single four-stroke trials mount of all time.

The combination of the all-alloy engine and new purpose-built lightweight frame was to prove a winner. In detail, the component parts of the frame were a large diameter

## Competition Models

### HT Trials 1954

| | |
|---|---|
| Engine | Air-cooled overhead valve single with alloy cylinder head; alloy barrel with nickel iron liner; double roller caged big-end |
| Bore | 81.8mm |
| Stroke | 95mm |
| Displacement | 497cc |
| Compression ratio | 5.6:1 |
| Lubrication | Dry sump, twin plunger pump |
| Ignition | Magneto |
| Carburettor | N/A |
| Primary drive | Chain |
| Final drive | Chain |
| Gearbox | Four-speed, foot-change, wide ratio |
| Frame | Fully brazed steel tubular construction; single front downtube |
| Front suspension | Telescopic fork |
| Rear suspension | Unsprung, rigid frame |
| Front brake | 7in single-sided drum, SLS |
| Rear brakes | 7in single-sided drum, SLS |
| Tyres | Trials pattern: 3.00 × 21 front; 4.00 × 19 rear |

**General Specifications**

| | |
|---|---|
| Wheelbase | 53in (1,326mm) |
| Ground clearance | 7in (178mm) |
| Seat height | 32in (813mm) |
| Fuel tank capacity | 2.5gal (11.4ltr) |
| Dry weight | 290lb (132kg) |
| Maximum power | 24bhp @ 5,800rpm |
| Top speed | 65mph (105km/h) |

### HS Scrambler 1954

| | |
|---|---|
| Engine | Air-cooled overhead valve single with alloy cylinder head; alloy barrel with nickel iron liner; double roller caged big-end connected by gears |
| Bore | 81.8mm |
| Stroke | 95mm |
| Displacement | 497cc |
| Compression ratio | 9:1 |
| Lubrication | Dry sump, twin plunger pump |
| Ignition | Luca racing magneto |
| Carburettor | Amal TT9 1³⁄₁₆ |
| Primary drive | Chain |
| Final drive | Chain |
| Gearbox | Four-speed, foot-change |
| Frame | Double cradle fully brazed steel tubular construction |
| Front suspension | Telescopic fork |
| Rear suspension | Swinging arm, twin Girling shock absorbers |
| Front brake | 7in single-sided, SLS |
| Rear brakes | 7in single-sided, SLS |
| Tyres | Front 3.00 × 21; rear 4.00 × 19 |

**General Specifications**

| | |
|---|---|
| Wheelbase | 56in (1,422mm) |
| Ground clearance | 6.25in (159mm) |
| Seat height | 31in (787mm) |
| Fuel tank capacity | 2.5gal (11.4ltr) |
| Dry weight | 318lb (144kg) |
| Maximum power | 34bhp @ 6,000rpm |
| Top speed | 80mph (129km/h) |

top tube, with a single front downtube and a pair of seat tubes. A massive tube connected the top and seat components to the swinging arm pivot and rear engine support, by plunging down vertically. The frame was 'open' under the crankcases so, in effect, the engine and transmission formed a stressed member. The frame was of all-welded construction. Rear suspension was by means of the standard all-welded box-section Ariel swinging arm pivoting on Metalastic bushes.

Compared to other 500cc-class trials bikes of the mid-1950s the first impression of riding one of the new Ariels was undoubtedly of extreme lightness. In fact, one rider said it was akin to riding 'a 197' – in other words, one of

## Competition Models

the lightweight Villiers-pioneered two-strokes such as James, Greeves or Francis Barnett.

### The HT5 Goes on Sale

In their 1 September 1955 issue, *The Motor Cycle* revealed: 'Two competition models – a trials machine and a scramble mount – are listed, detail specification of which will be available later. The trials model will have the sturdy but light diamond-type frame with pivoted rear fork, as employed by Ariel factory riders in the Scottish Six Days Trial and other important events.'

A year later came news of a new three-fifty trials mount, based on the by now established and successful five-hundred. The new model, the HT3, used an all-alloy 346cc (72 × 85mm) Red Hunter-type power unit. The HT3 had already been used in competition by Ron Langston and, in sidecar form, by George Buck. In appearance the bike was essentially the same as the 497cc-engined HT5. Transmission, apart from the overall gear ratios) and cycle parts were identical in each case and the two engines were of very similar design although the three-fifty was shorter in height, due to the cylinder barrel.

### Full-Width Hubs for the HS

For the 1956 model year the HS scrambler had received the new full-width, aluminium brake hubs, both front and rear, but was otherwise largely as before. Prices at the end of 1957 were: 347cc HT3 and 497cc HT5 £243 5s 3d; 497cc HS £268 4s 3d.

### The Most Famous Combination in History

If one had to name the most famous rider and motorcycle in trials history, it is a certainty that Sammy Miller and Ariel, registration

*Ariel Replica HT5 1957 owned by Nick Woolley, Classic Motor Cycle Show, Stafford, 2003.*

*Ariel HT5 engine, with all-alloy top end. Last of the big British thumpers before the lightweight two-stroke machines took over in the mid-1960s.*

number GOV 132, would be the top candidates. Actually, that famous number, GOV 132, first made an appearance back in 1947, but by the time Sammy won fame with it, just about all that remained of the original was the log book.

Sammy Miller first rode GOV 132 in 1956. He was already a star name in road racing, having raced Terry Hill's NSU Sportmax; works FB Mondial (1957) and works Ducati (1958) machinery followed, with works CZs in the early part of 1959. Thereafter he decided to concentrate efforts 100 per cent on his trials riding.

His first Ariel (in the 1956 Scottish Six Days Trial) was essentially a works version,

---

**HT3 Trials 1957**

| | | | |
|---|---|---|---|
| Engine | Air-cooled overhead valve single with alloy cylinder head; alloy barrel with nickel iron liner; double roller caged big-end | Front suspension | Telescopic fork |
| | | Rear suspension | Swinging arm, twin Girling shock absorbers |
| | | Front brake | 7in full-width drum, SLS |
| Bore | 72mm | Rear brakes | 7in single-sided drum, SLS |
| Stroke | 85mm | Tyres | Front: 2.75 × 21; rear 4.00 × 19 rear |
| Displacement | 346cc | | |
| Compression ratio | 5.6:1 | | |
| Lubrication | Dry sump, twin plunger pump | **General Specifications** | |
| Ignition | Magneto | Wheelbase | 53in (1,346mm) |
| Carburettor | N/A | Ground clearance | 7in (178mm) |
| Primary drive | Chain | Seat height | 32in (813mm) |
| Final drive | Chain | Fuel tank capacity | 2gal (9ltr) |
| Gearbox | Four-speed, foot-change, wide ratio | Dry weight | 285lb (129kg) |
| | | Maximum power | 17bhp @ 5,900rpm |
| Frame | Fully brazed steel tubular construction; single front downtube | Top speed | 60mph (96km/h) |

---

**HT5 Trials 1958**

| | | | |
|---|---|---|---|
| Engine | Air-cooled overhead valve single with alloy cylinder head; alloy barrel with nickel iron liner; double roller caged big-end connected by gears | Front suspension | Telescopic fork |
| | | Rear suspension | Swinging arm, twin Girling shock absorbers |
| | | Front brake | 7in full-width drum, SLS |
| | | Rear brakes | 7in single-sided drum, SLS |
| Bore | 81.8mm | Tyres | Front 2.75 × 21; rear 4.00 × 19 rear |
| Stroke | 95mm | | |
| Displacement | 497cc | | |
| Compression ratio | 5.6:1 | **General Specifications** | |
| Lubrication | Dry sump, twin plunger pump | Wheelbase | 53in (1,346mm) |
| Ignition | Magneto | Ground clearance | 7in (178mm) |
| Carburettor | Amal 376 Monobloc 1 1/16in | Seat height | 32in (813mm) |
| Primary drive | Chain | Fuel tank capacity | 2gal (9ltr) |
| Final drive | Chain | Dry weight | 290lb (132kg) |
| Gearbox | Four-speed, foot-change | Maximum power | 24bhp @ 5,800rpm |
| Frame | Fully brazed steel tubular construction; single front downtube | Top speed | 65mph (105km/h) |

standard production HT5. However, it did not remain standard for very long. Although many considered the Ariel light, Sammy realized that it could be much, much lighter, so he carried out a weight-cutting exercise, especially once he had begun work in the Competition Department at Ariel's factory in Selly Oak, Birmingham. As he was once to recall, 'I spent my first two months surrounded by turnings and filings, as the great lump of trials "horse" was turned into a racing thoroughbred.'

*Featherweight Five-Hundred*
In October 1960, Sammy Miller achieved what everyone had thought impossible by trimming a further 20lb (9kg) off what had already been nicknamed 'Britain's lightest five-hundred'. The new bike was named the 'Featherweight', and its competition debut came in the Alec Ross Trial.

Of Sammy Miller's own design, the frame was manufactured in Reynolds 531 tubing – a diamond pattern with single top, front-down and seat tubes. From below the seat nose, twin tubes separated to run rearwards to the rear shock absorber upper mountings. Additional tubes acted as struts between the base of the seat tube and the damper upper mountings. The engine and transmission were supported by dural mounting plates. The swinging arm remained as before, with the left fork serving as a rear chain oiler.

There was no separate oil tank. Instead, the seat tube – 2¼in (57mm) diameter by 16 gauge – served as an oil reservoir. A fabricated box at the top of the tube contained the filter. Lightweight materials and/or drilling played a vital role in the weight-reduction process, as did the use of fibreglass. For example, the complete primary chaincase now weighed half of the weight it had before. An upholstered seat with fibreglass base saved more. Even the competition number plate, registration plates and magneto shield were of plastic. A light-alloy crankcase shield replaced steel, whilst a rubber pad interposed between the shield and crankcase.

A German Megura all-alloy throttle assembly was used, and Sammy had drilled both wheel spindle ends to accept a tommy bar, whilst the single tank bolt was slotted for a coin – thus saving the weight of a spanner in the toolkit.

Using the steel top fork yoke as a pattern, an aluminium replacement was cast, whilst, as before, the wheels featured alloy rims built onto Leader (alloy) hubs. Water-excluding flanges were riveted to the shoe plates.

More attention to detail was spent making the bike as narrow as possible. To achieve this, Sammy modified the inlet tract and mounting flange, thus bringing the carburettor almost parallel with the frame tubes. Similarly, the exhaust pipe was even more tucked-in than previously. Weight in October 1960 was down to an incredible 250lb (113kg), but by the beginning of 1962 it had reached 242lb (110kg). Much of this reduction was achieved by using yet more fibreglass and even more drilling – there were even holes through the cylinder head and barrel fins!

*Engine Changes*
Sammy had also paid attention to the engine. The flywheels were standard (although others were tried), these being found to have an advantage in low-speed torque, and the compression ratio had been raised from 5.5:1 to 6.6:1. When interviewed in 1962, Sammy said the object was 'to get more complete combustion, plus a shade more top-end urge'. A special one-off cam and half-time pinion were also specified.

When Peter Fraser tested the latest rendering of GOV 132 for the 6 December 1962 issue of *The Motor Cycle*, he ended by saying: 'Good low-speed torque spells grip, and low weight ease of handling. By combining these two essentials to a novel degree, Sammy has produced what is probably the most successful trials machine of all time.' It was an Ariel. What more can be said?

# 7 Overhead-Valve Singles

By the late summer of 1925, Charles Sangster had gained the services of both Val Page and Vic Mole, as Chief Designer and Sales Manager respectively. These two men were to play a vital role in the growth of Ariel over the next few years. They were also to usher in a new era when Ariel was to be known as 'The Modern Motor Cycle' – a description coined by Vic Mole and brought about by the genius of Val Page's design work. The foundation of this success was the new breed of overhead-valve single cylinder machines.

## The New Designs

Essentially, Page came up with four models that were available in the amazingly short time of a few months, and were able to make their debut at the Olympia Show in London during November 1925. The newcomers were split between the Models A and B, that were both 557cc side-valves (described in Chapter 3) and the Models C and D using 497cc (81.8 × 95mm) overhead-valve engines. As Peter Hartley describes in his book *The Ariel Story*, published in 1980: 'Inevitably, in view of the short time available and Val Page's background, the new engines had many JAP-like features.' (As noted earlier, Page had quit JAP to join Ariel.)

Although the side-valve models were essentially workhorses intended to be fully capable of pulling a sidecar and members of the family, the new overhead-valve singles were designed to tempt the more sporting rider. To achieve this Page needed performance and, therefore, he plumped for details such as a hemispherical combustion chamber, higher compression ratio and a fiercer cam profile. Strictly speaking, the C was the sports model, the D for touring. However, in practice both new ohv machines offered a good turn of speed.

All the new Ariel models (the side-valves included) employed Druid-type sprung front forks and diamond-pattern (rigid) frames, both of which were largely carried over from the existing machines. However, that was all that was familiar, and Page had introduced a host of new features. These included:

- double-roller bearing big-end
- aluminium alloy, heat-treated two-ring piston
- ball race drive-side main bearing
- internally located mechanical oil pump; wet sump lubrication
- 7in (178mm) diameter internally expanding brakes on both wheels
- steering damper.

A particular feature of the new Val Page Ariel models for the 1926 season was the outstanding interchangeability of components that he introduced – including both the engine and cycle parts. This was a feature of the Val Page design philosophy – value-for-money engineering.

*Oil Pump Operation*
The oil pump operation saw it driven by a cam from the half-time shaft, its single plunger and cylinder being removable by two screws that secured the flange-mounted body of the

## Overhead-Valve Singles

*The 1926 Val Page-designed ohv single-cylinder engine with forward-mounted magneto, exposed valve gear and exposed pushrods.*

pump to the timing case. This design featured a disc valve that could be cleaned without the need of even removing the body of the pump. The pump drew in oil from the tank via a sight feed, the supply being regulated. Providing that an air-tight joint was kept between the drip-feed glass and its sealing, this was perfectly reliable in service.

### Fully Floating Gudgeon Pins

All the new engines employed fully floating gudgeon pins whilst a single camshaft sat in the crankcase, its two lobes operating exposed pushrods to the inlet and exhaust valves, these valves using double coil springs. As with the side-valve design, the ohv engine featured a cast-iron cylinder head and barrel, the former being detachable, with the valves being disposed at 70 degrees. The cylinder head had a four-bolt fixing, and the rocker gear was mounted on detachable pressed steel plates bolted to the head.

### Two Shock Absorbers

A pair of shock absorbers was specified for the transmission, one on the gearbox (final drive) sprocket, the other on the engine's crankshaft. There was also all-chain operation for both the primary and final drives.

### Improved Braking

Another feature was improved braking. The Model C Super Sport was equipped with a Bowden Servo Brake on its front wheel – its operation bringing into play the rear wheel brake – and thus Page and Ariel introduced one of the very earliest of linked braking systems for a motorcycle (some fifty years before Moto Guzzi introduced its highly publicized system in the mid-1970s).

A control lever on the offside (right) handlebar operated the front brake in the conventional manner, but the control was designed so that in the event of the rear brake cable breaking the front brake could not lock on. Instead, the anchor plate simply rotated until one of the stops made contact with the fork girder, when the brake operated in the normal way. The brake could be applied simply by using the little finger of the right hand on the brake lever and came into operation without snatch or vibration. In addition, no wheel locking occurred with this form of operation.

Considering that a road test in *The Motor Cycle* revealed a maximum speed of just over 80mph (129km/h) for the 1926 497cc ohv Ariel Super Sport Model C, it was just as well that the latest Ariels did have efficient braking, as the cycle-type rim brakes used previously were the weakest link in the outgoing model range. For an additional £5, Ariel would supply the customer with a certificate guaranteeing that his Model C would exceed 85mph (137km/h). When one considers that the maximum speed of the 1925 White & Poppe-engined Ariel five-hundred single was around 65mph (105km/h), this was a pretty impressive improvement.

With their higher performance, superior specification, competition successes (*see*

Chapter 6) and Vic Mole's publicity machine, sales of the 1926 Ariel model range soared ahead.

## The 1927 Models

After the great rush to complete his work on the 1926 model range in the short time available following his arrival from JAP, Val Page had a whole twelve months to make improvements in time for the 1927 model year. And some of the 'improvements' were of a major nature.

The new range was announced in the motorcycle press during September 1926, a few weeks before the London Olympia Show in November. It was not until the show itself that the brand new Model E was unveiled – this being essentially a 497cc Super Sport, but with a fashionable twin port head, and two separate exhausts.

*A New Frame*
One of the biggest changes concerned the frame, with the old diamond type replaced by a cradle type, a totally new innovation for Ariel. With the new design, the engine's crankcase no longer formed a stressed member as it had in the past. The engine and transmission were held in place in the new chassis by a series of plates. Saddle tanks were adopted for the first time, setting a fashion that was to embrace the entire motorcycle industry over the next few years.

Adding to an entirely new appearance were the girder-type front forks of triangulated design. These employed single barrel springs, replacing the Druid-pattern ones used previously. The friction steering and fork dampers of the 1926 models were retained, but new features were lugs at the top of the fork girders which acted as attachment points for the headlamp. Lamps, however, at this stage were still not standard equipment, remaining cost options. Ignition was by Lucas magneto, but unlike the 1926 model, this was now positioned at the rear rather than the front of the cylinder.

Braking was also revised, as the braking for the Model C, with its Bowden coupled system, had not proved successful, so was discontinued for 1927. As on the other models, the front brake was now hand-operated and the rear by foot pedal.

*A New Burman Gearbox*
A new Burman gearbox fitted to the 1927 models was specially manufactured by the Burman company – a tradition that would continue until the Leader and Arrow two-strokes were finally axed in the mid-1960s. The gearbox featured a large, easily removed inspection cover at the top. Lubricant could be poured in through this inspection hole. The friction area of the clutch plates was increased in capacity to cope with the significant increase in power output from the Page-designed engine.

## The Model E

Introduced at Olympia in November 1926, the Model E (and Model C) had an engine specification that included:

- polished exhaust and inlet ports
- domed, high-compression piston; 8:1 compression
- lightened connecting rod
- pushrod return springs
- balanced crankshaft.

Ariel noted that the Model E (and Model C) developed a minimum of 20bhp at peak engine revolutions. These power outputs were achieved using an Amal TT-type carburettor. It was also possible to buy a racing camshaft from the works.

## Mole Joins the Board

Thanks to the great success garnered by the new motorcycle, and record sales, Vic Mole, the Sales Manager of Ariel Works Ltd, was invited to join the board of directors, a position he took up in January 1928. During 1927 Ariel had spent a considerable sum of money on new tooling and machinery, thus making its factory one of the most modern in the industry. At the AGM of Ariel's parent company, Components Ltd, Chairman Charles Sangster was able to announce to the shareholders a profit for the 1927 trading year of over £31,000 (several million pounds sterling at today's value), which was a ten-fold increase over the previous year.

## The 1928 Model Range

The 1928 model range saw the same five Ariel models retained – A, B, C, D and E. However, there was a considerable number of changes. The most important of these were:

- enclosed valve gear on the ohv models
- redesigned frame
- improved engine quietness (a major complaint against the1927 models)
- bearing and rocker spindle surfaces increased in area by as much as 50 per cent
- wider teeth on cam-wheel
- wider camshafts
- enclosed pushrods
- Brooklands-style 'Fishtail' silencers
- pushrod return springs standardized on ohv models (formerly only on Super Sports versions).

## New 250cc Models

When advance details of the 1929 Ariel range were announced in September 1928, two new 248cc (65 × 75mm) single-cylinder models made their entrance – the only significant difference between the two lay in the engine units, one of which had a twin port ohv cylinder, the other a side-valve arrangement (*see* Chapter 3).

Except for the cylinder head and valve gear, the ohv engine was identical to the side-valve type, with a vertical cylinder, double-roller bearing big-end, a ball race for the drive-side main, a bearing for the timing side. The entire timing chamber was enclosed by an oil-tight magneto chaincase; the front of this case was extended to form a cover for the double-plunger oil pump. The latter item was driven by an eccentric on the end of the exhaust camshaft. Oil was cooled during circulation and also by deep cooling ribs on the crankcase. A changeover from wet-to-dry sump lubrication had been required for the new design of oil pump, which it shared with the larger bikes.

The ohv 248cc single (coded Model LF) put out 10bhp and could, Ariel claimed, reach 65mph, – the price was £38 10s, with extra charges for lighting equipment and speedometer. These new two-fifties were the first to bear the Colt name. Both the ohv and sv models were claimed to be within the 200lb (91kg) government taxation limit with the dynamo in situ, but without the speedometer. Special Burman gearboxes were needed for the two-fifties – these could be pivoted at their tops.

The 1929 Ariel range consisted of six models, including the pair of two-fifties already described. All had dry sump lubrication, whilst all three ohv models featured the fashionable, but less efficient twin port heads, the exhaust port arrangement having been discontinued at that time. The prices of the two larger ohv models were Model E Sports £47 10s and Model F de Luxe £50.

## New Super Sports Machines

A pair of new Super Sports models were announced when the 1930 Ariel range was made public towards the end of 1929. That the company felt confident to introduce new bikes had been helped by the huge sales generated that year – 19,000 in the eight months up to the end of August!

The newcomers were the 248cc LG and the 497cc G – both featuring specially tuned and bench-tested versions of the existing ohv single-cylinder engines. The ohv engines

*Above* Edward Turner's five-hundred Square Four of 1931. This ohc design created a sensation when it arrived.

*Left* The Ariel name can be traced back to 1847. The company's first powered motor vehicle, a tricycle, arrived in 1898. Ariel's original motorcycle debuted in late 1901; the model shown followed shortly afterwards.

The revised Red Hunter single-cylinder engine appeared for the 1938 season, with a new cylinder head and separate aluminium rocker covers. Oil leakage from the pushrod tubes was largely cured by the introduction of large 'O' rings.

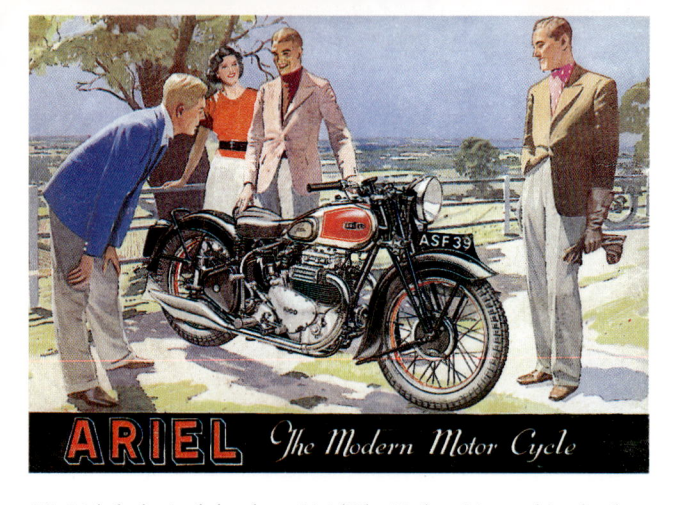

*Vic Mole had coined the phrase 'Ariel The Modern Motorcycle' a decade before the 1939 model range was announced. The magnificent 1000 4G Square Four headed Ariel's range at this time. It featured pushrod-operated valves, in place of the original overhead cams.*

*The 500cc Model VG ohv de Luxe, a twin-port single, cost £61 10s 1939. Features included deeply valenced mudguards, iron head and bar girder forks and rigid frame; plunger rear suspension was available at additional cost.*

*A November 1948 advertisement telling the world that Ariel were the only company offering single, twin and 4-cylinder models.*

**THE WORLD'S MOST *Comprehensive* SERIES**

# ARIEL
## ...THE *Only* RANGE OFFERING SINGLE·TWIN & 4 CYLINDER MODELS

1. Red Hunter 350 and 500 c.c. O.H.V. "Super Singles" DE LUXE 350 and 500 c.c. O.H.V. and 600 c.c. S.V.

2. Red Hunter and De Luxe 500 c.c. Vertical model KH and KG—the Aristocrat of Twins— Spring frame at extra.

4. SQUARE 4, the 1000 c.c. with the astronomical acceleration— the Monarch of the Multis.

ARIEL MOTORS LIMITED · SELLY OAK · BIRMINGHAM 29

'Choose your mount from the pedigree stable', showing the famous Ariel horse. The bike is a 1950 498cc KH Red Hunter ohv twin.

*Below left* The 1950 Ariel Red Hunter range showing, left to right: KH 500 twin, VH 500 single and NH 350 single.

*Below right* The famous Ariel 'Twins of 1931 and 1950' brochure, now a collector's piece in its own right, showing the KH and KG five-hundred ohv verticle twin models.

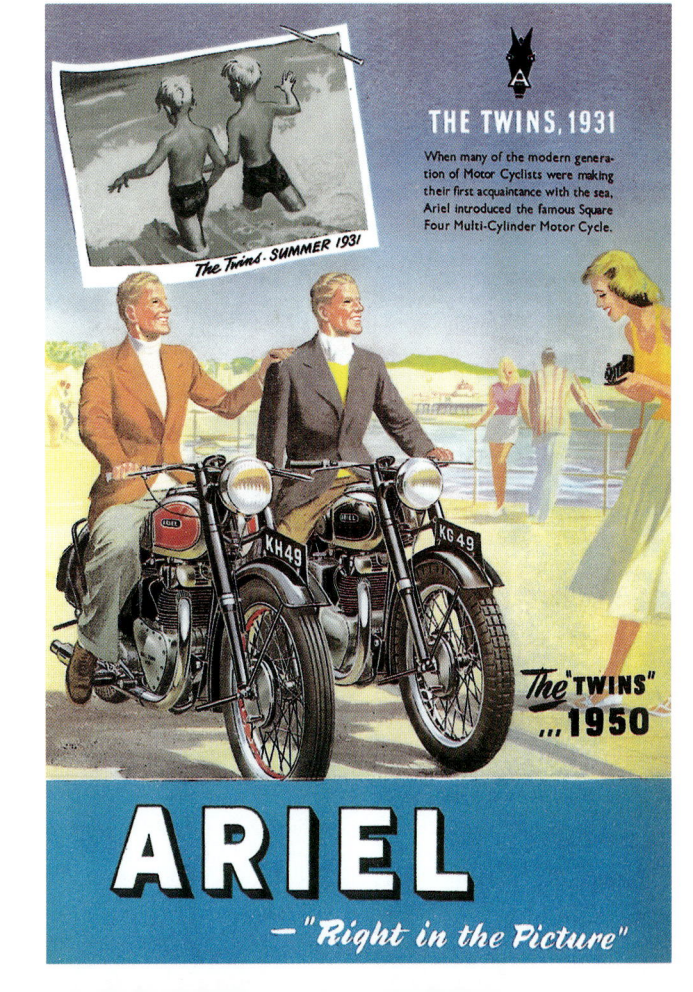

## Model HS Mark 1
# 500 c.c. SCRAMBLES RED HUNTER

### SPECIFICATION

**Engine.** Vertical O.H.V. 81.8 × 95 mm. = 497 cc. (3.22 × 3.74 = 30.4 cubic inches). Aluminium alloy cylinder barrel with nickel iron liner. Aluminium alloy cylinder head with valve seat inserts. Ground and polished inlet and exhaust ports. Polished flywheels, connecting rod and rockers. Super sports cams. Compression ratio 9.1. Amal "Monobloc" carburetter fitted with large capacity air cleaner. Straight through exhaust pipe. Certificate of performance, including bench test report, supplied with machine.

**Lubrication.** Dry sump. Oil circulated by dual plunger pump from separate oil tank, ½ gallon capacity.

**Ignition.** Magneto (Lucas waterproof).

**Frame.** Duplex cradle type, fully triangulated, combining light weight with strength and rigidity. Swinging arm rear suspension with hydraulic damping. Rubber bushed pivots.

**Forks.** Telescopic with hydraulic rebound and bump damping. Bearing surfaces automatically lubricated. Steering damper incorporated.

**Transmission.** Engine shaft shock absorber. Front chain ½" × .305" in polished aluminium oilbath chaincase. Rear chain ⅝" × ⅜". Four speed close ratio gearbox with three fabric clutch plates.

**Wheels.** Fitted with Dunlop sports tyres. 4.00 × 19" rear; 3.00 × 21" front. Plated rims. Full width light alloy hubs, front and rear, powerful central brakes 7" diameter. Fulcrum adjustment.

**Fuel Tank.** Steel, 2½ gallons capacity, finished in red with gold lines.

**Mudguards.** Light steel with wide clearance, chromium plated. (Aluminium alloy at extra charge.)

**Equipment.** Dualseat, complete tool kit and tyre inflator.

Price £200 0 0 plus Purchase Tax £48 0 0

### TECHNICAL DATA

| | |
|---|---|
| WHEELBASE | 56" |
| OVERALL LENGTH | 84" |
| HANDLEBAR WIDTH | 27½" |
| DUALSEAT HEIGHT | 31" |
| GROUND CLEARANCE | 6¼" |
| WEIGHT DRY | 318 lb. |
| ENGINE B.H.P. | 34 |
| ENGINE R.P.M. | 6,000 |
| COMPRESSION RATIO | 9.1 |
| GEAR RATIO, TOP | 6.02 |
| GEAR RATIO, THIRD | 7.9 |
| GEAR RATIO, SECOND | 10.2 |
| GEAR RATIO, FIRST | 16.1 |
| ENGINE SPROCKET | 18 tooth |
| ALTERNATIVE SPROCKETS AVAILABLE | 17-24 tooth |

*The definitive developments of the production 500 Scrambles Model HS ...*

## Model HT
# 500 c.c. TRIALS RED HUNTER

### SPECIFICATION

**Engine.** Vertical O.H.V. 81.8 x 95 mm. = 497 c.c. (3.22 x 3.74 = 30.4 cubic inches). Aluminium alloy cylinder barrel with nickel iron liner. Aluminium alloy cylinder head with valve seat inserts. Ground and polished inlet and exhaust ports. Specially tuned to develop high power at low R.P.M. All steel flywheel assembly mounted on two heavy duty roller bearings and one ball bearing. Large double row caged big end bearing. Amal "Monobloc" carburetter with gauze air filter.

**Lubrication.** Dry sump. Oil circulated by dual plunger pump from separate oil tank, ½ gallon capacity.

**Ignition.** Magneto (Lucas waterproof).

**Frame.** Specially designed short wheelbase, of great strength combined with light weight. High ground clearance. Swinging arm rear suspension with hydraulic damping. Rubber bushed pivots.

**Forks.** Telescopic with hydraulic rebound and bump damping. Bearing surfaces automatically lubricated.

**Transmission.** Engine shaft shock absorber. Front chain ½" x .305" in polished aluminium oilbath chaincase. Rear chain ⅝" x ⅜". Four speed wide ratio gearbox with two fabric clutch plates.

**Wheels.** Fitted with Dunlop Trials Universal tyres. 4.00 x 19" rear. 3.00 x 21" front. Plated rims. Full width light alloy front hub. Powerful 7" diameter brakes front and rear. Fulcrum adjustment.

**Fuel Tank.** 2 gallon capacity, light alloy, finished in red with gold lines.

**Mudguards.** Polished light alloy with wide clearance.

**Equipment.** Saddle, complete tool kit and tyre inflator.

Price £177 10 0 plus Purchase Tax £42 12 0

### TECHNICAL DATA

| | |
|---|---|
| WHEELBASE | 53" |
| OVERALL LENGTH | 80" |
| HANDLEBAR WIDTH | 27" |
| SADDLE HEIGHT | 32" |
| GROUND CLEARANCE | 7" |
| WEIGHT DRY | 290 lb. |
| COMPRESSION RATIO | 5.6 |
| GEAR RATIO, TOP | 6.02 |
| GEAR RATIO, THIRD | 9.46 |
| GEAR RATIO, SECOND | 14.7 |
| GEAR RATIO, FIRST | 19.3 |
| ENGINE SPROCKET | 18 tooth |
| ALTERNATIVE SPROCKETS AVAILABLE | 17-24 tooth |

## WHERE IT IS MOST NEEDED

*... and Trials Model HT appeared in swinging arm guise from the mid-1950s. The Trials model, in particular, ridden by the likes of Sammy Miller and Ron Langston, gained huge success.*

*The new four-pipe 1000 4G Mark II debuted for the 1953 season. This is typical Ariel publicity material from the period.*

## ARIEL
### Leaders of Design

**Built to LAST**

**COMPETITION HUNTER**
**SINGLE CYLINDER 500 c.c.** *Model* **VCH**

Specially designed for competition work in which light weight and ease of handling over the most arduous courses are the prime considerations.

*Running alongside the VH Red Hunter roadster of the early 1950s was the limited-production VCH competition model with rigid frame, telescopic forks and specially tuned 497cc ohv engine.*

**ENGINE:** Powerful O.H.V., fitted with polished aluminium alloy cylinder with wear resisting detachable sleeve. Polished aluminium alloy cylinder head with valve seat inserts. Designed to develop exceptional power at low speeds with high maximum speed. 81.8 × 95 mm. 497 c.c. (3.22 × 3.74 30.4 cubic inches). Forged steel flywheels. Large diameter mainshafts mounted on two heavy duty roller bearings and one ball bearing. Double row roller connecting rod big end bearing. Aluminium alloy piston, 6.8 compression ratio. (7.5 ratio supplied to order for use with 80 octane fuel). Ground and polished ports. Specially bench tested and tuned.

**LUBRICATION:** Oil circulates by dual plunger pump. Separate oil tank ½ gallon (2.26 litres) capacity.

**IGNITION:** Lucas racing magneto.

**GEARBOX:** Wide ratio gears, two plate Neoprene clutch (close ratio and three plate Neoprene clutch for scramble machines).

**FRAME:** Short wheel base, high ground clearance. Polished duralumin mudguards. Low level exhaust pipe with upswept silencer.

**WHEELS:** Dunlop Trials Universal tyres, 4.00 × 19 rear; 3.00 × 21 front. (Sports tyres to special order).

**FUEL TANK:** 2¼ gallons (11.25 litres) capacity, fitted with main supply and reserve tap with filter. Rubber knee pads.

Finished throughout in Deep Claret enamel, gold lining, chromium plating and polished aluminium. Magdyno lighting set optional extra; see separate Price List.

Spring frame with standard 56 inch wheel base, 5¼ inch ground clearance to special order at extra charge.

The new duplex frame made its debut for 1954. Shown here on the KH Hunter twin, it was eventually to be fitted to all Ariels of 350cc and above except the Square Four.

*Here is the 1954*
**ARIEL**
**500 c.c. K.H. HUNTER TWIN**

**WITH THE NEW DUPLEX CRADLE TYPE FRAME**

**SWINGING ARM REAR SUSPENSION**

**& FLUTED TANK**

ARIEL MOTORS LTD · SELLY OAK · BIRMINGHAM · 29

1955 KH 500 in completely original specification, including alloy head and cast-iron barrel, separate headlamp and cream-colour seat material.

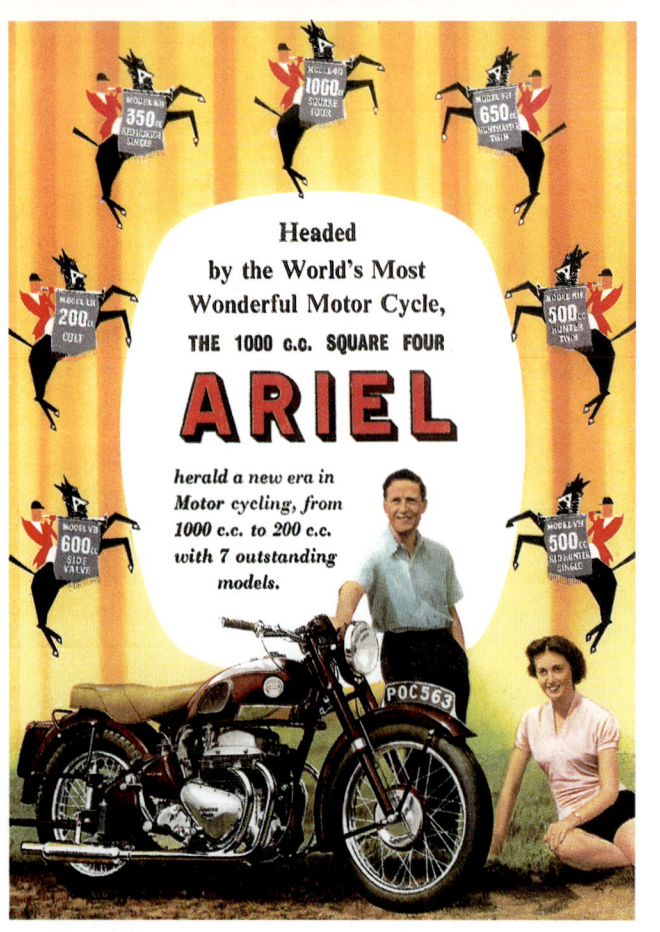

*The 1000 4G Mark II as it was in 1955. It then remained virtually unchanged until production finally came to an end in mid-1959, to bring the curtain down on a model series that ran for almost three decades.*

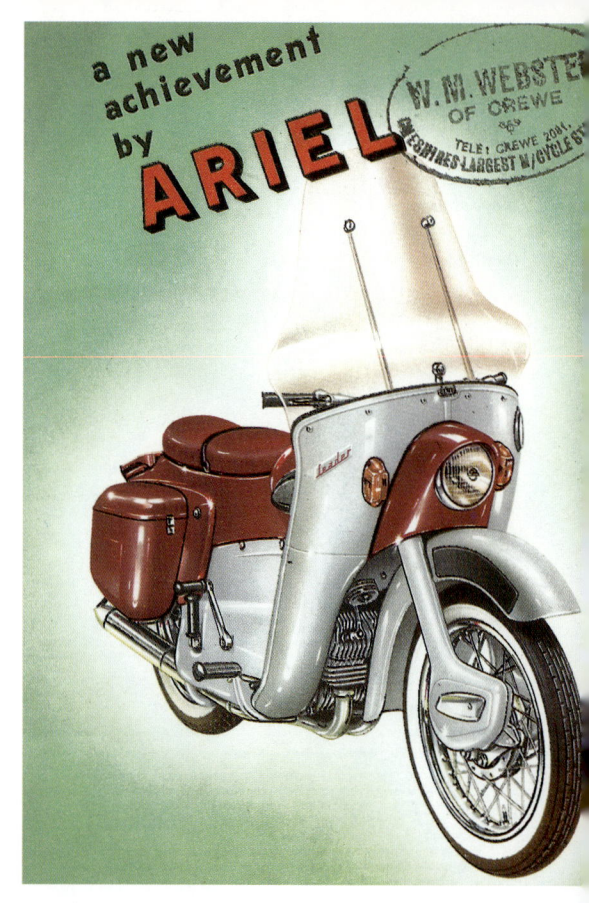

*Launched in July 1958, the twin-cylinder two-stroke Leader was a radical departure for the usually conservative Ariel marque. This rare brochure has the stamp of the famous rider/dealer W.M. (Bill) Webs* of Crewe, Cheshire.*

*A 1960 brochure co for the Leader/Arro range. It all looks to good to be true — an was, with motorcycle production ending in 1965 after a move Ariel's Selly Oak h to the BSA factory 1962.*

*Overhead-Valve Singles*

*During the late 1920s Ariel's publicity chief Vic Mole coined the phrase 'The Modern Motor Cycle'.*

*Lovely period advertisement, dated March 1928 – from an Ariel agent in Fleet Street, London.*

used by Ariel in its 1930 range were virtually identical to the 1929 units, but with their inlet guides lubricated from the crankcase. Redesigned engine shock absorbers were also specified, together with uprated oil feeds for both the primary and dynamo chains. Amal carburettors were now standardized throughout the range.

Both the Model G and Model LG came with highly polished ports and combustion chambers, plus deeper finning than the 'cooking' versions. Stronger valve springs were fitted together with higher compression alloy pistons. Completing the specification were high lift cams, larger bore carbs, ground-timing gears and racing-type Lucas racing magnetos. Interestingly, the two-fifty LG was officially known as the Colt, although the phrase had been almost universally adopted to describe all Ariel two-fifties made at that time.

*New Models Galore*
Ariel chose to launch a whole host of glamorous models on the eve of the 1930 Olympia Motorcycle Show, at a time when Great Britain, together with the rest of Europe, was beginning to feel the icy grip of the Great Depression, which was caused by the Wall Street stock market crash back in October 1929.

Besides the Square Four and the Sloper series (*see* Chapters 5 and 2 respectively), Ariel introduced the Model VG 31 de Luxe. This latter machine was not only the most expensive single cylinder in the line-up, but also the most technically advanced, with a vertical cylinder, four valves and a pent roof combustion chamber.

Page and Ariel were not the first to use four valves, but it was something of a technical coup for the marque. It came at a time when motorcyclists were demanding greater sophistication and performance than they had in the past; four-valve technology gave them both. Unfortunately, as with the other exciting Ariels introduced at the same time, it could not have been a worse time to put them on to the market. New models cost money to bring to the showroom – and within a few months Ariel would be in desperate straits.

As described in the side-valves chapter, Ariel introduced a centrifugal oil filter system – essentially a reservoir with a plug in the timing-side crankshaft flywheel. This was patented and was to remain a feature of the single-cylinder range for many years.

*A Redesigned Frame*
After experiencing problems with the rear section of the two-fifties' frame of the 1930 Colts, it was redesigned for 1931 (full details in Chapter 3), and they now featured inclined cylinders. The two vertical five-hundreds – the VB31 (side-valve) and VF31 (ohv) – were essentially the same machines as the Model B and F respectively from 1930. Thus, unlike the models with sloping and inclined cylinders, those with vertical ones retained the chain drive to the magdyno assembly. Like the 1930 Model G, the ohv Model VF31 employed rocker return springs instead of pushrod return springs.

Vic Mole had quit Ariel during 1931; his replacement was W R 'Big Bill' Wheeler.

## Return of the Vertical Cylinder Four-Valve Model

In September 1931, when Ariel announced its line-up for the 1932 season, it was seen that besides the four-valve Sloper (SE32), a return was made by a vertical cylinder four-valver (coded VG32). However, the real news came at the Olympia Show a few weeks later with the Model VH32, a Red Hunter tuned variant of the VG32, this too having a 499cc ohv four-valve engine. Features common to all 1932 models included:

- new silencer, with 'Fishtail' integral with body
- toolboxes in pressed steel
- redesigned front forks
- revised wheel spoking

- detachable sprockets
- revised handlebar controls
- improved brakes with revised adjustment.

The Model VG32, although having a vertical cylinder, had valve gear much as the 1931 Sloper VG31, but otherwise the remainder of the engine was considerably different. The pushrods now operated directly upon cam levers, whilst a downdraught Amal carburettor was used to achieve a straighter inlet tract. Other components within the engine had been beefed up; the result: the engine, running on a compression ratio of 6.24:1, put out some 24bhp.

Other features of the VG32 included a three-speed Burman hand-change gearbox, a new system of chain lubrication and a 2.5gal (11.4ltr) fuel tank.

*Three- or Four-Speed Gearboxes*
All 1932 Ariel models had hand-change except the new sports four-valve VH32, this featuring a foot-change. Interestingly, the Square Four and Slopers employed four-speeds; the others, including the vertical cylinder singles, only three. The new VH32, like the VG32, had an upright four-valve engine and was the first of the famous and long-lived Red Hunter family of ohv singles. The VH came with a tuned engine, close ratio gears, a racing magneto, racing-type carb, dropped handlebars, competition high-level exhaust pipes and cylindrical silencers. The VH32 was also the first to adopt the Red Hunter 'trademark' red top panel for the chrome-plated fuel tank and central red lining for the chrome-plated wheel rims. The Red Hunter cost £55 15s.

## Ariel Works (JS) Ltd

As outlined in considerable detail in Chapter 3, Ariel suffered a financial meltdown during the spring and summer of 1932, resulting from the collapse of its parent company, Components Ltd. The result was that the majority of the company's assets were purchased by Charles Sangster's son, Jack, and a new era began with the formation of a new company, Ariel works (JS) Ltd. Edward Turner had replaced Val Page as Chief Designer when the latter moved to Triumph (also to become a Jack Sangster company in 1935).

## Eight Models in 1933

The result was an eight-model range when the first details of the 1933 Ariel models were announced towards the end of October 1932. *The Motor Cycle* reported: 'Eight Main Models from 350cc to 600cc: Many Inconspicuous but Valuable Improvements: New Frame Common to Whole Range.' The new frame employed a series of large diameter tubes, with a single front downtube branching into a twin cradle underneath the engine.

*A 1932 ohv five-hundred twin port single with vertical cylinder.*

*Overhead-Valve Singles*

*1933 twin port Ariel single; note straight instead of angled pushrods compared to previous year. The company had been reformed at the end of 1932, following the collapse of the parent company Components Ltd. It now traded as Ariel Works (JS) Ltd, the new JS standing for Jack Sangster.*

## Red Hunter Revision

The Red Hunter five-hundred model had been extensively revised. Although it retained a vertical cylinder, it now featured only two valves and a new, almost square 86.4 × 85mm bore and stroke dimension, giving a capacity of 498cc. Each machine was delivered with two pistons: a low compression one for normal use; and the other giving a 7:1 ratio providing a power output of 28bhp and a claimed 90mph (145km/h).

An entirely new four-speed foot-change Burman was fitted. The gear change pedal was mounted on a serrated shaft so that it could be set in any position to suit the rider. By removal of the cover-plate, the foot-change mechanism, speedometer and kick-start components could be accessed.

Other features included an aluminium alloy oil bath for the primary chain, 7in (178mm) brakes, a 3.5gal (16ltr) fuel tank with instrument panel and an improved battery mounting; the VH five-hundred Red Hunter cost £57 10s. There were also touring versions with a choice of three- or four-speed gearbox, the VF3 and VF4 respectively.

*For 1934 the overhead-valve gear on all Ariel singles was enclosed, design work being carried out of Edward Turner.*

## A Trio of New Three-Fifties

A new 346cc (72 × 85mm) range of vertical cylinder models was introduced for the 1933 season; these were the NF3 (standard, three-speed), NF4 (standard, four-speed) and NH Red Hunter (four-speed). The most exciting and expensive of these was the NH Red Hunter at £47 10s. This featured a power output of 17bhp on a compression ratio of 6.9:1 and, except for the smaller engine, embodied all the features of its bigger brother the VH Red Hunter five-hundred.

## A Smoothness in Style

With Edward Turner as design chief, the Ariel range seemed to take on a smoothness in styling – a more modern look indeed – with rounded lines and an air of quality. For example, there were now recessed enamel badges with the Ariel name for either side of the fuel tank. A larger 8in (205mm) headlamp, now standardized, carried a built-in ammeter and switch, whilst the majority of the ten-model range for the 1934 season, when it was announced in October 1934, sported more modern-looking cylindrical silencers and on the sports models abbreviated mudguarding.

*Enclosed Valve Gear*
The biggest practical feature that Turner was to incorporate across the range for 1934 was the totally enclosed valve gear. In the case of the overhead valve models, the lower parts of the valve springs were surrounded by tubular thimbles, held in place by the springs themselves. The upper parts, including the rocker ends, were enclosed partly by an aluminium rocker housing and partly by quickly detachable visor-like covers that were held in position by spring clips.

With the above system, oil mist from the crankcase passed up the pushrod tubes, through the rocker box and was directed on to the valve springs and guides. Ariel carried out extensive testing before putting its fully enclosed valve gear design into production – the company worried that excessive wear might occur, particularly to the valve spring life. However, the design came through with flying colours.

Another improvement had been made in the timing gear cover, the two gear wheels now being housed in a close-fitting case, the crankshaft wheel being submerged in oil which could only pass into the upper section by way of the gear teeth. This ensured an oil 'cushion' between meshing teeth, and gave the added benefit of a quieter operation. Silence and rigidity had also been improved due to use of thicker and thus stiffened crankcase walls.

*Red Hunter Updates*
For the 1934 season there was a new two-fifty in the Red Hunter mould. This used a new 249cc (61 × 85mm) engine, the model being coded LH. There was a less expensive touring version, the LF, with three speeds and a lower state of engine tune. Both these motorcycles incorporated the 1934 design features described earlier, including the enclosed valve gear.

Forged steel flywheels, hardened and tempered so as to preserve the tapers into which the crankpin fitted were specified for all Red

*New for 1934, the 249cc LF twin port ohv single, three-speed, hand-change. It incorporated the new-for-1934 features such as enclosed valve springs.*

## Overhead-Valve Singles

*For the 1935 model year the Red Hunter five-hundred was given a new long-stroke 497cc (81.8 × 85mm) single-port engine.*

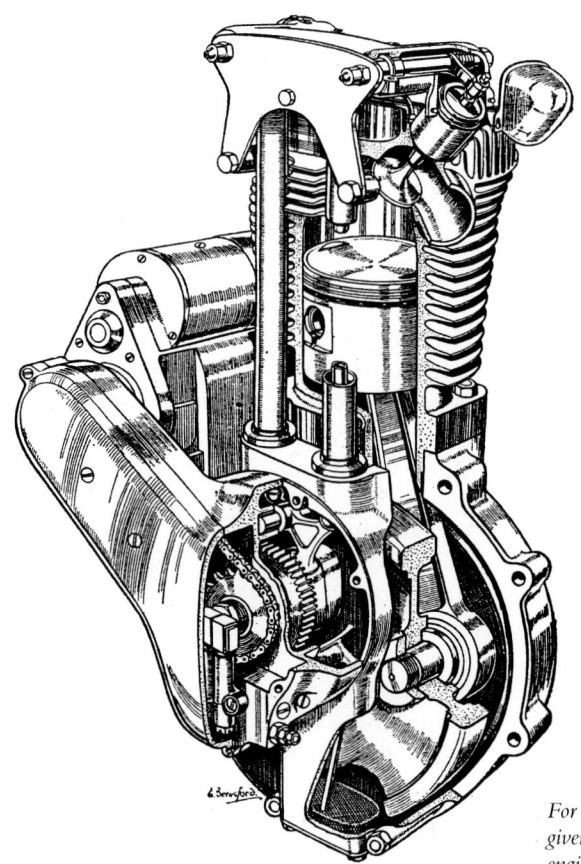

Hunters; 14mm spark plugs were now used. Improved induction ports and heads had been devised for the 350cc and 250cc versions, whilst the cylinder base of the 500cc model had been strengthened to withstand the stresses of full competition use, including road racing; this base now had a wall thickness of 1in (25mm).

There were also a number of detail improvements across the Ariel range, including rubber-mounted handlebars, a neutral indicator pointer fitted to the positive stop, foot-operated gear change, new front forks and a modified steering damper.

## A Redesigned Red Hunter for 1935

In September 1934 details of the 1935 Ariel model range were announced, the big news being the introduction of what amounted to a redesigned five-hundred Red Hunter. A prototype of the new machine had proved itself in the 1934 ISDT where, ridden by Len Heath, it came through the six days without losing a single point!

*A Long-Stroke with Single Port Head*
Previously, the Red Hunter engine had a short stroke (86.4 × 85mm), but the new VH had been revised with a new 487cc displacement and long-stroke 81.8 × 95mm dimensions. In addition, it now sported a single, instead of twin, port cylinder head, although the twin port remained on the touring version of Ariel's five-hundred. The combustion chamber was hemispherical, a 14mm plug was placed at an angle, whilst the offset inlet port, perfectly straight and highly polished throughout its entire

*1935 Ariel five-hundred Red Hunter girder forks and drum front brakes.*

length, was of the downdraught type. A similar 'mirror finish' was given to the exhaust port and to the whole interior surface of the head.

Externally, the new cylinder head was quite different, with the section of the finning being arranged, Ariel claimed, 'to provide much better cooling'. The roots of the fins were thick and tapered off more sharply than before, this feature being present on both the cylinder barrel and head. Another feature of the new head was that the lugs for the holding-down bolts had been reduced in height, thus allowing a free passage of air through the fins across the top of the head.

## A New Piston

The piston was of new design, featuring three rings – two compression and an oil scraper. Large diameter holes were bored through the gudgeon pin bosses, whilst the pin itself was sturdier than before. The standard piston gave a compression ratio of 6:1, but at no extra charge an alternative piston could be fitted at the factory to provide a ratio of 7.5:1, suitable for a 50–50 petrol-benzole mixture.

## The Connecting Rod

The connecting rod of the revised Red Hunter was made of high-tensile nickel-chrome steel and was polished all over; it was both light and strong and as before the big-end comprised a double row of caged rollers. Stronger main shafts were incorporated with forged steel flywheels; the main bearing on the timing side was a roller, while the drive-side had both roller and ball bearings – the outer bearing being of the latter type and providing support at a point much nearer to the end of the shaft than previously.

## A New Crankcase

To accommodate the flywheel assembly, a new crankcase had been designed. This was webbed both inside and out. Lubrication was still of the dry sump type, employing dual plunger pumps, the oil being carried in a tank of increased capacity. The centrifugal filter system was retained.

## Redesigned Brake Drums

On all 1935 Ariel models, except for the two-fifties, the front and rear brake drums had been completely redesigned. In place of the former pressings, the drums were now cast in chromidium; thanks to the improved quality of the materials and the external ribbing they were far less subject to distortion. A further feature lay in the fact that the spoke flange was an extension of the back plate, and not formed on the rim of the drum.

Other changes affecting all the 1935 ohv models were:

- quickly detachable rear wheel at extra cost
- hinged rear mudguard to aid wheel removal

*Overhead-Valve Singles*

- gearbox adjustment modified, making the operation simpler
- footrest position changed to improve riding position
- modified steering damper
- new horn.

## 1936 – Single or Twin Port?

For 1936, Ariel extended the choice of single or twin port for the Red Hunter models to include the 350 and 250cc versions. The single port head had been found to offer definite advantages for racing when a straight-through exhaust was used, and, for trials work, the reduction of the top-end weight (normally resulting from the elimination of one pipe and silencer) proved an asset. Ariel also offered a special Competition version of the 1936 Red Hunter series in 250, 350 and 500cc engine sizes at only a minimal increase in price over the series production roadster Red Hunter models.

Another important feature of the 1936 Ariel range was a new patented dry clutch of increased size. To prevent problems formerly found through clutch drag, the clutch assembly was now housed in a compartment completely isolated from the oil bath provided for the primary chain. Access to the clutch could now be gained without first having to remove the outer primary chain case cover.

Other improvements introduced for the 1936 series were:

- a new and larger brake pedal
- new steering head bearings
- gearboxes polished externally
- a new and enlarged toolbox of all-steel construction

*1935 Ariel RH 500 single port sports model.*

*Peter McPherson of Alness, Rosshire; owner of the 1935 Ariel Red Hunter single port sportster shown left.*

- four-speed gearboxes standardized throughout the range.

## Virtually No Change in 1937

Except for one or two very minor alterations and modifications, the 1937 Ariel range of single-cylinder models was unchanged from 1936. There were several reasons why the company decided on this policy. For one thing, sales of Ariel machines for 1936 were 25 per cent higher than they had been for 1935. In fact, demand far exceeded supply – quite simply, the Selly Oak works had been working at full stretch, but even then it had been impossible to build enough bikes. Also Ariel stated that orders received up to 1 September 1936 were precisely double those received by 5 September 1935 for 1937 models.

The changes were, therefore, restricted to a new type of knee-grip for the fuel tank, a 'water-tight' toolbox and, for all the singles except the 250 ohv Model LG de Luxe, a price increase of £1. The 1937 prices are listed below:

- Model LG de Luxe 250 — £50 10s
- Model LH Red Hunter 250 — £55 10s
- Model LH Red Hunter Competition 250 — £56
- Model NG de Luxe 350 — £54 10s
- Model NH Red Hunter 350 — £58 10s
- Model NH1 Red Hunter Competition 350 — £59
- Model VG de Luxe 500 — £61 10s
- Model VH Red Hunter 500 — £66 10s
- Model VH Red Hunter Competition — £67

## New Cylinder Heads and Modified Valve Gear in 1938

Considerable changes to the ohv single-cylinder engines were introduced for the 1938 model year, in regard to there being new cylinder heads and revised valve gear. Not only did this make an appreciable difference to the appearance, but also provided more efficient and oil-tight engines.

Both the Red Hunter and de Luxe ohv models were affected by these changes. A new cylinder head was introduced; in this, each valve with its rocker box was enclosed in a separate aluminium box, which was held down on to the head by four bolts. The joints between the rocker boxes and the head were made with gaskets to prevent oil leakage.

The rockers were mounted on hollow spindles to which a direct oil feed was taken. Surplus oil ran to the lowest part of the wells, in which the valve springs were contained, and from this point drained down the pushrod tubes on to the cams. At one side of each rocker box was a screwed cap, removal of which provided access to the tappet adjustment, that was at the end of the rocker arm.

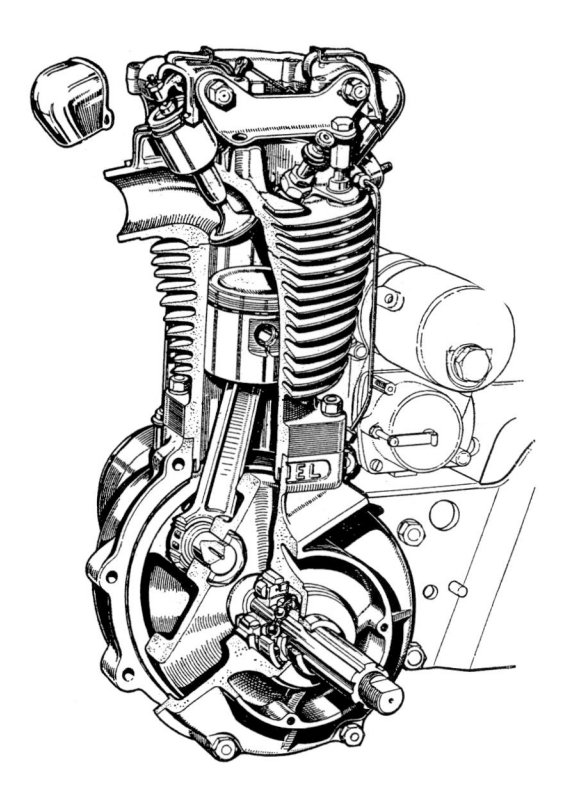

*The 1936 single port VH 500 Red Hunter engine, showing the modifications to the valve covers, valve guide lubrication system, plus crankshaft and big-end details.*

## LG 250 de Luxe 1937

| | |
|---|---|
| Engine | Air-cooled overhead valve single with vertical cylinder; twin port; cast-iron cylinder head and barrel; high-tensile steel connecting rod; double roller bearing big-end. |
| Bore | 61mm |
| Stroke | 85mm |
| Displacement | 249cc |
| Compression ratio | 6:1 |
| Lubrication | Dry sump, twin plunger pump |
| Ignition | Magneto |
| Carburettor | Amal |
| Primary drive | Chain |
| Final drive | Chain |
| Gearbox | Four-speed, Burman, foot-change |
| Frame | Tubular, all-steel construction; single front downtube |
| Front suspension | Girder fork |
| Rear suspension | Unsprung, rigid frame |
| Front brake | 7in single-sided drum, SLS |
| Rear brakes | 7in single-sided drum, SLS |
| Tyres | Front 3.00 × 26; rear 3.25 × 26 |

**General Specifications**

| | |
|---|---|
| Wheelbase | 54.5in (1,384mm) |
| Ground clearance | 4.75in (121mm) |
| Seat height | 26.5in (673mm) |
| Fuel tank capacity | 2.5gal (11.4ltr) |
| Dry weight | n/a |
| Maximum power | 10bhp |
| Top speed | 62mph (100km/h) |

## NH 350 Red Hunter 1937

| | |
|---|---|
| Engine | Air-cooled overhead valve single with twin port (NH2) or single port (NH1) optional twin port; Totally enclosed valve springs; valve guides automatically lubricated; polished flywheels, special polished alloy steel connecting rod; double roller bearing big-end. |
| Bore | 72mm |
| Stroke | 85mm |
| Displacement | 346cc |
| Compression ratio | 7:1 (7.5:1 option at extra cost) |
| Lubrication | Dry sump, twin plunger pump |
| Ignition | Magneto, 6-volt |
| Carburettor | Amal |
| Primary drive | Chain |
| Final drive | Chain |
| Gearbox | Four-speed, Burman, foot-change |
| Frame | Tubular, all-steel construction; single front downtube |
| Front suspension | Girder forks |
| Rear suspension | Unsprung, rigid frame |
| Front brake | 7in single-sided drum, SLS |
| Rear brakes | 7in single-sided drum, SLS |
| Tyres | Front 3.00 × 26; rear 3.25 × 26 |

**General Specifications**

| | |
|---|---|
| Wheelbase | n/a |
| Ground clearance | 4.75in (121mm) |
| Seat height | 27.5in (721mm) |
| Fuel tank capacity | 2.5gal (11.4ltr) |
| Dry weight | n/a |
| Top speed | 67mph (108km/h) |

Oil leakage from the ends of the pushrod tubes was eliminated by providing special 'O' ring seals, because it had been found in the past that after the engine had been dismantled, it proved difficult to achieve an oil-tight seal with the washer formerly fitted.

*A Revised Gearbox Casting*
The Burman-made gearbox had also received attention. Internally this was unaltered, but the casting had been cleaned up considerably, sharp corners having been removed, and the nuts securing the cover now had domed

heads. A further refinement was that the whole of the clutch operating lever was now covered by a moulded rubber sheath.

*Other Changes*
A modification had been made to the front brake, to provide maximum braking power whilst placing a minimum load on the operating cable. Other changes included a headlamp with a domed glass, the fitting of a chrome-plated instead of enamelled instrument panel and a revised damper knob.

Prices had risen slightly, the VH Red Hunter now costing £70 10s, for example.

## 1939 – A Sprung Frame

The next change, which came in time for the 1939 model year, was the introduction, as a cost extra, of a sprung frame. This was the work of Frank Anstey, who had replaced Edward Turner as Chief Designer (earlier, Anstey had joined Triumph from Rudge, and then transferred to Ariel from Triumph after Jack Sangster had moved Edward Turner to the Coventry-based concern). All quite complicated! Anstey's design employed plunger boxes, but in such a way as to ensure that the chain tension remained unaltered throughout the entire travel of the rear wheel. Its design features are fully covered in Chapter 5.

*Auxiliary Fork Damping Springs*
A modification common to all models, except the two-fifties, was the fitting of auxiliary damping springs to the front forks. There were also detail changes to the handlebars, rear number plate, tail lamp and, on the singles only, a new front chain case with a streamlined front boss giving a more pleasing style. The five-hundred singles also featured a modified saddle position, the seat being mounted slightly further rearwards than before. On the Red Hunter and the de Luxe five-hundreds a bolder sweep had been introduced to the top of the fuel tank

The 250cc Red Hunter and de Luxe machines now boasted a new frame of orthodox pattern. The downtubes were more vertical, and the frames were lighter than previously, providing a slightly shorter wheelbase. The 250 engine was of the single port type, although a twin port head was available at an extra charge. The engine units had been updated to keep in line with the larger ohv singles. The 250s were now coded OG de Luxe and OH Red Hunter.

## War Stops Play

When Ariel finally announced its 1940 model range at the beginning of November 1939, there were no changes in specification except

*A 1938 346cc (72 × 85mm) Red Hunter single, with upswept exhaust, chrome tank, tank-top speedometer and central spring girder forks.*

## Overhead-Valve Singles

some slight variations in price. Then came a break while normal civilian life was left on hold until Mr Hitler and his cronies were dealt with. So, it was not until the late summer of 1945 before Ariel could announce details of its model range to the public once again.

There is, however, no doubt that the Second World War came at the wrong time for the Ariel concern. During 1938 and 1939 the Selly Oak company had chalked up record sales and, in fact, besides a healthy home market, it was exporting to no fewer than an astounding sixty-eight countries, and had brochures printed in some fifteen languages. The most popular foreign destinations for Ariel motorcycles at that time were: Continental Europe (notably Germany!); the British Commonwealth countries (in particular Australia, Canada, South Africa and New Zealand); plus the United States of America.

*The American Market*

In the USA, Ariel had become the first British marque to employ a full-time factory representative in that vast country; his name was C E Hopping of Haddon Hall, Bronxville, New York. On the other side of the States in Pasadena, California, Bill Johnson, himself a motorcycle enthusiast, had fallen in love with the Ariel Four Square; he wrote to Edward Turner (the original designer) and the result was that Johnson became Ariel and Triumph importer for the western seaboard of the United States in the years after the war had ended.

## Page Replaces Anstey

In May 1939, Frank Anstey left Ariel to join the Wolverhampton-based Villiers company; his position at Selly Oak was taken by none

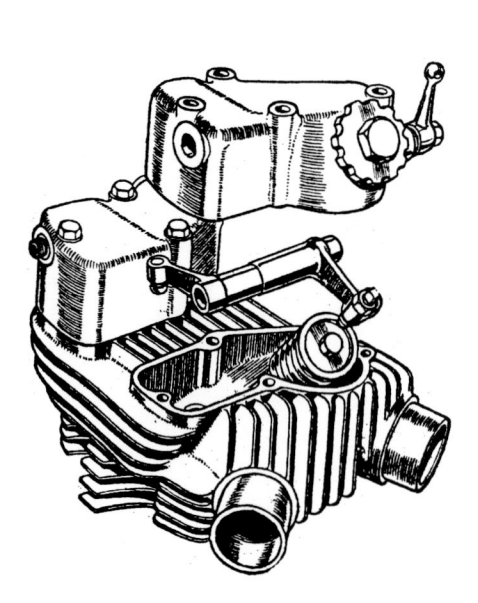

*The new cylinder head fitted to the ohv singles for the 1938 season. Not only did it make an appreciable difference, but it was also more efficient and oil-tight.*

*American Bob McKeever Junior with his plunger framed 1939 five-hundred Red Hunter, circa early 1940s, before being enlisted for military service during the Second World War. He later rode a Manx Norton at Daytona in March 1948, finishing fourteenth. Bob, now in his mid-80s, lives near Washington, DC.*

other than Val Page, who had joined Triumph in the early 1930s and subsequently left for BSA.

During the course of the long years of war, Jack Sangster decided to sell his shares in Ariel to the giant BSA Group. This news, when it came during late 1944, did not go down well in the Selly Oak workplace. They feared it would result in their becoming second-class citizens compared to BSA workers – and that the loss of independence would spell trouble ahead. In the long term, they were to be proved right, although this took many years to happen. In the meanwhile, Ariel remained at Selly Oak and got on with meeting the vast demand for its products fuelled by the coming of peace.

## Post-War Developments

As for the single-cylinder ohv Ariel range, the only big news for the remainder of the 1940s was the development and introduction of new telescopic forks (*see* Chapter 5), these providing the post-war Ariels with a more up-to-date appearance, at least when used with the optional Anstey plunger rear suspension. At first, this was restricted to a brand new five-hundred ohv twin and later on the updated Square Four. With the singles – which were actually the biggest singles – it was very much a case of trying to meet the demand rather than carrying out any more developments. There were also considerable sales of either new or reconditioned War Department models, notably the 346cc W/NG ohv single (*see* Chapter 4). A major issue was prices, these having risen by a large amount compared to pre-war days. For example, when the 1947 programme was announced in August 1946, the ohv single ranged from the NG de luxe 350 at £132 1s 7d to the VH Red Hunter 500 costing £156 4s 3d (both these prices including the recently introduced UK purchase tax).

The first major change to the ohv single-cylinder line came for the 1950 model year, when Ariel launched an alloy-engined Competition Red Hunter, coded VCH. (Details of this machine and its development history are contained in Chapter 6.) The other ohv singles continued much as before, though prices had steadily increased, with the VH Red Hunter 500 now costing £173 19s 10d.

## Additions and Subtractions in 1951

The 1951 model year was one of additions and subtractions for Ariel's long-running three-fifty and five-hundred ohv single family. In order to simplify the production problems caused by over-demand, two models had been axed. These two, the 497cc Model VG and its 347cc counterpart the NG, both with specifications similar to the Red Hunter versions, Ariel said: 'would no longer be manufactured and an increase in the output of the Hunter models VH and NH was anticipated'.

*Revised Instrumentation*
A feature of the 1950 Square Four and five-hundred vertical twin-cylinder models had been the revised instrumentation, with the speedometer relocated from the tank top position to a steel bridge between the fork legs, and the headlamp switches transferred to the front top panel. However, for 1951 the ohv singles (as well as the four- and twin-cylinder models) featured a new light-alloy speedometer mounting that formed an attractive fork-top facia. Additionally, the other switches, ammeter and so on, were relocated back to the headlamp shell. The fuel filler cap was now moved to a central position atop the tank.

*A New Cam Gear*
As *The Motor Cycle* of 21 September 1950 reported: 'It is in the three single-cylinder machines, the 497cc VH, Competition VCH and the 347 NH, that the most interesting technical modification is found.' A new cam gear had been evolved, dispensing with the two separate cams used formerly, and employing a single cam of double width. A forked cam follower arrangement enabled vertical

Overhead-Valve Singles

*As this November 1945 advertisement shows, the immediate post-war civilian Ariel production began essentially where it had ended following the outbreak of war. This is a three-fifty NH Red Hunter single-port model.*

*A 1946 497cc VH Red Hunter single port, with low-level exhaust.*

*Overhead-Valve Singles*

*An NG350 with the Val Page-designed telescopic front forks – introduced for the 1948 model year – after first appearing on the Square Four a year earlier.*

*An American export VH 500 Red Hunter with teles, twin port head, hi-level exhausts and rigid frame; 1949.*

*A UK spec 1949 VG de Luxe; single port, low-level exhaust, rigid frame, single saddle and pillion pad, valanced front mudguard.*

*Overhead-Valve Singles*

*1949 Ariel advertisement proclaiming the economy of the VG500 de Luxe and other single-cylinder models in the range. Petrol rationing was still in force in Great Britain.*

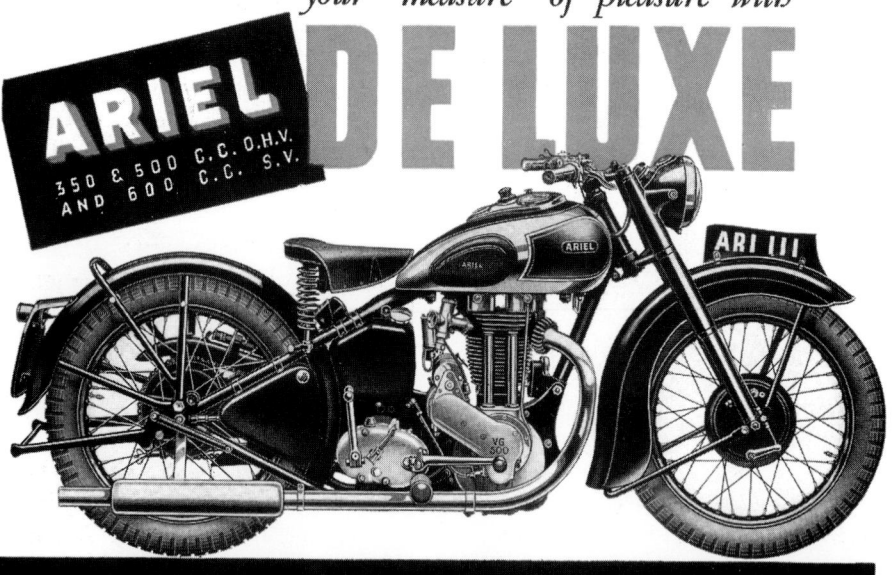

| NG 350 1945 | |
|---|---|
| Engine | Air-cooled overhead valve single with vertical cylinder; single or twin exhaust port; iron cylinder head and barrel; forged steel connecting rod; roller bearing big-end; vertically split aluminium crankcases. |
| Bore | 72mm |
| Stroke | 85mm |
| Displacement | 346cc |
| Compression ratio | 6:1 |
| Lubrication | Dry sump, twin plunger pump |
| Ignition | Magneto |
| Carburettor | Amal 275 7/8in |
| Primary drive | Chain |
| Final drive | Chain |
| Gearbox | Four-speed, Burman CPI, foot-change |
| Frame | Tubular, all-steel construction; single front downtube |
| Front suspension | Girder forks |
| Rear suspension | Unsprung, rigid frame |
| Front brake | 7in single-sided drum, SLS |
| Rear brakes | 7in single-sided drum, SLS |
| Tyres | 3.25 × 19 front and rear |
| **General Specifications** | |
| Wheelbase | 56in (1,422mm) |
| Ground clearance | 6in (150mm) |
| Seat height | 28in (152mm) |
| Fuel tank capacity | 2.5gal (11.4ltr) |
| Dry weight | 348lb (158kg) |
| Maximum power | 13bhp @ 5,000rpm |
| Top speed | 71mph (114km/h) |

thrusts to be centralized and, as these permitted follower pads of double width to be used, Ariel claimed cam and follower wear to be considerably reduced by this means – and production of the camshaft was a simpler machining operation.

*Detail Changes*
Fuel tank capacity had been increased by 0.5gal (2.3ltr), the mudguards now had integral (instead of bolted) lugs for the attachment of tubular stays; front number plates were of alloy castings with a concealed fixing; the battery clamp had a two- instead of a single-bolt fixing; all saddles came with barrel-shaped helical springs, which gave a more progressive action; piston design had also changed.

## Testing a 1951 VH Red Hunter

When *The Motor Cycle* tested a 1951 VH Red Hunter five-hundred ohv single, it found that the outstanding features 'were the supreme comfort of the riding position, ease of starting, particularly smooth transmission and excellent low-speed torque'.

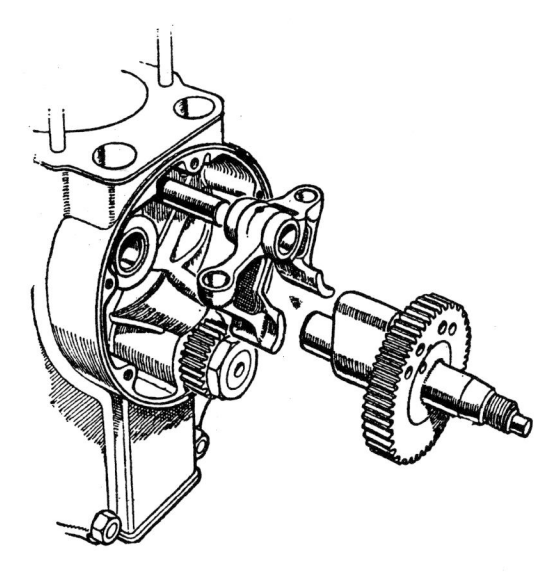

*From the 1951 season, the ohv single cylinder engines employed a single wide camshaft lobe, rather than the former two-lobe design.*

Magdyno-equipped (as, indeed, the VH was to the very end of its life in the late 1950s), the machine had manual ignition control and this had to be used in conjunction with the throttle if the best results were to be obtained. At idling speeds valve-gear and piston were audible if the ignition was fully advanced. On full retard, with the tickover as slow and reliable 'as a steam engine', the piston was all but silent. *The Motor Cycle* tester found that: 'Pick-up was clean-cut and brisk'. Minimum non-snatch speed in top gear was 17mph (27.4km/h); and: 'A 70mph cruising speed in no way extended the engine's capabilities. Slight vibration could be felt at speeds above 60mph.' Weighing in at 385lb (175kg) with lubricant and 1 gal (4.6l) of fuel the maximum speed achieved was 85mph (137km/h).

## A Light-Alloy Cylinder and Head for 1952

The big story for the 1952 model year was the adoption of a new light-alloy head and cylinder barrel for the 497cc, coded VHA and costing £207, compared to the existing iron top-end VH model which cost £194 9s 5d (both included UK taxes). Low expansion silicon light alloy, with a pressed-in iron liner, was used for the cylinder barrel of the new Red Hunter. A square base with a five-point fixing was employed, with the deep finning completely covering the upper portions of the cast-in 'Y' alloy, which maintained its structural strength at high temperatures. Pressed-in valve inserts were of stainless steel. The alloy top end accounted for a reduction in engine weight of 12lb (5.4kg).

*A New Oil Tank*
Together with the side-valve single and ohv twin, the 1952 model Ariel ohv singles had new oil tanks, mounted so as not to obstruct the fitting of a sidecar. Previously the oil tank filler cap did not permit sufficient clearance for the sidecar fixing below the saddle, and an extension bracket had to be employed. In

## Overhead-Valve Singles

addition to having the filler cap further to the rear, the new tank had more rounded corners than previously. The Red Hunter five-hundred singles also featured a small increase in depth at the rear of the fuel tank (a feature shared with the side-valve VB 600).

All 1952 Ariels came with a new spring-up prop stand fitted to the nearside (left) of the motorcycle, slightly forward of the former position.

### Very Little Change in 1953

Very little change to the ohv singles occurred when the 1953 model range was announced at the beginning of November 1952. The

# ARIEL
## it's their staying power that makes them such a good proposition to-day
### — and tomorrow

**THE ARIEL RED HUNTER 500 c.c. MODEL V.H.**
Universally acknowledged as the world's finest Sports Machine. Robust and big hearted, the exceptional stamina of this Red Hunter Single Cylinder makes it ideal for either solo or sidecar.

Send for 1952 illustrated literature to
ARIEL MOTORS LTD · SELLY OAK · BIRMINGHAM, 29

*January 1952 advertisement for the five-hundred Model VH Red Hunter.*

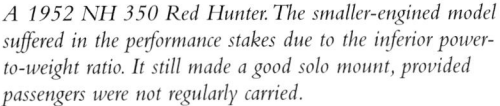

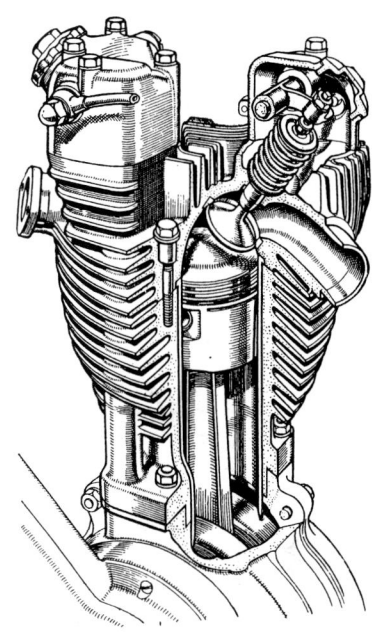

*A 1952 NH 350 Red Hunter. The smaller-engined model suffered in the performance stakes due to the inferior power-to-weight ratio. It still made a good solo mount, provided passengers were not regularly carried.*

*All-alloy top end from the 497cc Red Hunter from the end of 1952 with integral pushrod tubes cast in the barrel. Five-stud crankcase and head, held by five sleeve nuts.*

three-fifty NH Red Hunter was brought into line with the other models by having the revised 6pt (3.4ltr) oil tank fitted. Oil feed to the rockers on all the ohv singles was now taken from a point on the return pipe near its entry into the oil tank. A new Lucas stop and tail lamp was specified for the five-hundred Red Hunter, but not the smaller-engined model. The sprung frame and QD rear wheel were still listed as cost extras.

## Six-Fifty Twin in 1954

In October 1953 Ariel launched its 1954 model range, the big news being a six-fifty twin (*see* Chapter 8) and more significantly for this chapter, a new duplex frame with pivoted fork rear suspension. This frame and the design are fully discussed in Chapter 8.

The alloy barrel/head VHA Red Hunter was dropped for 1954, its place being taken by the standard VH model, but with an aluminium alloy head replacing the former cast-iron component. The swinging arm five-hundred Red Hunter cost £198 including UK taxes; the three-fifty NH model, now with swinging arm but retaining its iron head, retailed at £180.

A major feature of the new swinging arm framed models (which meant everything except the Square Four and VB 600 sv) was a styled oil tank, designed to blend in with the lines of the rear sub-frame, and a matching toolbox at the opposite side, a new centre stand and an oil-impregnated air cleaner. The centre stand had elliptical feet that allowed the bike to be rolled on to the stand with a minimum of effort.

## Ariels for 1955

For the 1955 season there were no radical changes, it being very much attention to detail. The new Amal Monobloc 376 replaced

115

*January 1953 NH 350 Red Hunter single and view of the Selly Oak factory.*

*October 1954 advertisement for the duplex frame five-hundred Red Hunter with swinging arm suspension. In that year's ISDT, the Ariel works team, riding similar bikes, completed the six days without loss of marks, thereby gaining a Manufacturers Team Award and three special Gold Medals.*

MODEL VH
500 c.c. HUNTER SINGLE

**ENGINE:** Vertical O.H.V. 81.8 × 95 mm. = 497 c.c. (3.22 × 3.74 = 30.4 cubic inches). Cast iron cylinder and polished aluminium alloy cylinder head with valve seat inserts. Large diameter mainshafts mounted on two heavy duty roller bearings and one ball bearing. Double row roller big end bearing. Amal carburetter with air cleaner. Dual plunger oil pump. Lucas manual ignition control.
**FRAME:** Duplex cradle type, fully triangulated, ensuring great strength and rigidity, with lugs for sidecar attachment either side. Swinging arm rear suspension with hydraulic damping. 3½ inch wheel movement. All pivot points rubber bushed. Easy-lift spring-up central and strong tubular front stands, also prop stand.
**MUDGUARDS:** Wide D section with tubular stays. Back end of rear guard detachable for easy wheel removal.
**BRAKES:** Ariel design of great power, ensuring positive and progressive action. 7 inch diameter front and rear. Car type fulcrum adjustment.
**LIGHTING EQUIPMENT:** 7½ inch headlamp incorporating lighting switch and ammeter. 56 watt voltage controlled magdyno. 6 volt battery. Stop and tail lamp. Electric horn.
**FINISH:** Superbly finished throughout in best quality Deep Claret enamel.

*Extract from the 1954 Ariel range catalogue showing the VH 500 Red Hunter, with alloy head and iron barrel.*

| VH 500 Red Hunter 1954 | |
|---|---|
| Engine | Air-cooled overhead valve single with vertical cylinder; single port; alloy head and cast-iron barrel; forged steel connecting rod; roller bearing big-end; vertically split aluminium crankcases. |
| Bore | 81.8mm |
| Stroke | 95mm |
| Displacement | 497cc |
| Compression ratio | 6.8:1 |
| Lubrication | Dry sump, twin plunger pump |
| Ignition | Magneto |
| Carburettor | Amal 376 Monobloc 1 1/16in |
| Primary drive | Chain |
| Final drive | Chain |
| Gearbox | Four-speed, Burman GB6, foot-change |
| Frame | Duplex cradle, all-steel construction |
| Front suspension | Ariel telescopic fork |
| Rear suspension | Swinging arm, twin shock absorbers |
| Front brake | 7in single-sided drum, SLS[1] |
| Rear brakes | 7in single-sided drum, SLS[1] |
| Tyres | Front 3.00 × 20[2]; rear 3.25 × 19 |
| **General Specifications** | |
| Wheelbase | 56in (1,422mm) |
| Ground clearance | 5.5in (140mm) |
| Seat height | 31in (787mm) |
| Fuel tank capacity | 4gal (18ltr)[3] |
| Dry weight | 375lb (170kg) |
| Maximum power | 26bhp @ 5,000rpm |
| Top speed | 85mph (137km/h) |

[1] 1956 full-width front and rear.
[2] 1955 3.25 × 19.
[3] 1957 4.5gal (20ltr).

the old, separate float bowl 276 type, on all models except the Square Four. The NH 350 had a 1in (25mm) as before, whereas the VH 500 now sported a 1 1/16in (27mm) instead of the former 1 1/8in (29mm) size. There was also the introduction of a Yale-type steering lock, this being a cylindrical unit with a co-axial, 5/16in (8mm) diameter plunger.

On the two single-cylinder engines, flexible oil delivery and return pipes superseded the copper pipes previously employed. On the five-hundred single, the exhaust valve head diameter had been reduced from 1 3/4 to 5/8in (45 to 41mm). This modification lowered the normal running temperature of the valve, thus, Ariel claimed, 'reducing any tendency toward detonation'; the valve was manufactured in G2 austenitic steel.

Together with other Ariel models, 1955 saw the introduction of a Vacrom piston ring. This was fitted as the top compression ring due to it being the most highly stressed. As well as reducing ring-wear generally, the Vacrom ring was claimed to double the serviceable life of the cylinder bore. Another innovation was a screwed plug in each rocker box to permit insertion of a feeler gauge when checking the valve clearance. Removal of the rocker box cover-plate and cap provided access to the adjuster.

After a couple of years when there was a selection of colour schemes, the entire Ariel range reverted to the marque's traditional deep claret with chrome-plated tank panels (flutes) and wheel rim centres. All models, except the rigid frame VB 600, came with the following as standard equipment:

- dual seat
- centre and prop stands
- air cleaner
- pillion footrests
- speedometer.

Prices for the 1955 ohv singles were as follows:

- NH350  £186
- VH 500  £198.

Both prices included UK taxes.

*Overhead-Valve Singles*

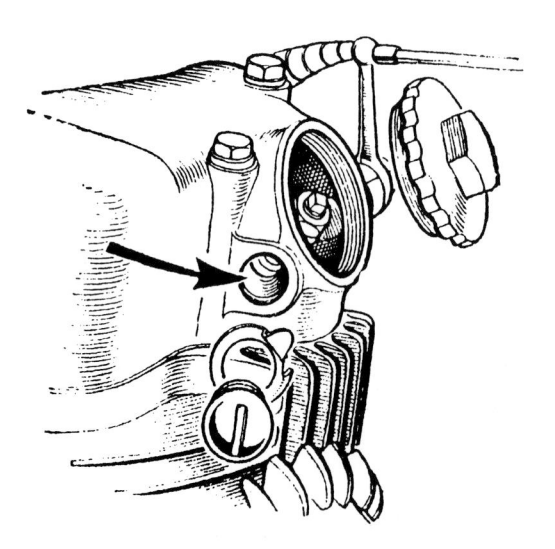

*Access hole and cap lock introduced on 350 and 500 ohv singles from the 1955 model year.*

## Testing the VH 500

When *The Motor Cycle* tested the latest VH 500 in its 28 April 1955 issue it began by saying: 'A mainstay of the Ariel stable since the early 1930s, the 497cc overhead-valve Red Hunter is an outstanding example of the type of high performance, single-cylinder mount, notwithstanding the popularity of vertical twins, that still has many advocates and commands a large following.'

Engine performance of the test model 'was in the best single-cylinder tradition'. It went on to record: 'Speedometer readings in the 70s were habitually obtained during out-of-town journeys; indeed, when conditions permitted, a gait of 70mph was adopted as a cruising speed'. 'Powerful' and 'tireless' were two words used. The tester also found that: 'After being driven hard for mile after mile, it remained oil-tight, retained its tune, and gave no signs of overheating.'

On the score of rider comfort, the Red Hunter single 'earned full marks'. In every way the machine gained nothing but praise; in fact, the only complaint centred around the difficulty of inspecting the fuel level when the tank cap was removed!

## Full-Width Hubs for 1956

Full-width aluminium brake hubs, a headlamp nacelle and the choice of having a final drive case with automatic oiling (the latter as a cost option) were the highlights of the 1956 Ariel 350 and 500 ohv singles. There is no doubt that the new brakes were much admired – and BSA even chose to fit the Ariel-designed brakes on some of its most expensive models – a rare compliment from Small Heath to its Selly Oak brothers.

The new cast-aluminium full-width hubs incorporated 7in (178mm) diameter centralized brakes equipped with 1.5in (38mm) linings. They are fully described in Chapter 8, as are the full chain enclosure and headlamp nacelle.

*A Redesigned 350 Barrel and Head*
Another innovation for the 1956 model year was a redesigned cylinder barrel and head on the NH Red Hunter three-fifty – thus at last bringing it in line with its larger counterpart. The cast-iron cylinder barrel employed cast-in pushrod tunnels instead of the separate pushrod tubes formerly used. Replacing the iron cylinder head was a deeply finned aluminium-alloy head with cast-in valve seat inserts of nickel iron. The compression ratio was now 7.5:1, as compared to the former 6.2:1.

## Minimal Changes for 1957

The most noticeable change for 1957 was a new, larger capacity fuel tank of 4.5gal (20.5ltr) of a more rounded form. As described elsewhere in this book, the method of construction of this tank had also been changed – it was now built of two steel pressings welded along the centre line. These welds were concealed under a bright metal strip. There was also a new design of front mudguard, with a single stay at the rear. The only new Ariel model that year was the HT3 three-fifty trials mount (described in Chapter 6); otherwise the changes are best described as minimal.

*The attractive 1955 Model VH 500 Red Hunter; the final year of separate headlamps before the nacelle was adopted. Also note single-sided brakes.*

> Over the Hills and
> **FAR AWAY THE LIVELIEST "SPORTING" SINGLE – SOLO or SIDECAR**
>
> **ARIEL**
> V.H. 500c.c. RED HUNTER
>
> Write for full colour catalogue to:
> ARIEL MOTORS LTD., SELLY OAK, BIRMINGHAM, 29
>
> Full Range:
> 1,000c.c. SQUARE FOUR, MODEL H.G.
> 650c.c. HUNTMASTER TWIN, MODEL F.H.
> 500c.c. HUNTER TWIN, MODEL K.H.
> 500c.c. RED HUNTER SINGLE, MODEL V.H.
> 350c.c. RED HUNTER SINGLE, MODEL N.H.
> 600c.c. SIDE VALVE, MODEL V.B.
> 200c.c. COLT, MODEL L.H.

1956 P.R.F. MODEL – SHOWING FULLY ENCLOSED REAR CHAIN.

*1956 saw the arrival of several changes, notably full-width aluminium brake hubs front and rear, headlamp nacelle and, as a cost option, a fully-enclosed final drive chain.*

## PETROL 2/- A GALLON ★

★ IF YOU split the increased price of petrol THREE ways on an

**ARIEL** The 350 c.c. **RED HUNTER SINGLE** MODEL N.H.

Bernal Osborne, "Motor Cycling," writing of the Red Hunter 350 c.c. Solo says...

"It was a wet, gusty night, one which more or less enforced a moderate speed, but the 6.4 : 1 top gear provided the facility for real 'top-only' running up-hill and down-dale with little need to open the throttle more than quarter-distance.

"Apart from observing halt signs, such as that at the A5 crossing, no stop was made; in fact the model would proceed in the traffic stream at Ashby and Tamworth right down to speeds of approximately 10 m.p.h. and the result was an m.p.g. figure of nearly 126."

Write now for full colour catalogue to
ARIEL MOTORS LTD · SELLY OAK · BIRMINGHAM 29

*Advertisement dated February 1957 for Model NH 350 Red Hunter. Now with aluminium cylinder head and headlamp nacelle.*

## No Changes for 1958

There were no specification changes for 1958 – this was a break with tradition, as previously, except for the Second World War period, Ariel had always had its yearly updates. Of course, unbeknown to the general public this was because of the imminent launch in July of that year of the new and radical Leader – a twin cylinder two-fifty two-stroke (*see* Chapter 11). The arrival of this motorcycle and the related Arrow series was in fact to be instrumental in the BSA Group's decision to axe *all* Ariel's four-stroke models a few months later by mid-1959.

From then on, in the author's opinion, Ariel's fate was sealed. But the long-running four-stroke singles refused to go quietly away. And there was that man Sammy Miller and his immortal GOV132 HT5 five-hundred trials bike, the full story of which is recorded in Chapter 6. Suffice it to say that until the Spanish Armada finally landed in Britain in 1965, the big Ariel thumper continued to crush the opposition as it had in the 1950s.

*An early 1980s photograph showing the Ariel specialists Draganfly Motorcycles, then based in East London (now in rural Suffolk). A mid 1950s Red Hunter awaits its owner outside; a 1970s Yamaha TZ four-cylinder two-stroke racer fills out the window display.*

# 8 Overhead-Valve Twins

In May 1939 Frank Anstey had been succeeded as Chief Designer by Val Page, who had quit BSA and returned to the Selly Oak company after an absence of almost seven years. Later, by the end of 1943 when it was becoming obvious that the Allies would win the war, Ariel owner Jack Y Sangster began to study the prospects when peace finally returned. Taking into account how difficult things were in the aftermath of the First World War, he decided to dispose of his interest in Ariel Motors to the BSA Group, leaving himself free to concentrate upon Triumph.

When news of Sangster's intentions reached the Ariel workforce, a sit-down strike (organized by sales boss Tom Davis) took place. This only ended when it was discovered that a condition of the sale was that Ariel would remain at its Selly Oak works and would 'retain its individuality, identity and regime for as long as it was considered economically viable'.

## Ariel Joins BSA

The merger with the BSA Group was finally completed in December 1944 and James Leek, then the BSA General Manager, became the new Managing Director of Ariel Motors. As Peter Hartley reveals in his book *The Ariel Story*: 'Two further conditions of the sale were: that Jack Sangster was to remain Director of the concern with which he had been associated for so long and secondly, if at any time in the future he wished to dispose of the Triumph concern he should give the BSA Group first refusal.'

## Peace Returns

When peace finally returned in 1945, Val Page and Ariel attempted to get back on track. Besides putting back into civilian production the model range it essentially had when war had broken out some six years earlier, Page had two major development projects already under way: the company's new telescopic front fork; and the design of a brand new five-hundred ohv twin. The latter had largely, as with the rest of the British industry, been inspired by Edward Turner's Speed Twin of 1937, and a prototype had run by the end of 1944.

## Work on the New Twin Begins

Val Page and his team spent much of 1945–47 in the development of the new parallel twin. In fact, as early as September 1946 one of the works test riders, Len Moss, had ridden an early prototype machine from the Birmingham factory to Brands Hatch (then a grass track circuit) in Kent, thus giving a sneak preview of what lay ahead. However, it was not to be for many months more that details of the new design were officially to be announced in the press, in late 1947.

There is no doubt that in Val Page, Ariel not only had a designer of premier league status, but also one well-voiced in parallel twins. For example, when the original ohc Square Four project had begun, Page had been design chief at Ariel and deeply involved with the stillborn 250cc twin produced by using the rear half of a Square Four engine with a 360-degree

## Overhead-Valve Twins

crankshaft, purpose-built camshaft and crankcase assembly. Page had then moved to Triumph where he designed and built the six-fifty twin of 1933. Later still, whilst at BSA he had been involved in the design of two experimental twins built by the Small Heath concern during the late 1930s. He was, of course, extremely familiar with Turner's Speed Twin. This, combined with an early start on the new twin, gave Ariel a major advantage over their rivals, who strove to put a twin into production during the immediate post-war period.

### A Suitable Chassis

Another major advantage was that Ariel already had in existence cycle parts which could more than cope with a five-hundred twin, thanks to its wide experience with the 600 and 1000 four-cylinder models.

So it was that when the new 498cc (63 × 80mm) twin was announced in November 1947, it was a particularly well-developed machine. Certainly, it was less of a hurried launch than rivals such as AMC, Norton, Royal Enfield, BSA and the like.

### A One-Piece Crankshaft

Val Page plumped for a one-piece, rather than a built-up crankshaft, reasoning that the former would be more rigid. This was forged in chrome-molybdenum steel of 65-ton tensile strength heat-treated prior to grinding. The shaft measured 6.38in (162mm) between main bearing centres and weighed in at 9.75lb (4.4kg). On the timing side, a 1¼in (32mm) diameter journal ran in a white-metal-lined phosphor bronze bush, whilst on the drive-side the diameter of the shaft in the single row 10 × 10mm roller bearing was 1⅛in (27mm). This roller bearing was of the single-lip variety, allowing the inner race to move laterally relative to the outer race to compensate for expansion of the die-cast aluminium crankcase.

### RR56 Light-Alloy Connecting Rods

The connecting rods were manufactured in RR56 light alloy. These were polished on the outer faces of the H-section to prevent scratches that could, potentially, have otherwise caused a fracture at a later date. The big-end eyes of the rods were split, with the caps retained by 5/16in (8mm) bolts equipped with self-locking nuts. Detachable steel-backed white-metal shell bearings were employed, measuring ⅞in (22mm) in width.

With the crankshaft at tdc (top dead centre), the big-end nuts could be unscrewed through the crankcase mouth – thus, replacement shell bearings could be fitted without dismantling the crankcase assembly.

*1948 five-hundred KH ohv vertical twin with rigid frame and Ariel's own telescopic front forks.*

## Phosphor Bronze Small Ends

The small ends of the con-rods were phosphor-bronze bushes, taking $^{11}/_{16}$in (18mm) taper-bored gudgeon pins, the latter in case-hardened nickel steel of 50-tons tensile; the gudgeon pin being ground and lapped was retained in the piston bosses by wire circlips.

## Specialloid Full-Skirt Pistons

Specialloid full-skirt light-alloy pistons were employed. They were produced by a hot-pressing process which, Ariel claimed, ensured that there was no porosity in the aluminium. In comparison with conventional cast pistons, hot pressings had the advantage of higher tensile strength – around 28–30 tons – and increased elasticity. There were two compression rings and a single slotted oil scraper ring.

## Timing Sprocket

A keyed, parallel fit to the crankshaft, the timing sprocket drove two camshafts by means of an 8mm duplex chain. On the normally 'slack' rim of the chain (between the crankshaft sprocket and the inlet camshaft sprocket) was a Weller-type spring tensioner with an adjustable stop to prevent chain whip. The three sprockets each had extractor threads on their bosses to aid removal.

## One-Piece Camshafts

One-piece camshafts were employed, forged in case-hardened mild steel, and were machined all over. Supporting each camshaft on the timing side was a $^7/_8$in (22mm) diameter by 1in (25mm) long phosphor bronze bush, whilst on the drive-side the bush dimensions were $^5/_8 \times {}^5/_8$in (16 × 16mm). The camshafts were set as close as possible to the bearings to reduce whip in the shaft. Page incorporated quietening curves on the cams – 15 degrees of crankshaft rotation taking up the valve gear clearance slowly before the valves were lifted.

In a similar manner to the crankshaft, the camshafts were located by the timing side bushes. On the drive-side of the engine the camshaft bushes were, in effect, of the blind variety (plugs in the crankcase sealing the outer ends), thus allowing lateral movement as required to accommodate crankcase expansion.

## A Fibre Pinion

Riveted to the rear of the inlet camshaft sprocket was a fibre pinion, meshing with the magneto pinion. The latter component incorporated the automatic mechanism for the BTH Type KC2 or Lucas AC53 magneto. Both these makes of magneto were of the three-sided flange type, bolted and sealed against the face on the rear of the timing chest and were fitted with ignition cut-outs.

To the rear of the exhaust camshaft sprocket was another fibre pinion – this drove the Lucas dynamo. The rear face of the sprocket was ground and pressed against the fibre pinion; on the other side of the pinion was a ground steel washer and then a flat steel spring washer held in place by a boss of the sprocket being spun over. This assembly operated as a friction clutch that slipped when the drive was under extreme load. The dynamo was driven at $1^1/_3$ times crankshaft speed. A special dynamo endplate was employed that was robust enough to take three of the timing case screws, ensuring that a sound oil seal was maintained between the dynamo and the rear of the timing chest. The dynamo itself was supported in a cradle formed in the timing-side half of the crankcase and was held in position by a metal strap.

## A Cast-Iron Cylinder Barrel

A total of eight studs held the one-piece cast-iron cylinder barrel assembly on to the crankcase. The cylinders were sunk into the crankcase mouths and featured cutaways to provide clearance for the connecting rods. Page and his team had provided sufficient air passages between the cylinders, and the integral pushrod tunnels were placed at the four outer corners of the barrel. These tunnels connected with those in the cylinder head, whilst cast-iron tappet guides were fitted in the base of the cylinder barrel tunnels.

## Flat-Base Type Tappets

The tappets were of the flat-base type and were a particularly interesting design. Each tappet stem was hollow and in two sections. Inside the hollow stem was a coil spring of sufficient strength to ensure that the valve operating mechanism above the tappet was at all times in contact; consequently, the valve clearances were literally between the faces of the two parts of the tappet stem, where lubrication was at its best and where noise was deadened by the guide and the cylinder barrel. To aid maintenance when dismantling or assembling the cylinder, the tappets were held in their guides by small circlips.

## Integral Rocker Boxes

The cylinder head was also a one-piece cast-iron assembly including a quartet of integral rocker boxes. Page had given special attention to cooling and there were thus no blind spots between the exhaust ports; the air stream through the finning travelled to the rear with outlets above and below the inlet port. The head carried eight high-tensile studs of $^5/_{16}$in (8mm) diameter with register ends for easy fitting of the nuts, and there was a copper-asbestos gasket between the cylinder head and barrel assemblies.

## A Single Induction Flange

A single induction flange branched internally within the head to feed each cylinder. The combustion chambers were of the conventional hemispherical shape and 14mm sparking plugs were specified. To reduce heat transference to the Amal 276 carburettor, a thick, plastic insulating gasket was fitted between the carb and head.

## Tulip Inlet Valves

Manufactured in 3 per cent nickel steel, the tulip inlet valves measured 1$^5/_{16}$in (33mm) head diameter, the KE965 exhaust valves having a diameter of 1¼in (32mm). The ends of the inlet valve stems were case-hardened to withstand rocker impact, but since KE965 is an austenitic steel, and thus cannot be hardened, the stems of the exhaust valves were Stellite-tipped. The angle between the valves was 80 degrees, with the valve seatings at the usual angle of 45 degrees. Each valve had two coil springs, the outer exerting 83lb (38kg) pressure and the inner 36lb (16kg) when the valve was closed. The valve guides, which were a pressed-fit in the head, were of cast iron.

## Rocker Spindles

Case-hardened steel was used for the rocker spindles, which were a tight fit in the outer bosses of the rocker boxes and were pulled up against a shoulder by cap nuts at the inner ends; between the nuts and the face of the rocker box inner bosses were the banjo unions of the oil feeds. The spindles were hollow for lubrication purposes, and featured screw plugs at their outer ends.

Operating directly on the spindles, the nickel-chrome steel rockers were of the straight-line variety. Each rocker was locked laterally by a coil spring between it and the face of the inner rocker box boss.

## Valve Gear Clearance

Valve gear clearance was set by a ball adjuster in each rocker which bore on the valve. This adjuster was of the socket type and was tight in the threads of the rocker boss. The rocker featured a saw cut from the boss along the arm and, at right-angles through the saw cut, the rocker arm was drilled and tapped to take a socket screw that acted as a clamp to hold the setting of the adjuster. A common socket size was employed for the adjuster and the clamp screw.

At the other end of the rocker arms were hardened-steel ball ends that operated in the forged-on cups of the solid pushrods. An incidental, but nonetheless important, feature of the Ariel twin rocker gear design was that with the head on the bench the rockers did not have to be dismantled before removal of the valve springs and valves when, for example, the engine was being worked on.

A common light-alloy cover was used for each pair of exhaust and inlet rocker boxes. There were vents to allow air flow between the rocker boxes.

*A Gear-Type Oil Pump*

A departure from Ariel practice in the past came with the fitting of a gear-type oil pump located in a small sump to the rear offside of the crankcase and was operated at approximately one-fifth crankshaft speed by a vertical shaft skew gear drive, from the inlet camshaft. The vertical shaft was supported by a phosphor bronze bearing in the crankcase and was kept pressed downwards in engagement with the pump drive spindle by a spring-loaded ball at the top. This ball was located in a plug in the crankcase just behind the cylinder barrel, and the plug also formed the union for the crankcase breather, the oil mist from the breather being led away by a pipe to the final drive chain.

*High-Pressure Lubrication*

A modern high-pressure lubrication system was employed, with a ball valve at the end of the crankshaft on the timing side that ensured a constant 40lb per sq in pressure. In practice, this saw around 15 per cent of the oil supply available being forced to the bearings, the remainder passing the valve and returning to the sump. An idea of the capacity of the supply side of the pump can be appreciated from the figure of 11gal (50ltr) per hour at 4,000rpm.

*A Centrifugal Filler*

From the pump, lubricant was forced through an oilway in the timing side of the crankcase to the main bearing. The oil then entered the hollow crankshaft, before passing through the timing side web and so to the big-end bearings. The feeds through the big-end journals were on the inside so that any sludge or foreign body in the oil did not reach the bearings; instead, it was thrown outwards by centrifugal force to the walls of the hollow journals and could therefore be removed during overhauls.

There were screwed plugs in the crank webs to provide access to the sludge traps.

Cylinders, small-ends, drive-side main bearing and camshaft bearings were lubricated by oil flung out from the big-end bearings. Oil passing the ball valve in the end of the timing side of the crankshaft escaped into the timing chest and thereafter to the sump. However, the overflow hole between timing chest and crankcase was located so as to provide a pre-determined level of oil in the timing chest into which the timing chain dipped.

*Valve Gear Lubrication*

To facilitate lubrication to the overhead rocker there was a tapping in the crankcase from the main pump supply. An external pipe led up to a five-way union between the rocker boxes. From this union there was a lead to each banjo union on the rocker spindles and a lead to the pressure gauge in the tank-top panel. Oil passed along the drilled rocker spindles to the bearing surfaces and escaped past the ends of the bearing bosses; it then went down the pushrod tunnels, lubricating the valve guides – also passing through grooves in the guides that formed oilways between guides and the cylinder barrel. By this method the oil reached the sump after passing over the tappets and cams.

*A Mesh Filter*

At the base of the sump was located a mesh filter which surrounded the pump, held in position by a coil spring seating on a detachable plate in the bottom of the sump. Oil was drawn by the return gears of the pump, which had a larger capacity than the supply gears, and then fed back to the 5pt (2.8ltr) tank on the offside (right) of the machine. The pump body was manufactured as a zinc-base aluminium casting, which, without bushes, formed the bearings for the gear spindles.

The oil tank had been designed to permit the very high-pressure return without leakage past the filler cap. The returning oil entered the tank before flowing along a platform to a detachable mesh filter. It was thus possible, as the oil poured into the filter, to view this operation if the filler cap was removed; the filter could be withdrawn through the filler cap orifice for cleaning purposes.

*Pear-Shaped Crankcase*
A deep, pear-shaped, vertically split crankcase was an extremely clean aluminium die-casting that required the very minimum of machining. The total weight of the engine with its accessories was 98lb (44.5kg) – just 1lb (0.454kg) heavier than the existing ohv single-cylinder assembly.

The new five-hundred twin was made available in two guises: the KG500 de Luxe (with a compression ratio of 6.8:1); and the more sporting KH Red Hunter (with a higher ratio of 7.5:1). Prices (including UK taxes) were £196 17s and £185 8s 5d respectively. Cost options were spring frame £19 1s and speedometer £5 1s 8d. Both models were equipped with Ariel's new telescopic front fork as standard equipment. The cycle parts were almost completely shared with the existing single-cylinder models, which provided a good power-to-weight ratio and an interchangeability of components.

*The new 499cc (63 × 80mm) twin went on sale in early 1948; it could be supplied in Red Hunter (KH) or de Luxe (KG) forms. This machine had the optional (extra cost) plunger rear suspension.*

### KG 500 de Luxe 1948

| | | | |
|---|---|---|---|
| Engine | Air-cooled overhead valve parallel twin with cast-iron cylinder head and barrel assemblies; one-piece crankshaft rod with plain bearing big-ends. | Front suspension | Telescopic fork |
| | | Rear suspension | Unsprung, rigid[1] |
| | | Front brake | 7in drum, SLS |
| | | Rear brakes | 7in drum, SLS |
| | | Tyres | Front 3.25 × 19; rear 3.50 × 19 |
| Bore | 63mm | **General Specifications** | |
| Stroke | 80mm | Wheelbase | 56in (1,422mm) |
| Displacement | 499cc | Ground clearance | 5in (127mm) |
| Compression ratio | 6.8:1 | Seat height | 28in (711mm) |
| Lubrication | Dry sump, gear pump | Fuel tank capacity | 3.25gal (15ltr) |
| Ignition | Magneto, 6-volt | Dry weight | 375lb (170kg) |
| Carburettor | Single Amal 276 15/16in | Maximum power | 24bhp @ 6,000rpm |
| Primary drive | Chain | Top speed | solo: 78mph (126km/h); sidecar: 62mph (100km/h) |
| Final drive | Chain | | |
| Gearbox | Four-speed, Burman CP, foot-change | | |
| Frame | Tubular, all-steel construction, single front downtube | [1] Plunger as an option. | |

## Testing the New Twin

*The Motor Cycle* carried out a comprehensive test of the new twin (a KG de Luxe) in its 20 November 1947 issue. This machine was tested in both solo and sidecar forms. The test began by revealing:

> Contrary to the usual secrecy enshrouding the long and patient development of a new design, the evolution of the Ariel twin has received a fair measure of publicity. Pressmen were among the numerous fortunate enthusiasts who had experienced many enjoyable miles on prototypes. Therefore, the Model KG de Luxe submitted for test was not an entirely unknown machine, but it was now in the sense that it was the very first production model to be completed.

*Performance*
In solo trim, the KG de Luxe recorded a maximum speed of 78mph (126km/h). However, these bare figures do not really tell the story, because the new Ariel twin had the ability to average relatively high speeds with a smoothness not found in many half-litre parallel twins. As revealed by *The Motor Cycle tester*:

> The smoothness of the power output from the twin cylinder engine, coupled with its lively acceleration, makes town riding a pleasure. The engine pulls a high gear comfortably and for meandering could be used as a top gear machine at about 18mph, from which speed it would easily and lightly accelerate away provided the throttle was used intelligently. As a machine for the sporting rider interested in high averages, the new Ariel is among the best in its class. Its top speed is high enough, but the strong characteristic is the liveliness of its acceleration up to the seventies and the capacity of the engine to maintain that figure, it seemed indefinitely, without any manifestation of stress. There was no perceptible vibration and no particular speed which might be termed best.

A further example of the machine's pleasant, easy-going nature was the following: 'For mile after mile, the speedometer needle (which was reading slightly fast) could be kept hovering between 70 and 75mph with the engine humming smoothly and tirelessly.'

Mechanically, the engine was found to be 'reasonably quiet', with the tester commenting: 'There was the hum of well-oiled mechanical movement with the tick tick of the valve gear just identifiable. There was no piston slap once the engine was warm. The silencers give a pleasant, almost musical, cadence as the throttle is manipulated.'

Unlike the Square Four 4G 1000 of the same era (*see* Chapter 5), the riding position was judged 'first class' and 'proved to be as suitable for town work as for high-speed riding on the open road'. In fact, the tester went on to say:

> It would be difficult to suggest any improvements. The footrests are a taper fit on the hangers and may therefore be adjusted over a wide range; the handlebars are clipped to the steering head lug forward of the steering column and may be adjusted for angle; saddle height at the rear may be varied by means of the fixing bolts at the bottom of the long saddle springs.

Although the brakes were adjudged 'particularly powerful', they were criticized on two points. The first was that to be kept to the highest level of efficiency 'frequent resetting of the excellent fulcrum adjusters was necessary'; secondly, the exhaust pipe under the brake pedal limited the range of pedal movement – in consequence, 'rear brake adjustment was critical'.

*A Third Wheel is Added*
After something over 1,000 miles (1,600km) as a solo the KG de Luxe was fitted with a sidecar and, in effect, retested. The only changes carried out to the machine were the fitting of stronger front fork springs, and a nineteenth-tooth engine sprocket to lower the gearing. Maximum speed dropped to 62mph (100km/h). However, the tester was impressed

by the 'liveliness and high cruising speed of the outfit'. In fact, except for a reduction in maximum speed compared to solo trim, the Ariel five-hundred twin still impressed.

*93mph*

*Motor Cycling* tested one of the KH 500 Red Hunter models, this being the more sporting model with the higher compression ratio, achieving a maximum speed of 93mph (150km/h). This made the new Ariel twin one of the very quickest of British-built five-hundred twins. At this time, with customers clamouring for every machine that rolled off the production line, it was very much a seller's market. Quite simply, Ariel could have sold every bike it built several times over. Many potential customers had to go without, just to fulfil export demand, because the British economy needed every dollar, franc or deutschmark it could get.

## 1949 Saw Limited Changes

Partly due to 'getting it right first time' and partly because of the sheer weight of demand, when the 1949 Ariel range was announced in October 1948, the KG/KH models were little changed. Indeed, the changes were described in the motorcycling press as 'refinements'. The exact details were as follows:

- rake and trial of front fork altered, to improve steering lock
- new prop stand, which pivoted on the nearside frame member
- new longer Lucas 3in (76mm) dynamo with a 60-watt output
- new Lucas headlamp with 36-watt bulb (against 24-watt of previous assembly)
- chrome plating for moving fork members and front brake plate.

## A Larger Tank in 1950

For the 1950 model year, the KH Red Hunter was given a new, larger fuel tank. With a capacity of 3.5gal (16ltr), it was some 2in (50mm) deeper. The new depth of the tank not only visually separated the KH from its cheaper KG brother, but enhanced the general appearance, filling the space that previously existed above the engine. As on the Square Four, the speedometer was now mounted at the top of the forks, rather than in a panel on the tank top. Prices had also gone up, the KH Red Hunter now being £201 18s 8d, and the KG de Luxe £190 10s 1d, both including UK taxes.

## The 1951 Model Year

When the 1951 model year Ariel range was announced, it was seen that certain modifications were common to all models – Ariel sources saying these had been introduced to

*Engine from a 1950 KH Red Hunter twin. Like all the early twins, this had a one-piece cylinder head (with integral rocker boxes) and a one-piece barrel, both in cast iron. Tappet covers were in aluminium.*

improve appearance and ease servicing tasks. These included a new die-cast alloy fork top bracket that supported the speedometer. The tank was now devoid of an instrument panel. This had enabled the filler cap to be moved to the centre; the small oil pressure gauge was mounted to the rear of the tank top. Rear mudguard stays had been revised to provide a much neater appearance. A wide chrome-plated metal strap, secured by two pinch bolts, replaced the narrow hinged fitting that formerly located the battery, whilst the front mudguard plate/bracketing were now of aluminium with concealed fittings. Increased seat comfort had been obtained by the use of chrome-plated barrel springs, which replaced the former parallel coil assemblies. Piston design had been changed to prevent slap and thus help overall quietness, whilst a shorter gear pedal gave a crisper change.

*Engine Modifications*
Both the KH and KG engines had been quite extensively modified in light of service conditions. The cylinder head and barrel finning depth had been increased, giving the top end a more chunky appearance. There were also new, rounder profile exhaust header pipes.

Internally, a new flywheel assembly with a weight increase of some 20 per cent was claimed to have provided a smoother engine and transmission without affecting acceleration or pick-up. Increased rigidity in the rocker box covers ensured superior oil tightness at the top of the engine. Prices remained unchanged.

## A New Side Stand in 1952

Little change occurred for the 1952 season, with only a new side stand making an appearance. This new stand was still fitted to the nearside of the motorcycle, slightly forwards of the previous position. It folded back closer to the frame and pivoted on a lug set at an angle of 45 degrees to the horizontal, so that it swung outwards and downwards. The return spring operated as soon as the stand was relieved of its load, akin to a mousetrap. The KH now cost £222 6s 8d, the KG de luxe having been discontinued.

## 1953 and an Alloy-Engined Sports Model

When the yearly round of changes was announced in November 1952, it was seen that a new light-alloy version of the five-hundred twin had been added, to run alongside the old iron-engined model. Coded KHA (A for Aluminium!), the newcomer featured a power unit similar to the one used by Cecil Martin (Bob) Ray to win a Gold Medal in the 1952 International Six Days Trial. The comprehensively finned cylinder barrel was cast in

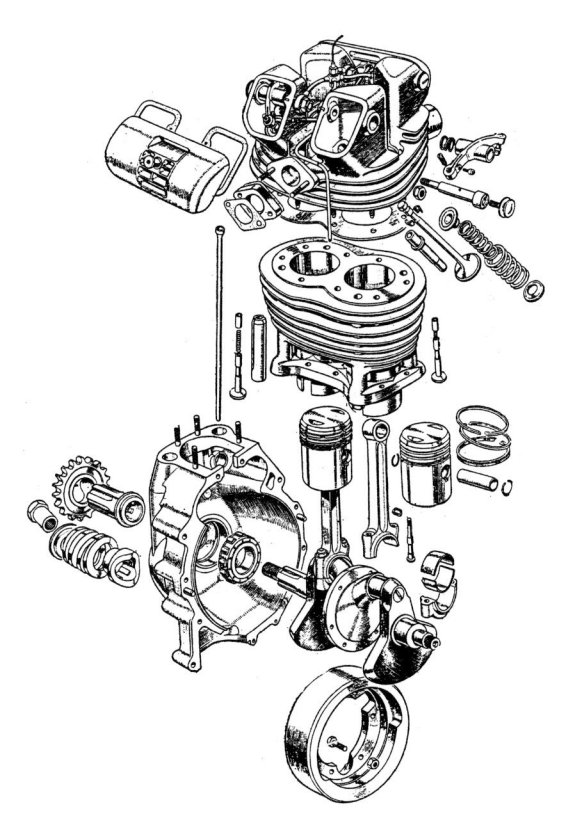

*Val Page-designed five-hundred vertical twin. This featured a one-piece forged crankshaft, plain bearing big-ends and split-cap connecting rods.*

*Advertisement showing the 1952 KH Red Hunter twin with the optional plunger rear suspension.*

### KHA 500 1952

| | | | |
|---|---|---|---|
| Engine | Air-cooled overhead valve parallel twin with aluminium cylinder head and barrel assemblies, the latter with cast-iron liners; one-piece crankshaft; plain bearing big-ends. | Frame | Tubular, all-steel construction; single front downtube |
| | | Front suspension | Telescopic fork |
| | | Rear suspension | Unsprung, rigid |
| | | Front brake | 7-inch single-sided drum, SLS |
| | | Rear brakes | 7-inch single-sided drum, SLS |
| Bore | 63mm | Tyres | Front 3.00 × 20; rear 3.50 × 19 |
| Stroke | 80mm | | |
| Displacement | 499cc | **General Specifications** | |
| Compression ratio | 6.8:1 (7.5:1 as an option) | Wheelbase | 56in (1,422mm) |
| Lubrication | Dry sump, gear pump | Ground clearance | 5.5in (140mm) |
| Ignition | Magneto, 6 volt | Seat height | 30in (762mm) |
| Carburettor | Single Amal 276 1in | Fuel tank capacity | 4gal (18ltr) |
| Primary drive | Chain | Dry weight | 370lb (168kg) |
| Final drive | Chain | Maximum power | 28bhp @ 6,200rpm |
| Gearbox | Four-speed, Burman GB, foot-change | Top speed | 93mph (150km/h) |

Lo-Ex silicon alloy (also used on the alloy-engined Square Four) and featured pressed-in iron liners. Eight through-bolts, that screwed into bronze inserts in the head and rotated in steel thrimbles in the crankcase, held down the head and barrel assemblies. Two out-of-step hexagons (permitting twelve spanner holds per rotation) were provided on each bolt to facilitate tightening-down operations. Buyers had the choice of either 6.8:1 or 7.3:1 compression ratios, depending upon the octane rating available in a particular country. Ariel's official power output figure for the KHA was 28bhp at 6,200rpm.

The bottom end of the engine was shared with the KH iron unit. A new Lucas stop-and-tail lamp was also introduced that year, plus the improved Burman B52 gearbox (replacing the BA type).

Finally, several new colour schemes were made available. One was Wedgwood Blue with white-lined fuel tanks and blue wheel rim wells. The KH twin was finished in Ariel's traditional claret, with a gold-lined tank. Prices were: KHA £235 2s 3d; KH £222 6s 8d (both inclusive of British purchase tax).

For most, the first chance to see the new alloy-engined KHA came at the London Earls Court Show in November 1952. This bike attracted considerable attention, helped not only by the complete motorcycle, but also by the display of an electrically driven, sectioned model of the engine.

## Major Changes for 1954

The *Motor Cycling* headline in the 15 October 1953 issue proclaimed 'Swinging Fork Frames and a New '650' are Added to the Established Range of Multi- and Single-cylinder Ariels'. This, in effect, was a major turning point in the history of Ariel's ohv twin cylinder family.

### The Swinging Arm Frame

The new frame, with modern swinging arm and twin shock rear suspension, was to be

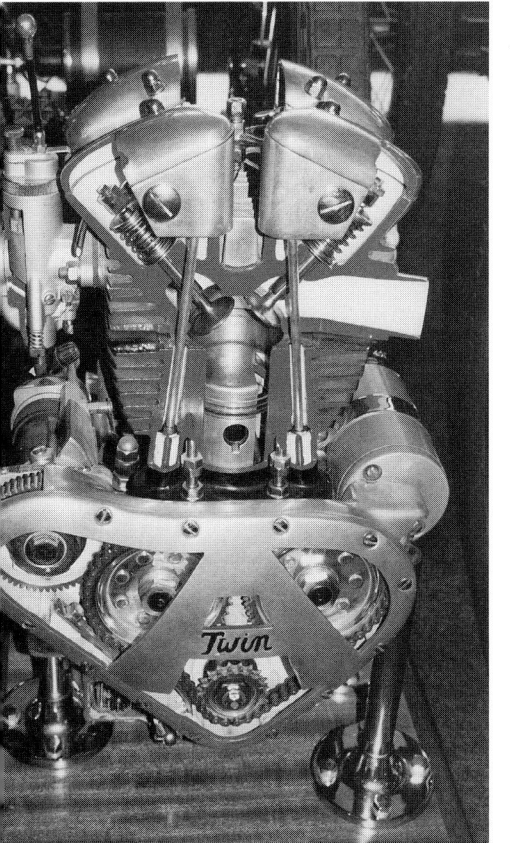

*Short-lived all-alloy engine based on works prototype ridden by C M (Bob) Ray in the 1952 ISDT, gaining a Gold Medal.*

*An assortment of Ariel engines including: an alloy-head five-hundred twin; an iron top-end five-hundred twin; VB six-hundred side-valve single; and an assortment of other sv and ohv singles.*

fitted to all 1954 models, with the exception of the 4G Square Four that retained the Anstey-designed link plunger type. *Motor Cycling* said of the swinging arm frame: 'This somewhat radical change'. It introduced a full duplex loop frame of part-brazed, part-welded construction with swinging arm and hydraulically damped rear suspension

The front down tubes of the new frame were 1 1/8in (29mm) diameter at the steering head, tapering to 1in (25mm) and they swept round to form an engine cradle and then continued upwards at an angle of 45 degrees to blend with a forked, cross-braced top structure carrying two welded anchorage lugs for the damper units. The forward end of this structure was formed by a forked malleable lug through which ran the top tank rail. This was then swept downwards aft of the gearbox to form a vertical saddle pillar and was forked at its extremity to join the two lower frame members. Midway, the saddle pillar carried a substantial welded steel bucket bracing the pillar and upswept rear frame members, and acted also as a fulcrum point for the swinging arm frame.

A feature of the swinging arm fork, which was of the conventional 'U' shape pattern, was the particular strength of its root derived from the welded-box construction of the fork arm members. As for the dampers themselves, these were bought-in from Girling and provided two-way damping and featured provision for adjustment under varying degrees of loading.

*The Huntmaster 650*
Ariel's ohv twins fall into two distinct categories – the original Val Page 500 KG/KH design, and the 650 FH Huntmaster, which was essentially Ariel's version of the BSA A10 Golden Flash.

As Steve Wilson pointed out in his *British Motor Cycles Since 1950*, 'A BSA motor may have been the beginning of the erosion of marque identity', which Ariel was to suffer from the mid-1950s onwards. Even so, Bert Hopwood's excellent single camshaft (the Page five-hundred had two cams), 646cc A10 power unit, and outwardly modified, combined with the excellent Ariel duplex frame and front forks, high standard of finish (compared with BSA), conspired to produce a well-loved motorcycle. Also the Burman gearbox, compared to BSA's own box on the A10, was another gap between the two bikes.

The engines for both the BSA and Ariel versions were constructed at BSA's Small Heath works, and from 1953 the A10 (and smaller A7 five-hundred) had departed from the original semi-unit engine and gearbox construction, thus permitting the marriage of the BSA engine and Burman gearbox. It should also be pointed out that the engine used in the Ariel was the iron cylinder head and barrel type with the narrow cylinder base flange, as the later alloy head versions only made an appearance on A10s (initially the Super and Road Rocket types) in 1957. Only in 1958, the year prior to the Huntmaster's demise, was the thicker base flange (and therefore more robust and tunable engine) introduced for BSA's production.

*Engine Specifications*
When the Huntmaster was launched in October 1953, no mention was made of BSA or the A10; instead, *The Motor Cycle* simply reported: 'The 646 Huntmaster Twin is based on sound, well-tried principles of vertical twin-cylinder design.' As already detailed, technically the Ariel used the BSA engine. This meant a forged steel crankshaft, with integral bob-weights and bolted-on central flywheel member. Wide, pressure-lubricated indium-flashed (lead-bronze) big-end liners were used, whilst the timing-side 'main' took the form of a 1 3/8in (35mm) white-metal plain bearing, the drive-side of the crankshaft being supported by a 2 1/2in (64mm) caged roller bearing. The connecting rods were of RR56 forged aluminium alloy. The pushrods, which were housed in tunnels cast integrally with the cylinder barrel, were operated by a gear-driven single camshaft (which incorporated an

"The new Fork mounted Speedometer on the 1951 ARIEL certainly appeals to me"

*The traditional Ariel tank-top instruments and switches were transferred to the headlamp shell — and a special speedometer bracket between the fork legs as the 1950s dawned. Incidentally, only the twins and the Square Four retained the oil pressure gauge, set in the tank top just aft of the filler cap.*

THE NEW 1951 RANGE INCLUDES

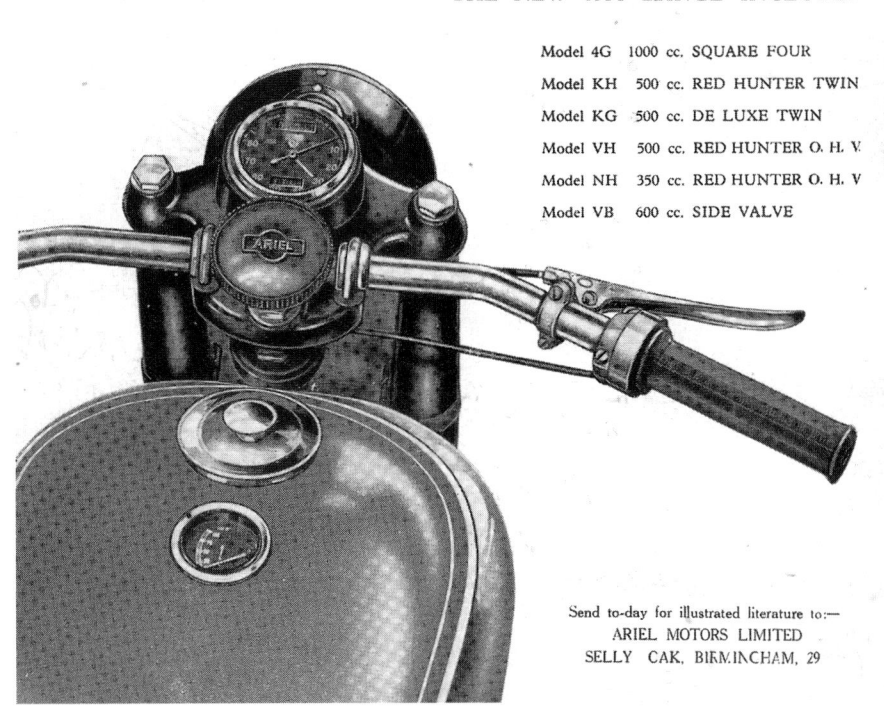

Model 4G   1000 cc. SQUARE FOUR
Model KH   500 cc. RED HUNTER TWIN
Model KG   500 cc. DE LUXE TWIN
Model VH   500 cc. RED HUNTER O. H. V.
Model NH   350 cc. RED HUNTER O. H. V.
Model VB   600 cc. SIDE VALVE

Send to-day for illustrated literature to:—
ARIEL MOTORS LIMITED
SELLY OAK, BIRMINGHAM, 29

automatic engine breather) located at the rear of the engine and supported in a trio of bronze bushes.

### Details

Bolted to the cylinder head, a one-piece, cast-alloy rocker box was fitted, embodying inspection covers to provide access for valve clearance adjustments. In addition, at the top of the rocker box there was a circular inspection plug, removal of which allowed the fitting of the pushrods.

A twin-gear oil pump was skew-driven from the engine shaft and delivered lubricant to the timing-side main bearing, the big-end bearings, the timing gear wheels and the

## Overhead-Valve Twins

camshaft and, by means of an external feed pipe, the overhead rocker spindles. A simple ball-and-spring pressure release mechanism was housed in the lower section of the crankcase casting.

Electrical equipment comprised a Lucas K2F magneto with automatic ignition advance mechanism. This was gear-driven from the crankshaft, and a chain-driven 56-watt dynamo was frontally mounted.

The Huntmaster was equipped with a four-speed Burman GB33 gearbox, providing solo ratios of 4.35, 5.7, 7.4 and 11.5:1 or, for sidecar use, 4.7, 6.45, 8.4 and 14:1. With a claimed power output of 40bhp at 6,200rpm, the Huntmaster shared its frame with the KH Hunter twin and two singles, the NH 350 and VH 500 Red Hunter ohv models.

Costing £230 8s (against £216 for the five-hundred twin), the new Ariel six-fifty was the most expensive model in the company's line-up bar the Square Four.

### An Alloy Head for the 500

For the 1954 model year an iron barrel and alloy cylinder head were used on the latest 500 twin, the KH Hunter – which effectively replaced the KH and KHA models, both of which had been axed. Bench-tested and tuned, the alloy head KH developed 'a guaranteed 28bhp at 6,200rpm' on delivery. This model also used the duplex, swinging arm frame.

*Ariel FH Huntmaster 650 twin arrived for the 1954 model year. It featured a swinging arm frame right from the beginning of its life.*

### ARIEL Range & Prices.. 1954

| MODEL | PRICE | PURCHASE TAX | TOTAL |
|---|---|---|---|
| | £ s. d. | £ s. d. | £ s. d. |
| 4G  1,000 c.c. Square Four | 245 0 0 | 49 0 0 | 294 0 0 |
| FH  650 c.c. Huntmaster Twin | 192 0 0 | 38 8 0 | 230 8 0 |
| KH  500 c.c. Hunter Twin | 180 0 0 | 36 0 0 | 216 0 0 |
| VH  500 c.c. Hunter Single | 165 0 0 | 33 0 0 | 198 0 0 |
| NH  350 c.c. Hunter Single | 150 0 0 | 30 0 0 | 180 0 0 |
| LH  200 c.c. Colt | 110 0 0 | 22 0 0 | 132 0 0 |
| VB  600 c.c. Side Valve | 142 0 0 | 28 8 0 | 170 8 0 |
| Spring Frame Model VB | extra 16 0 0 | 3 4 0 | 19 4 0 |

ARIEL MOTORS LIMITED · SELLY OAK · BIRMINGHAM 29 · ENGLAND

*Ariel range and price list for the 1954 season.*

## Overhead-Valve Twins

*Nearside view of the new-for-1954 Huntmaster twin.*

*Details of the 646cc (70 × 84mm) Huntmaster engine – essentially an iron BSA A10 unit with modified outer casings.*

## Detail Improvements for 1955

For 1955, several detail improvements arrived. The new Amal Monobloc (Type 376) carburettor made its appearance, with a 1in (25mm) on the KH500 and a larger 1¹/₁₆in (27mm) instrument specified for the FH650. This carburettor replaced the old Type 276, which had a detachable float chamber. An anti-theft steering lock was now fitted, together with a screw-in horn button; 3.25 × 19 ribbed pattern front tyre; repositioned oil filler cap (to be out of the way of the rider's leg) and the tail of the rear mudguard extended 3in (76mm) to below wheel spindle height.

Later, from June 1955, on the KH500 only, the primary chain tensioner was modified; this was now a hardened steel tensioner blade, raised or lowered by an adjustable wedge, secured by a nut and lock washer to a stud in the timing case.

## 1956 – Full-Width Aluminium Brake Hubs

Full-width aluminium brake hubs, rear chain enclosure and a combined headlamp cowl and instrument panel were among a raft of progressive new features unveiled when the 1956 Ariel model range was launched at the beginning of September 1955.

*Overhead-Valve Twins*

| FH 650 1954 | | | |
|---|---|---|---|
| Engine | Air-cooled overhead valve parallel twin with cast-iron cylinder head and barrel assemblies; one-piece crankshaft with plain bearing big-ends | Frame | Duplex, all-steel construction |
| | | Front suspension | Telescopic fork |
| | | Rear suspension | Swinging arm, twin shock absorbers |
| | | Front brake | 7in single-sided drum, SLS |
| Bore | 70mm | Rear brakes | 7in single-sided drum, SLS |
| Stroke | 84mm | Tyres | Front 3.00 × 20; rear 3.50 × 19 |
| Displacement | 646cc | | |
| Compression ratio | 6.5:1 | **General Specifications** | |
| Lubrication | Dry sump, gear pump | Wheelbase | 56in (1,422mm) |
| Ignition | Magneto, 6-volt | Ground clearance | 5.5in (140mm) |
| Carburettor | Single Amal 276 1¹/₁₆in (376 Monobloc from 1955) | Seat height | 31in (787mm) |
| | | Fuel tank capacity | 4gal (18ltr) |
| Primary drive | Chain | Dry weight | 410lb (186kg) |
| Final drive | Chain | Maximum power | 35bhp @ 5,750rpm |
| Gearbox | Four-speed, Burman GB33, foot-change | Top speed | 100mph (160km/h) |

*1955 Ariel KH 500 twin with aluminium cylinder head.*

*1955 650 Huntmaster – compare this with the original 1954 model.*

136

## Overhead-Valve Twins

The new cast-alloy full-width brake hubs incorporated 7in (178mm) diameter centralized brakes equipped with 1½in (38mm) wide linings. Internally, the hub featured integral stiffening webs; externally, it was finning for brake cooling. The brake drum was a cast-iron liner. The brake shoes and shoe plate were aluminium alloy castings.

Both front and rear hubs were similar except for the driving studs and an associated strengthening flange on the rear hub. Wheel spindle diameter in both cases was 1in

*Left: A 1955 KH twin. Alloy cylinder head and integral rocker boxes gave it a more purposeful look than the earlier iron engine; note duplex frame and chrome, detachable cover for dry clutch.*

*Below: The 1955 KH 500 twin was, and still is, a much underrated motorcycle, providing as it does an excellent blend of performance, handling and comfort.*

(25mm) – an increase of ¼in (6mm) over the earlier Ariel component. The greater diameter was intended to increase lateral rigidity at the fork ends. Both brakes retained the ratchet-type fulcrum adjustment that had been a feature of Ariel brakes for many years. In addition, normal finger-operated cable adjusters were fitted; that for the front brake was at the handlebar end of the cable.

A by-product of these new brakes was that in service they needed considerably less adjustment, although actual braking performances were similar.

*Chain Enclosure*
Full enclosure of the final drive chain by a pressed-steel case was available as an optional extra on all models sporting the swinging arm frame (which in reality meant everything except the Square Four and Colt 200 for 1956).

Manufactured in 20-gauge pressed steel, the rear chain case comprised four sections. The forward portion enclosed the gearbox sprocket and a short length of chain, and was bolted to the frame and gearbox. The upper and lower middle sections were bolted to lugs on the swinging arm, while the rear section that covered the rear wheel sprocket was attached to the middle section by two screws. Metal-to-metal, tongue-and-groove joints were employed between the two middle sections and also at their junction with the rear section. To allow for the pivotal movement of the rear fork, the middle sections overlapped the fixed, forward section of the chain case and there was a small clearance at the joint faces.

Removal of a rubber plug in the lower middle section uncovered an inspection hole through which the chain tension could be checked. Screwed-type chain adjusters were fitted and the wheel spindle protruded through a slot in the chain case; hence chain tension could be adjusted in the conventional manner.

*Automatic Chain Lubrication*
Automatic lubrication of the final drive chain was provided whenever the engine was running. Oil spouting from the return pipe inside the filler neck of the oil tank was directed on to a short, tubular wick. This 'wick' conveyed a small amount of lubricating oil into a pipe which was led out through the base of the oil tank and through a rubber grommet in the back of the forward section of the chain case; oil issuing from the pipe was directed on to the lower run of the chain. Under normal running conditions oil was supplied to the chain at a rate of two or three drips a minute. Excess oil from the case escaped on to the tarmac via the clearance at the lower forward joint. Introduction of the rear chain case required the rear brake cable to be transferred to the offside (right) of the motorcycle.

As described in Chapter 6, the one-piece steel pressing for the new headlamp cowl replaced the previous fork shrouds and lamp brackets. The cowl is best described as being a nacelle, similar to that found on Triumph and Royal Enfield models at the time. The 7in (178mm) diameter pre-focus light unit was a new Lucas component featuring an arrangement whereby the dipped beam was also offset to the left (on UK market machines).

Other changes for the 1956 model year were: a new, quickly-detachable rear wheel as standard; a single bolt fixing for the fuel tank (replacing the previous four-bolt set-up); deletion of the chrome plates on the tank; tank badges were now chrome yellow and black (previously red and gold); and dual seats could be specified in a fawn-coloured vinyl. On the KH Fieldmaster only, the oil gauge was deleted from the tank box; on the FH Huntmaster only, wheel rims were now fully chromed and overall gearing was reduced by clutch sprocket with two teeth less (a twenty-four instead of a twenty-two component).

**Testing the Huntmaster**

*The Motor Cycle* carried a three-page road test of the Huntmaster in its issue dated 1 December 1955. The headline read: 'High

*1956 KH 500 Fieldmaster twin. New that year were the brakes and nacelle. The optional fully enclosed rear chain is not fitted to this machine.*

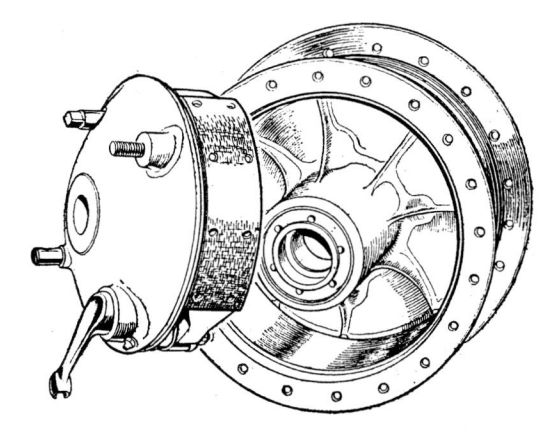

*Internal and external webs were a feature of the full-width brake hubs introduced for 1956. Parent company BSA also used them on some models.*

Performance Combined with Remarkable Tractability and Notable Fuel Economy: First Class Steering and Braking'.

On the open road, it was found that 'a cruising speed of 80mph was well within the Huntmaster's capabilities, and that with throttle to spare'. A certain amount of vibration was 'perceptible', being most noticeable 'in the region of 50mph in top gear and at corresponding speeds in lower gears'. Vibration was also noted at higher speeds 'through the petrol tank'.

The clutch was 'light to operate' and 'took up the drive firmly and showed no sign of distress after repeated full throttle standing starts', whilst 'engagement of bottom gear from neutral with the machine stationary and the engine idling was accompanied by a slight clonk'. Gear changing itself required 'a brief pause in pedal movement when changing upwards and a momentary increase in engine speed when changing downwards'. In contrast, 'steering was first class. The readiness with which the Ariel responded to the slightest handlebar torque or body lean quite belied the machine's weight of over 400lb', whilst 'bend swinging was effortless and delightful at all speeds'. The first thing to ground when heeled over was the 'centre stand'. The tester noted that 'The steering damper was never brought into use, even at a speed of 100mph.' The riding position of the Huntmaster proved 'extremely good for the low and medium speeds'; the tester commented 'for high-speed riding, a more rearward setting of the footrests would have been preferred'.

Engine starting proved 'a first kick affair whether the unit was hot or cold'. With a cold engine the procedure was as follows: 'liberal flooding of the carburettor, closing the air lever (choke) and rather less than one-eighth throttle opening'. Then it was simply 'a lusty swing of the kick-starter; no preliminary starting drill was needed when the engine was warm'.

It was also noted during the 800-mile (1,300km) test that 'a film of oil formed in the vicinity of the joints of the primary chain case, the timing chest and the exhaust rocker box, and also on the gearbox end cover'.

At the conclusion of the test, *The Motor Cycle* said: 'Finished in maroon enamel, the Huntmaster is a handsome model possessing a remarkable combination of high performance and fuel economy, and is endowed with excellent steering and braking.'

Maximum speed was found to be exactly 100mph (160km/h). The cost in December 1955 was £252 19 3d (including UK taxes); the rear chain case was an additional £3 2s 6d.

## Little Change for 1957

There was little change to the Ariel twin-cylinder model for 1957. The most noticeable was an increase in fuel tank capacity from 4gal (18ltr) to 4.5gal (20.5ltr). This new tank was manufactured in two sections and joined beneath and above with a medial strip; chrome bands hid the welds. There were smaller knee grips. Another change was a new front mudguard that featured a deeper section and had no forward mounting stays.

The Huntmaster's only mechanical change, as on the Square Four from this year, was to the clutch drum's innermost plate, which, previously plain and located against a shoulder of the clutch centre, now had four friction material segments riveted to it, and the first plate bore on them.

## Final Months

The KH Fieldmaster five-hundred ceased production in August 1957 – sales having fallen drastically after the larger twin had been released. From then, until production of all the remaining four-stroke models came to an end in the summer of 1959, the FH Huntmaster six-fifty continued unchanged.

*A 1958 FH Huntmaster, little changed from 1956 – production ended (together with all Ariel's range of four-stroke models) in the middle of the following year.*

*This 1958 Huntmaster was turned into a café racer by owner Mike Trail during the late 1960s and early 1970s. Others succumbed to the chopper craze that hit Britain in the mid 1970s.*

# 9 The Arrow Racer

July 1958 saw the launch of the radical Leader. To a conservative industry the new Ariel was a major departure from the norm, not only because of its twin-cylinder two-stroke engine, but also the full enclosure (including leg shields and screen) pressed-steel frame and a host of other unique features.

At first glance, a more unlikely candidate to form the basis for a competitive racing motorcycle would have been hard to imagine. However, when Ariel undressed the motorcycle to produce the Arrow, everything changed. A similar thing happened in Italy when the Aermacchi Chimera was stripped of its tinware to form the basis for the Ala d'Oro racer.

## Piston Port

The piston port 247cc twin with square bore and stroke dimensions of 54 × 54mm had its cylinders inclined forwards at 45 degrees with the firing interval at 180 degrees. The engine porting was conventional for the time with the inlet at the rear of the cylinder, exhaust at the front, transfers to each side of each bore and all timings piston controlled. On the roadster there was only one carburettor, and the crankcase design was to prove a real nuisance to the many Arrow tuners who were to appear over the years.

The engine and gearbox were assembled into a single light-alloy casting and this formed the main crankcase. The gearbox was a four-speed Burman, whilst the primary drive was by Simplex chain. The original cylinder barrels were cast iron, with alloy heads.

The Arrow arrived in time for the 1960 season. Officially the Selly Oak factory did not make racing motorcycles. But unofficially things were very different, with various factory personnel actively beginning work on a racing conversion. This was to continue well into the 1960s, with changes including twin carburettor crankcases, alloy cylinders, specially cast heads, close-ratio gear clusters and even a batch of racing crankshafts made by the Alpha concern.

Most of this 'illegal' factory race development was carried out by quite an impressive array of talent including Peter Inchley, Hermann Meier, Sammy Miller, Roger Barlow and even Val Page. Of course, by this time Ariel was owned by the BSA Group, and heaven knows what its corporate bosses would have done had they found out! But this clandestine activity was to benefit several riders, not only Peter Inchley himself, but also Robin Good, Michael O'Rourke and Cecil Sandford, to name just three.

## The Meier Machine Makes its Debut

The very first to appear was the O'Rourke machine which, entered by London dealer and former TT winner and lap record holder, Harold Daniell – and tuned by Hermann Meier – made its debut at the Silverstone Hutchinson 100 meeting in early April 1960. In the event, after being a highly impressive fourth fastest in qualifying, O'Rourke lay tenth in the race until a piston tightened on the fourth lap. If this was a disappointment,

# The Arrow Racer

*A set of standard crankcases complete with front engine mount, but fitted with rev counter drive on clutch cover . . .*

*. . . compare to this pukka race engine with modified crankcase and twin carb conversion.*

what followed certainly was not. First, at Brands Hatch in mid-May O'Rourke took the Meier-tuned Arrow past Dan Shorey and Fred Hardy on NSUs and then the mighty Mike Hailwood's works twin cylinder Desmo Ducati, to lead the 250cc race. Even though he was eventually forced back to fourth, O'Rourke had opened more than a few eyes with this breathtaking performance.

## The Racing Conversion

Meier had spent considerable time and energy in carrying out an effective conversion to twin Amal GP carburettors with these being fitted on to an aluminium block bolted to the crankcase. To allow this to take place, the original inlet port and mounting flange had to be removed and filled in by weld. This effectively also removed a main engine support, so new racing cylinder heads were made which incorporated lugs that bolted to new fixed brackets of the frame beam. The rest of the engine work was one of careful preparation with special attention being given to the porting and exhaust.

A weight-saving exercise was also carried out with all the unnecessary road gear being removed, plus any unwanted lugs and the like.

*Standard Arrow crankshaft (front) with special Alpha racing assembly at the rear, with its wider and heavier flywheels.*

The wheels were rebuilt with 18in (457mm) aluminium rims and racing tyres, expansion chamber fitted and a full dolphin fairing helped streamline the bike. Actually, it was a remarkably standard motorcycle, with the frame, forks and brakes all being standard Arrow production components.

*The original Meier-tuned engine in 1960 as ridden by Michael O'Rourke; it finished a magnificent seventh in that year's Lightweight TT.*

*Arrow cylinder heads. Left to right: factory racing 12:1; central plug post 1960 10:1; non-squish pre-1960 8:1.*

*Arrow restoration project on display at Donington Park 27 July 1986; claimed to be the actual Meier machine – complete with history board.*

*Single-cylinder 125 Arrow. Silverstone practice day, March 1960.*

## The TT

Then came the TT in June, where the Ariel twin created a sensation when O'Rourke proved its speed and reliability not only by being the best-placed British machine, but finishing seventh at an average speed of 80.18mph (129km/h), – only 30sec behind the sixth-placed man, Naomi Tanaguchi, on a factory four-cylinder Honda – and in front of some glamorous foreign marques including Bianchi, MV Agusta and NSU.

## Thruxton

The reliability of the Ariel under racing conditions was emphasized later that month when Cecil Sandford and Sammy Miller came second in the 250cc class of the Thruxton 500-mile (805km) endurance race. Another

## The Arrow Racer

Arrow finished third. In fact, if Miller had not fallen in the early stages and damaged the bike, it would probably have won comfortably.

A year later, Robin Good and Peter Inchley finished runners-up, with another Arrow fourth, but Sandford and Miller were forced out after sixty-five laps with an engine seizure.

In 1962, victory once more eluded the Selly Oak factory when Good and Inchley again finished runners-up, with Sandford and 'new' co-rider Michael O'Rourke, third.

## Specials

The Ariel engine was also used in a number of privately built, but nevertheless highly interesting specials. One notable machine was the Ernie Earles-built 496cc four cylinder

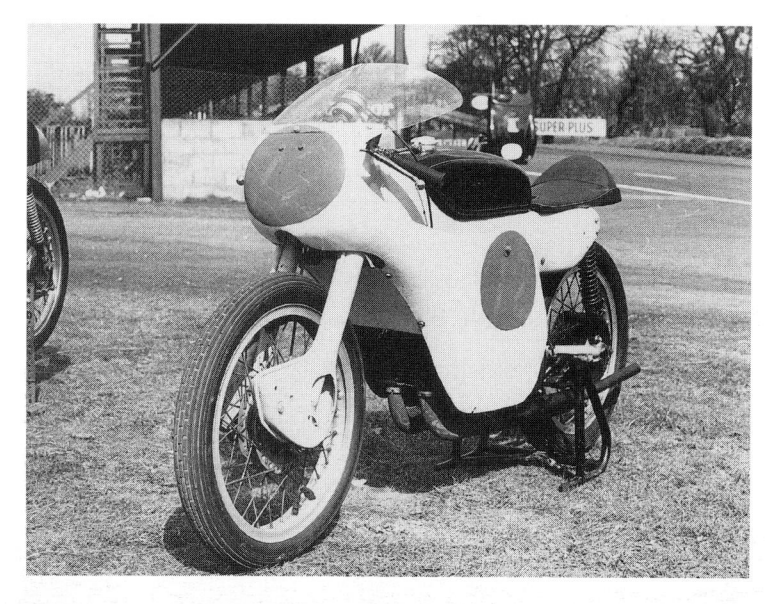

*George Salt Arrow racer at Oulton Park 1962. This was successfully raced by Robin Good in both 1962 and 1963, at national and international level.*

*Peter Inchley, factory development engineer and unofficial factory Arrow racer, Mallory Park 1962.*

*Period photograph of a privately built Arrow racer; early 1960s. Lots of similar bikes were built around this time following the success of the Meier/O'Rourke machine.*

(using what amounted to a pair of Arrow units side by side). Although hugely fast when it kept going, it was extremely unreliable. Raced by the highly experienced Birmingham-based Bill Boddice, the Earles Arrow sidecar outfit first appeared in 1960 and was campaigned, with limited success, until the end of 1962.

Technically, it was of considerable interest, with a Norton racing gearbox that was driven off a central coupling between the two engines. Both engines were fitted with twin Amal GP carburettors. Coil ignition was employed with a battery in the sidecar nose and a distributor on the offside of the offside engine.

Another four was the later machine built by brothers Gerald and Michael Piper. Unlike the Earles design, this was a solo and the engine configuration was entirely different. The engines were mounted one above the other in a similar fashion to the Yamaha four-cylinder works machines, which were ridden by Phil

*The Ernie Earles-built 494cc four-cylinder for sidecar use (two Arrow engines alongside each other with central chain drive), on the test bed at the Ariel factory, August 1960. Officially Ariel did not support racing!*

Read and Bill Ivy during the late 1960s. However, on the five-hundred MGP (Michael and Gerald Piper), the cylinders were not mounted on a common crankcase as on the

145

## The Arrow Racer

Japanese design, but retained their separate crankcases. In place of the standard issue Ariel Burman gearbox, was a racing Norton type. The carburettors – one per cylinder – were a quartet of Amal Monobloc instruments. Cycle parts were largely Norton, except the one-off space-type frame (although even this was effectively a modified Featherbed).

Other home-brewed Arrow projects included a three-cylinder model raced by Harry Price and even half an Arrow – a single-cylinder 125 (which retained the square 54 × 54 bore and stroke dimensions) having made its debut at a Silverstone practice day in early 1960. Another Arrow (a 250) was even converted to disc valve induction.

*The MGP Special, a privately built four-cylinder Arrow five-hundred racer, 1968.*

*MV-framed Arrow racer at the twentieth anniversary CRMC meeting at Brands Hatch, August 1999. Frame has been heavily modified to accept low slung Arrow engine.*

## Sprinting the Arrow

Vincent specialist George Brown of Stevenage, Hertfordshire, won much acclaim for his sprinting efforts aboard the likes of Nero and Super Nero. However, the Brown family, George and his son Antony, also achieved considerable success with a specially adapted Arrow-engined machine that broke both the standing and flying start quarter-mile British records. This tiny bike was capable of in excess of 130mph (209km/h) and took the record at 126.44mph (203.44km/h).

## A Missed Opportunity

But in the end the full potential of the Arrow as a racing motorcycle was missed. Without 'Big Brother' BSA, Ariel would no doubt have been in an ideal position to build and sell a competitive and affordable racer. Instead, the opportunity to cash in on the over-the-counter racing boom that occurred as the 1960s unfolded was left to smaller rivals such as Greeves, Cotton and DMW with their Silverstone, Telstar and Hornet machines respectively. One can only speculate on what might have been. In the author's opinion, with a concerted effort, fully backed by the powers above, Ariel would surely have emerged victorious against those much smaller concerns.

For the last quarter of a century, converted Leaders and Arrows have made their mark in both Vintage and Classic racing circles. In many ways they are an ideal machine, being simple, cheap to buy and maintain – and easy to tune.

*One of the most common modifications for classic racing is to replace the original Ariel pistons with Suzuki items (on left of picture). Standard piston is on right.*

*Mike Hose (in leathers third from left) with team members and Arrow racer, CRMC Cadwell Park, October 2002.*

*Racing veteran Ray Boughey with his Arrow special, CRMC Cadwell 2002.*

# 10 Colt

The original Ariel Colt (coded L) was a very light (for its day) two-fifty single cylinder machine, its name coined by publicity guru Vic Mole during the late 1920s. It was produced in both ohv and side-valve guises and its design and development are discussed earlier in the book. In this chapter we are concerned with the 'modern' Colt offered by Ariel in the years 1954–59.

The Colt of the 1950s was very much a product of increasing BSA Group influence on Ariel's design and production at that time. Although not quite as blatant a badge engineering exercise as say, AMC's AJS and Matchless products, the LH Colt was nonetheless heavily influenced by BSA cycle components and its engine construction 'a dead ringer for the BSA CIIG 250cc', as Roy Bacon described it in his 1983 book, *Ariel, The Postwar Models*.

## The Newcomer

The new 198cc Colt was first announced in the press during early October 1953, making its public debut on the company's stand at the London Motor Cycle Show at Earls Court between Saturday 14 November and the following Saturday 21 November. In its Show Guide issue *The Motor Cycle* commented: 'It seems certain that many old-timers will visit the Ariel stand with the express purpose of reliving happy memories of a famous model, popular some 20 years ago.' Total attendance for the seven days (the show was not open on a Sunday) was 187,096 – of which a staggering 51,129 made their visit on the first day.

Although, as already mentioned, very similar to BSA's own CIIG (which was only offered in 1954 and 1955), the LH Colt had a different bore and stroke measurement of 60 × 70mm, compared to the larger 249cc BSA's 63 × 70mm dimensions.

*The Engine Design*
The aluminium (Y-alloy) cylinder head (iron on the CIIG) of the Colt incorporated valve seat inserts of austentic iron, cast into position. The combustion chamber was of elongated hemispherical shape, a feature adopted so that valve head diameters of no less than $1^{7}/_{32}$in and $1^{5}/_{32}$in, inlet and exhaust respectively, could be adopted by the Colt's designer, Val Page. A shallow rocker box was formed integral with the head casting. The single rocker spindle operated in a pedestal bolted to the head. The valve mechanism was enclosed by a deep, one-piece, light-alloy rocker box cover. As on the CIIG, the Colt featured crossed pushrods, retained from the original ohv CII engine of the late 1930s.

Featuring a 7.5:1 compression split-skirt cast-aluminium piston with a slightly domed crown and three rings (two compression and a single oil scraper), the gudgeon pin ran in the small end of a forged-steel connecting rod, with a phosphor-bronze bush. Meanwhile, at the base of the con-rod the big-end bearing was of the double-row, crowded-roller pattern, employing $^{1}/_{4}$in diameter × $^{1}/_{2}$in hardened rollers. Supporting the built-up crankshaft assembly was a ball race bearing on the drive- (clutch) side, with a plain phosphor-bronze bearing on the timing side housed, in traditional British fashion, in a pair of vertically split crank cases. A double acting, gear-type oil pump for the dry sump lubrication system was situated in the timing chest and driven by spiral gearing from the crank mainshaft. The capacity of the oil tank was ½gal (2.3ltr).

The iron cylinder barrel was held down by six studs. The barrel featured a cast-in tunnel on the right (offside), thus making the valve gear totally enclosed. A head gasket was fitted and the nuts for the head studs fitted between the barrel fins as on the Ariel five-hundred twin. Each valve was operated by a pair of coil springs.

*The Timing Side*
The timing side of the Colt engine was extremely simple, and because of an alternator instead of a mag/dyno was very compact. Much as on the larger Ariel singles, it featured a pinion on the crankshaft which meshes with another gear above it on the camshaft (the latter ran in bushes – one in the timing case, one in the crank case). Above these gears was a fixed pin and on that the pivotal pair of bell-crank cam followers, one for each valve. These were laid out so that the outer cam had a follower positioned ahead of the camshaft line and was for the inlet valve.

The pushrod lay back at an angle and was thus in line with the valve itself when viewed from the side. The exhaust followed a similar pattern with the pushrod tilted forwards so that, as already mentioned, the two rods crossed over. Incorrect assembly is impossible as the crankcase top has two holes drilled for the pushrods – so they could only be placed in the correct position.

*The new 198cc (60 × 70mm) Colt was first announced in the press during October 1953. It was the product of the BSA 'parts bin', rather than a true Ariel. For example, the engine was a smaller version of the CIIG, whilst many of the cycle parts were Bantam (including the silencer on this machine from the first batch).*

*Colt*

*Coil Ignition*
The end of the camshaft was taper bored and to this was fitted the ignition centrifugal advance and retard mechanism, with the contact breaker points cam, the latter with a pin to key the components together at the correct position. The circular timing case carried the points and condenser on a backplate – this could be rotated for fine adjustment of the timing. The outer cover was embossed 'Colt 200'. An ignition coil supplied the sparks.

*The Alternating Generator*
The alternating generator was of Wico-Paco origin and fitted at the opposite end of the crankshaft to the contact breakers. Situated within the primary chaincase, it was impervious of oil and produced a 54-watt output. The rotor was mounted on the crank's mainshaft, whilst the six-pole stator was mounted on studs projecting outward from the chain case; thus, the chaincase cover could be removed without disturbing the generator.

Incorporated in the headlamp-mounted ignition switch was an emergency starting position, so that the engine could be started by means of the kick-starter if the battery became discharged. The battery was a 6-volt/8-amp hour type and charged via a conventional rectifier.

*Clutch and Gearbox*
Also situated in the primary chaincase was the five-plate clutch, consisting of two plates with cork inserts and three main plates. Running in oil and incorporating a synthetic-rubber, vane-type transmission shock absorber it proved light in operation and hard wearing in service. The primary chain was of the simplex type, whilst the chaincase itself was of pressed steel.

A new Burman-made gearbox, the GB30, was specially created for the Colt and was extremely compact. The employment of short, yet robust shafts, ensured considerable rigidity. At the time of the Colt's launch, Ariel sources claimed 'A saving in space and weight has been affected by a redesigned form of selector mechanism'. Located behind the gear train, the selector mechanism differed from the normal Burman type in that a cam plate, actuated through long trip plates, replaced the quadrant mechanism normally employed. Overall gear ratios were: top, 6.43:1; third, 8.5:1; second, 11.6:1 and first, 17.5:1.

*Kick-Start*
As with the gearbox, the kick-starter drive assembly, in which the starter operated on a sleeve-cum-spindle bearing directly on the layshaft, was designed with a view to weight- and space-saving. At its outer end, the sleeve was reduced in diameter to become a solid spindle, and was supported in a phosphor-bronze bush in the outer end cover; the spindle and layshaft were thus concentric.

The sleeve section of the spindle carried a spring-loaded pawl, which, when the kick-start lever was operated, engaged with a ratchet formed integrally with the layshaft bottom-gear pinion. When the kick-starter lever was in its normal position, the pawl was automatically forced out of mesh by cam-type profiling of the inner edge of the phosphor-bronze bush supporting the spindle.

*Carburettor*
For the first year of the LH Colt's production life, an Amal 275 $^{13}/_{16}$in carburettor was specified, this being normally equipped with a 75 main jet and a 5/3 slide. But, from the beginning of 1955 until production came to an end in 1958, a new 375 instrument was fitted, with a larger 90 main jet and a slide number 3½.

*The Chassis*
As with the engine, the Colt's frame was very much BSA-inspired. Of all-welded-steel construction, it was of the open-diamond type and featured plunger rear suspension. This assembly was very much as the CIOL. The front forks were again of BSA origin, coming from the CIIG, and had coil springs and hydraulic damping, together with 4in (100mm) of movement.

And just to show the Colt as being a 'parts bin special', the rear hub was from a Bantam, with the same narrow sprocket. This meant that the Colt was unusual in having the odd feature of a final drive chain being a narrower section than the primary chain! Brake diameters were 5½in (140mm) front and 5in (127mm) rear; 19in tyres were specified front and rear.

*Balance of the Specification*
Other features of the Colt included comprehensive (steel) mudguards; a steel pressed cowl, streamlining the 6in (152mm) diameter headlamp (this cowl was soon dispensed with for more conventional ear-type headlamp brackets); rubber knee grips; steel panelling between the engine and gearbox; plastic circular period Ariel tank badges and an 80mph Smiths' speedometer. Also part of the standard 'as supplied' specification was a rear stop lamp, centre stand, dual seat, pillion footrests, tyre inflator, a rider's handbook and toolkit.

The first pre-production examples were finished in black enamel and gold pin striping with chromium brightwork such as wheel rims, exhaust and handlebars. However, the production version was finished in Brunswick Green in place of the black.

Other changes from the 1953 Earls Court Show models included narrower 2.75 instead of 3.00 section tyres and a conventional Burgess-type silencer instead of the flat Bantam DI component. At its official launch in the autumn of 1953, the new Colt cost £132. When sales finally ground to a halt at the end of 1959, the price had risen to £150 15s 8d.

## Road Testing the Colt

In the spring of 1955 *Motor Cycling* tested an example of the Colt. With the bike fully equipped with fuel and oil the weight was 256lb (116kg). Out on the road this meant a maximum speed of 63mph (101km/h), and fuel consumption averaged around 90mpg (3.14/100km) throughout the test.

Generally the *Motor Cycling* tester found the little Ariel single to his liking, saying that it was 'well finished' and 'well suited to its tasks'. As for the latter, this really meant commuting to work and back, plus touring. When the Colt was first put into production the

| LH Colt 1954 | | | |
|---|---|---|---|
| Engine | Air-cooled overhead valve single with vertical cylinder; crossed pushrods; roller bearing big-end; aluminium cylinder head; cast-iron barrel | Frame | Tubular steel construction, with single front downtube |
| | | Front suspension | Telescopic forks |
| | | Rear suspension | Swinging arm, twin shocks |
| | | Front brake | 5.5in single-sided drum, SLS |
| Bore | 60mm | Rear brakes | 5in single-sided drum, SLS |
| Stroke | 70mm | Tyres | 2.75 × 19 front and rear (1955 onwards 3.00 × 19) |
| Displacement | 198cc | | |
| Compression ratio | 7.5:1 | **General Specifications** | |
| Lubrication | Dry sump, double gear type pump | Wheelbase | 51.5in (1,308mm) |
| Ignition | Coil, contact breakers; 6-volt battery | Ground clearance | 5.5in (140mm) |
| Carburettor | Amal 275 or 375 1³⁄₁₆in with separate float chamber | Seat height | 29.5in (749mm) |
| | | Fuel tank capacity | 2.5gal (11.4ltr) |
| Primary drive | Chain | Dry weight | 270lb (123kg) |
| Final drive | Chain | Maximum power | 10bhp @ 5,600rpm |
| Gearbox | Four-speed, Burman, foot-change | Top speed | 63mph (101km/h) |

Selly Oak-built two-hundred was by no means the smallest or the least powerful motorcycle on the British market. As Triumph had discovered with their 150cc Terrier, a small four-stroke could be a top seller, offering as it did several advantages over far more common rivals usually powered by Villiers two-stroke power units from a myriad of small producers including James, Francis Barnett, Sun, Tandon, Excelsior and Norman.

The engine proved an easy starter and was quite capable of cruising between 45 and 50mph (72–81km/h). It could also cope with a pillion passenger. However, this showed up the bike's biggest failing: the largely ineffectual and undamped plunger rear suspension. Although the standard dual seat was useful and necessary for carrying a passenger, a single, sprung saddle would have been preferable in the comfort stakes.

The *Motor Cycling* tester had criticisms regarding the handlebar shape and gear-change pedal, but otherwise Ariel's smallest came in for considerable praise, particular mention being made of the willing engine, front forks and front brake.

*Little Change*

Many view the number of changes, or the lack of them, as a way of judging if the design team got things right or not. In the Colt's case the model has to be adjudged a success, if for no other reason than an almost total absence of changes during its first few months of production; what few there were centred around cosmetic details: silencer, headlamp mounting and colour scheme, as already outlined.

## The 1955 Model Year Changes

But, as with every mechanical vehicle, changes were introduced over time, the first 'updates' coming towards the end of 1954, in time for the 1955 model year. The first was the change from an Amal 275 (with separate float chamber) to Amal 375 (Monobloc) carburettor. Internally, the engine had a ramp cam form adopted – this retained the existing timing figures, but eased the way the clearance was taken up – whilst the pushrod diameter was increased. Another area of modification centred on clutch adjustment. This was revised so that the pressure plate had its central screw axed in favour of relocation into the clutch worm on the right. The Ariel development team saw fit to replace a hardened pad between the adjusting screw and the clutch pushrod, with the housing only needing to fit into a single position in the end cover, thus resulting in an easier method of adjustment.

Strangely, the Ariel team reverted once more to the larger 3.00 section tyres. At the same time the mudguards, particularly the rear, were altered. Originally, the latter were quite heavily valanced, but on the revised rear mudguard this valancing was largely removed and it was given a circular section similar to the front. The stays for the rear mudguard were changed and now featured a single tube each side bent to run out to the mudguard again. The right (offside) tube was made detachable to ease rear wheel removal.

## The 1956 Update

When the 1956 Ariel range was announced at the beginning of September 1955 it was seen that the LH Colt had been the subject of three detail modifications. The Amal 375 Monobloc carb was now mounted transversely and was provided with a right-angle induction pipe to impart turbulence to the gas flow; Ariel claimed that the new induction layout resulted in improved flexibility and sweeter running of the engine.

Superceding the original combined ignition and lighting switch in the headlamp were two separate switches: one controlling the ignition – including that for emergency starting – and the other for the lighting system. Finally, whereas previously a dry-type battery was fitted, this had been replaced by an orthodox wet type of 9-amp hour rating.

## Cosmetic and Electrical in 1957

The annual range of small modifications came around again at the beginning of September 1956, in time for the 1957 season's model. This time the updates were minor to say the least, with only electrical and cosmetic changes being introduced. A two-tone colour scheme was adopted; whilst the frame, forks and mudguards were still Brunswick Green, the tank was now finished in a light shade of pastel green. Engine appearance had been improved by polishing the timing chest and the fins of the aluminium cylinder head.

In line with the larger displacement Ariel models, the fuel tank was altered. The method of construction was changed. Each side of the new tank was a single pressing and the two

*One component specially made for the Colt was the Burman GB30 gearbox and it was an extremely compact assembly. This 1955 model has minor changes from the first batch; these being mainly confined to the silencer and rear mudguard brackets, plus carb and air filter. When Motor Cycling tested an example during the same year the maximum speed was 63mph (101km/h).*

*Official factory photograph showing the 1956 two-hundred Colt. The 1956 model differed by having separate switches to replace original combined lighting and ignition assembly. The previous dry charge battery was replaced by an orthodox wet type.*

## Colt

were joined by a strip along the top and by the tunnel roof underneath. Concealing the welds between sides and medial strip was an aluminium band. In the author's opinion this was, unfortunately, largely a cost-cutting exercise with the fingerprints of the BSA Group accountants clearly showing. This new tank also meant the end of the traditional and distinctive Ariel chromed tank flutes, which had given the Selly Oak machine a touch of class. On the electrical side, an ammeter had been added to the headlamp and was centrally mounted between the two switches. A new Wipac-sourced rear light was now fitted.

From then on until production, together with that of other four-stroke models, came to an end as the 1950s became the 1960s, the Colt soldiered on unchanged. Like the Square Four, the Colt was never to be given a swinging arm frame. Actually, in the Colt's case, this move would have been easy because a suitable frame had already been produced by BSA for its C12 model (made from 1956 until 1958).

An so the Colt died – effectively killed off by a combination of the new Ariel two-stroke Leader/Arrow family and BSA's increasing grip on Ariel's affairs and thus independence. Sad, but nonetheless true.

*A July 1956 advertisement saying 'Colt – the pedigree 200cc'; when it was actually anything but, thanks to its mixed parentage!*

# 11 The Futuristic Leader

The Ariel Leader (originally called the Glida before production began in late 1958) was in many ways a revolutionary, forward-looking design; one which attempted to progress the motorcycle a stage further. Unfortunately, as history proves time and time again both before and after the Leader, motorcyclists are notoriously conservative, often shunning innovative new designs.

## Ariel's First Two-Stroke Since 1914

The Leader was Ariel's first two-stroke since 1914, but this was only one of many unusual features of the machine, because when it was announced in the press on 17 July 1958 the Leader started tongues wagging with its entire design. The styling was controversial to say the least, as was the full enclosure of the engine-gearbox unit and comprehensive, in-built weather protection. In fact, Ariel claimed in its official press release: 'In all but extremes of bad weather the Leader can be ridden without the need for special clothing. Steel pressings are employed for the frame and bodywork and the side panels are readily removable to provide access to the power unit.'

## Ingenious Practical Features

As *The Motor Cycle* said in its 30 October 1958 issue, 'Ingenious, practical features abound'. For example, the headlamp beam setting could be adjusted merely by moving a short lever projecting upwards through the instrument console. The primary and final drive chains could be adjusted within record-breaking time. Similar careful attention by the design team headed by Val Page was clearly evident in many other directions, too. For example, the design and layout of the Leader had been aimed at providing owners with probably the best small capacity motorcycle suitable for all forms of touring ever conceived. For proof of this, even today the Ariel could, one imagines, be suitably 'grown' into a large-capacity model of say 1000cc and passed off as a twenty-first century luxury touring mount to equal anything on the market. Of course, tyre technology, braking design and an electronic engine-management system would play their part in the update of this fifty-year old design – but the basics were all there at the Leader's launch. Also, today the majority of motorcycles feature comprehensive enclosure, so modern riders now appreciate the benefits which the new Ariel design offered back in 1958, unlike riders at the time.

However, the Leader offered so much more than just enclosure and rider protection. It was a notable design for a myriad of other reasons. Chief designer Val Page and his team were, thankfully, given a free hand in their design brief, the only stipulations being that the new model had to be a two-fifty with built-in weather protection and a good performance. The project, which began during 1955, took three years from the initial drawing work through to the completed motorcycle, ready for production.

To understand *why* the Leader emerged as it did one has to study the motorcycling world as it was during the mid-1950s. Unlike the beginning of the twenty-first century, the

# The Futuristic Leader

*When the Leader was announced in July 1958 it created a vast amount of press interest, due to its revolutionary concept – and the departure for Ariel of having a twin cylinder two-stroke engine.*

requirements of half a century ago were completely different. Then, bikes were not seen as purely leisure-time toys for the well-off; instead they were everyday transport, doubling up as ride-to-work transport during the weekdays with touring to the country on high days and holidays.

## A Unified Design

A key part of the Leader's design was that it had been conceived very much as a whole, unified structure, not as a collection of components as was usually the case with more conventional machines. In many ways it was akin to a grown-up scooter rather than a traditional naked motorcycle. As Steve Wilson recalled from personal experience in his *British Motorcycles Since 1950* series: 'Back in 1960, the parental decree for me, illogical but firm, was that as far as two wheels were concerned I could only go to scooters – motorbikes were out. Yet I almost succeeded in persuading them to get me a Leader, passing it off as a sort of *big scooter*. And I was not really disappointed when I failed because that was really how I, and a lot of other 16-year old would-be rockers, thought of it.' As Steve Wilson went on to relate, this was 'unfair, given the excellent handling and an eventual top speed of around 80'.

The above comments rather go to prove that somehow, even though in many ways the Leader was far ahead of its time, the potential buyers had not been consulted as to whether they would, in fact, have been willing to own such a different machine to the run-of-the-mill types already in existence.

## The Engine Type

Maybe Ariel did not research who would buy the motorcycle as an entire unit, but the company certainly carried out researches into 'customer requirements' as to what type of engine should be used. They found there was a strong body of opinion in favour of a two-fifty two-stroke twin. Val Page openly admitted when interviewed in August 1958 that 'without this preliminary investigation' the design team might well have settled upon a different engine type. However, this posed a considerable challenge, as Ariel had not built a two-stroke since the pioneer days, whilst Page said he 'welcomed the opportunity of designing a two-stroke again', because the last one for which he had been responsible had

156

*A launch date (July 1958) Esso Two-stroke Oil advertisement – recommended by Ariel.*

# Two-Stroke
# LEADERS!

For their revolutionary new 250 c.c. Twin Two-Stroke 'Leader', Ariel naturally recommend Esso Two-Stroke Motor Oil

**Esso**

## TWO STROKE
### MOTOR OIL

*World Leader in Two-Stroke Motor Oils*

*'Motor cycling de luxe' was very much how Ariel's publicity department saw the new Leader. However, several of its touring aids were expensive cost options. Nonetheless, fully equipped it could perform the touring role in fine style.*

*motor cycling de-luxe*

## The Futuristic Leader

*A lovely period photograph taken of a Leader negotiating Hyde Park Corner, London, circa spring 1961.*

*This view of the Leader shows the smooth flowing lines with the accessories in place. However, for many, it was all too scooter-like. Actually, it was ahead of its time – by some thirty years!*

been when he was with JAP in the early 1920s.

Because of this long gap in both the company's and the design chief's experience, it had been necessary not only to study current two-stroke designs from the other companies – notably the German Adler marque (*see* the box on page 160), but also look at the knowledge acquired by Ariel's parent company BSA, with its Bantam (which had, of course, itself largely begun life as a German design, the DKW RT125).

Even so, during the 1958 interview Val Page had wanted to make it clear that 'the final design was entirely an Ariel matter', and one in which his Assistant Designer, Bernard Knight, had played a vital role – adding that the bench and road testing during the development of the Leader project had been carried out by Clive Bennett. However, there is little doubt that the Adler two-fifty twin *did* play a big role in the design. For example, not only did the two designs share the same 54 × 54mm bore and stroke dimensions, but the cylinders were inclined 45 degrees.

The loop scavenging Adler and Ariel engines featured pistons that were interchangeable. Also both engines shared an unconventional feature which saw each crank chamber made accessible via what Steve Wilson described as a 'door'. This feature allowed each outer bearing to be removed and the engine dismantled without having to remove it from the frame.

But even though the Adler and Ariel engines were similar, they were certainly not the same. The German design would, quite simply, have been too expensive, and, as Val Page's instructions had been 'to produce an economical power unit', there were several features which showed how the Selly Oak factory's design saved money over the German one. For example, there was chain instead of the more costly geared primary drive and only three main bearings instead of four.

The German engine was much neater in appearance, although some of this was due to the Leader's engine being fully enclosed, rather than open to full public view as on the Adler. However, when undressed to provide the Arrow series, this untidiness became apparent. It is also interesting to note that on the Adler the clutch was mounted on the crankshaft, which, as Yamaha discovered, was not the best place to put it, whereas on the British engine it was located in the more conventional position in line with the gearbox.

*One-Piece Crankcase*
The basis of the Leader's engine gear unit was a one-piece die-casting which comprised the

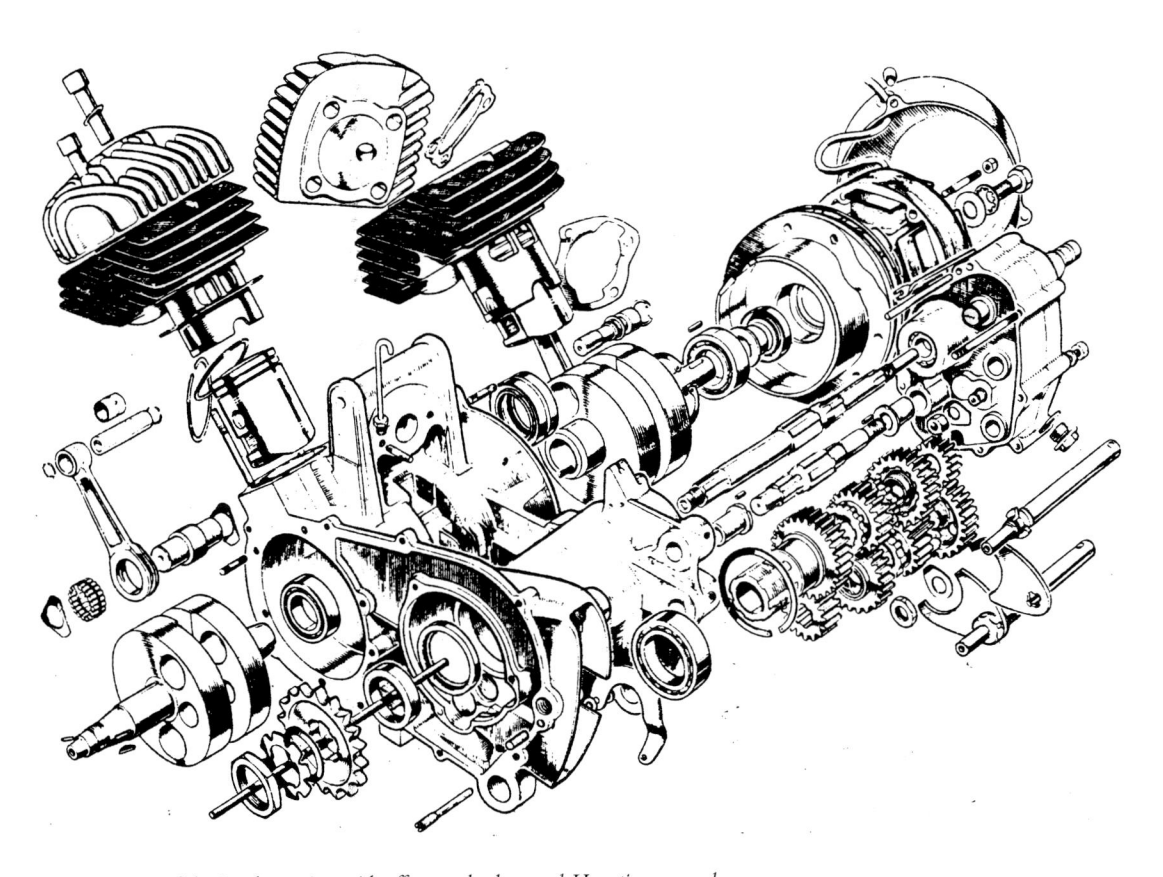

*Earliest version of the Leader engine, with offset spark plugs and H-section con-rods.*

## The Futuristic Leader

### German Influence

As is described in the main text, the engine design of the Ariel Leader (and thus its Arrow derivatives) owed much to the German Adler MB250. In fact, not just the Birmingham company used the Adler as its inspiration, so did the Japanese Yamaha company, but that is another story.

Originally established by Heinrich Kleyer as Adler Fahradwerke AG in 1886 to manufacture bicycles, the company then went on to become a major producer of typewriters (1895), cars (1899) and motorcycles (1902). But unlike its other products the motorcycle side was forgotten for over four decades, until 1949, when in the boom years of the immediate post-war period the German motorcycle industry was reborn.

The first of the new Adler motorcycles, the M100 single-cylinder two-stroke, designed by Hermann Friedrich, made its bow in 1950. Following hard on the M100's heels came the M200 – a 195cc twin.

But the really important breakthrough came with the launch of the new M250 twin in 1952. This machine was to form the basis of the Adler's success over the next few years. Not only was it to prove the company's most popular and best-selling model, but at its heart was a superb 247cc (54 × 54mm) parallel twin-cylinder engine unit. Like the M200, the M250 sported piston port induction with loop-scavenging, as well as aluminium heads, cast-iron barrels and slightly inclined cylinders.

At the end of 1953 the improved MB250 arrived together with the MB250S (Sport), but it should be pointed out that the 'improvements' were actually to machine specification and tuning, rather than the overall design of the power unit. The MB250S developed 18bhp and was good for 72mph (116km/h). One also has to bear in mind that not only was this an excellent, class-leading performance, but the two-fifty Adler twin was a heavy bike, weighing in at 320lb (145kg) with a tank of fuel. Even then this was only half the picture, because the Adler twin was sufficiently well engineered that it could accept considerable tuning for competition work.

Both air- and water-cooled versions were built for racing – mainly by privateers in Germany. With over 30bhp on tap, the twin-cylinder Adler remained competitive well into the 1960s, even at international level. In addition, the MB250 formed the basis for a line of successful motocross and endurance machines. Whether it was for touring, fast road work, racing, motocross or Six Days Trial work, the Adler could more than cope.

The German marque's brochure for the twin cylinder *wünder* bike read thus: 'Very low minimum speed without jerks, vibration-free throughout all speed ranges! High maximum speed, unlimited full-throttle capacity and – as a special feature – unrivalled, powerful acceleration! MB250, QUICK, POWERFUL, QUIET!' No wonder that others, including Ariel, were impressed by the Adler design.

Ultimately, both Adler and Ariel, if not Yamaha, were to suffer from the advent of the small affordable car explosion that began at the end of the 1950s. The German motorcycle industry felt the effects first and Adler, like many other rivals, was forced to close. In July 1958 the giant Grundig Corporation acquired a controlling interest in Adler. This act was to seal the fate of Adler motorcycles, and shortly afterwards senior management was instructed to concentrate its efforts solely upon office equipment, including typewriters and the like.

*Although not a direct copy, Val Page and his team (like Yamaha, too) used the twin-cylinder German Adler as a template in creating their 247cc (54 × 54mm) power unit.*

crankcase (manufactured in DTD 424 aluminium alloy) inner half of the primary chain case and gearbox shell. This was in fact quite a complex moulding, the die having no fewer than sixty-eight components. As already mentioned, because it was originally designed to be almost entirely concealed by the bodywork, no concessions had been made to appearance. As proof of this, the crankcase was merely a liberally finned box, absolutely no bigger than needed to house the crankshaft – on exposed engines in more conventional motorcycles of the era, styling of the crank cases/outer covers was taken into account – not so with the Ariel.

Because of the way the engine assembly was mounted in the frame, the main casting (the aforementioned crankcase die-casting) being literally 'hung' from the frame beam, the crankcase unit had to perform functions other than would normally be asked of it, and usually looked after by the frame itself. Another example of the unconventional nature of the Ariel design was that below the gearbox were two lugs into which a steel sleeve was pressed which formed a pivot for the centre stand. Within the sleeve lay the crossover shaft for the rear brake pedal, all this showing both the unity of the design and at the same time the economy of material by Page, Knight and the remainder of the development team.

## *A Divided Crankshaft*
As on the Adler, a 'split' crank was selected so that the engine could be dismantled *in situ*, which meant that the crankshaft had to be of divided construction. This was achieved in the following way: integral with each of the inboard full-disc crank webs was a short shaft. The left (nearside) shaft fitted through the inner race of the middle main bearing and featured a male-taper end with an internal thread. In the right (offside) shaft was a matching female taper and a captive drawbolt to pull together or separate the crank assemblies. Angular location of these two assemblies was by means of a radial keyway on the male shaft which engaged a captive dog, or end-key, retained between the head of the drawbolt and a collar. The bolt was provided with a hexagon-socket head, accessible through the hollow right-hand (offside) outboard mainshaft with the aid of a long hexagonal bar.

## *The Outer Crank Webs*
The outer crank webs were also of the full-disc variety and integral with the mainshafts. The crankpins were shouldered, with $^{7}/_{8}$in (22mm) diameter roller tracks, and were a parallel press-fit in the webs, which were balanced by holes and reduction in width over half in which the pin was located. To minimize the rocking couple inherent with a 180 degree twin, the cylinders were set as close together as possible; the distance between the axes was only $3^{5}/_{8}$in (92mm). Clearance between the crankwebs and case was kept down to $^{1}/_{32}$in (0.8mm) to ensure a high primary ratio.

## *A Lucas Alternator*
Positioned outboard of the right (offside) crankcase chamber plate and enclosed by a pressed steel cover, was a Lucas RM 13/15 alternator. Its stator was spigot-mounted on to the plate, whilst the rotor was pressed on to the mainshaft, with a Woodruff key location. On the other mainshaft, in addition to the twenty-two-tooth engine sprocket, was an external $5^{3}/_{8}$in (137mm) diameter flywheel, to supplement the relatively small diameter internal wheels. The mainshaft extended through an oil seal in the outer wall of the chaincase and carried the cam for the externally mounted twin contact breaker points that also featured a pressed steel cover.

## *Crowded Roller Big-Ends*
Crowded roller bearings were employed for the big-ends. There were two rows of $18\,^{3}/_{16} \times {}^{3}/_{16}$in rollers per bearing, separated by a steel spacing washer. During the 1958 interview Val Page had been asked why crowded rollers had been selected. His reply was that: 'inadequate guiding rather than skidding of the crowded

rollers was more often to blame for failures' and that 'if the rollers were kept square-on by means of hardened-steel spacer and end washers in conjunction with the minimum of end clearance, would give good service'. In fact, Val Page said that: 'the big-end in the Leader engine was the most durable of the several patterns tried'. He also pointed out that the end washers had a triangular, not circular, periphery to enable oil to get to the rollers.

*Mechanical Quietness*
Because of the full enclosure of the engine unit, Page and his development team realized that mechanical quietness was important. With this in mind, it was decided that the gudgeon pin axis should be offset $1/16$in (1.6mm) to the rear of the cylinder axis. The offset had the same effect as *de saxé* of the cylinder relative to the crankshaft: the movement of the piston across the bore from the non-thrust to the thrust face at tdc (top dead centre) was softened and thus piston slap was kept to the minimum. Page decided to offset the gudgeon pin rather than the cylinder to provide greater simplicity of machining, the small amount involved having been found to have a markedly beneficial effect on piston noise without any disadvantage at the bottom of the stroke where, of course, the piston tended to move across more rapidly with no offset.

*Bronzed Bush Small Ends*
Bronzed bush small ends were employed, each connecting rod having five lubrication holes. At their base the connecting rods were ribbed for stiffness and slotted for lubrication (at the big-end eye). The piston crowns were slightly domed, each piston having two narrow rings, with ports in the skirt of both pistons to register transfer ports in the cylinders. Compression ratio of the Leader was 8.25:1.

*Separate Cylinders and Heads*
There were separate cylinder barrels (cast iron) and cylinder heads (light alloy, pressure die castings). The barrels were short and their spigots were ported because the lower portions of the transfer passages were in the crankcase. Of unusually wide pitch, the square finning was at 55 degrees to the cylinder axes. When questioned about whether the barrels had been designed like this from the start, Val Page said: 'Oh no', going on to reveal, 'although the original design had the wide pitch finning this was at right angles to the bore. But we suffered bother through local overheating in the exhaust port region and changed over to the present scheme which has proved absolutely satisfactory.' Page then went on to point out that 'the exhaust tract in each barrel was longer than normal and also had a high heat capacity which accounted for the trouble with the earlier finning. The length was necessary, though, to give an easy change of section from rectangular at the port to circular at the pipe, and to permit as simple a pipe shape as possible.'

*Cylinder Head Finning*
Finning of the cylinder heads – extremely clean due to pressure die casting in LM2M light alloy – was originally straight. Then tests carried out on the direction of the actual air flow over the heads on a prototype bike resulted in the cranked fins being adopted which, like the barrels, improved the cooling.

*Combustion Shape*
The combustion chamber shape was part-spherical (unmatched thanks to the accuracy possible with pressure die casting). When asked if any experiments had been done with other shapes (such as the squish type used on the then current Lambretta TV175), Val Page replied that: 'combustion chamber design was another aspect where BSA knowledge had been helpful', going on to say, 'Where economy and medium rpm torque were the aims, rather than the maximum top-end power, BSA experience was that the part-spherical form was the most suitable.'

However, alternative spark plug positions had been extensively tested, to the sides and rear of the cylinder axes, but the 25-degree forward inclination adopted had proved to be the best, this fact being attributed to the particular flow pattern of the transfer streams. Another advantage was accessibility due to the extensive enclosure of the Leader's design.

*Exhaust Pipe Length*
During the mid-1950s, motorcycle engineers were just beginning to appreciate the importance of exhaust pipe length and silencer characteristics to the performance of the two-stroke engine. So during the development of its new machine Ariel devoted considerable time to this subject. Amongst the layouts tried and rejected was the Siamesed exhaust pipe type, Page and his team finding that 'no satisfactory results could be achieved therewith in spite of ringing changes to the variables'. The pipe length finally selected (using a separate exhaust header pipe for each cylinder), was 20½in (521mm) to the initial expansion cone of the silencer, and the diameter being 1⅝in (41mm).

Design of the cylinder passages was officially based 'on Bantam experience', with Val Page saying 'little experimental work was needed to achieve satisfactory results'. But, as with many other areas, the author is absolutely sure that considerable attention was also given to the existing Adler design.

*The Transmission*
The gearbox internals were essentially those of the heavyweight Burman CP (fitted to the larger Ariel four-strokes), but with narrower gears to suit the twin-cylinder two-stroke engine. Since the shaft sizes were unchanged, their reduced length in the Ariel design resulted in the bonus of having less shaft movement and thus reduced gear whine. However, it was necessary to modify the four-speed CP design to bring the gear pedal further rearward, so the cam barrel and selectors were relocated from ahead of to the rear of the gear clusters. Also the kick-start mechanism was moved to the top to provide for increased ground clearance for the gear lever. Internal gear ratios were: 3.2, 1.86, 1.31 and 1.

*Primary Drive*
As already mentioned earlier in this chapter, one of the major differences in the Adler and Ariel designs was that the British one used a primary chain, while the German one used gears. The primary drive chain was a ⅜ × 0.225in simplex one and maximum chain life was ensured by the employment of a leaf-spring tensioner faced with synthetic rubber and adjusted by means of a drawbolt extending through the front of the chaincase. Val Page and his team used this set-up as it believed that: 'The rubber facing wears the link plates of the chain much less than would a steel facing and is itself worn extremely slowly.'

The clutch ran in oil and was an interesting departure from conventional practice in that teeth – not torques – were used to transmit the drive. Instead of featuring the normal slots, the drum had twenty-four corrugations and the two plain driving plates were similarly profiled on the periphery. The clutch centre unit, incorporating a rubber vane-type shock absorber, was externally toothed to accept the serrations of the three driven plates which had bonded-on Neolangite friction segments, the first driven plate bearing on the back face of the clutch drum. There were three springs and the pressure plate was a dished steel pressing.

Final drive was by a ½ × 0.305in chain that was enclosed in a pressed-steel case manufactured in two halves with the overlapping joint horizontal. At the forward end the case fitted round an extension of the main engine casting, which embraced the gearbox sprocket. This case was attached by screws to the left (nearside) arm of the pivoted fork – the chain being lubricated from the primary chaincase. Chain tension was checked by the removal of a rubber inspection plug.

*The Cycle Parts*
If the engine assembly of the Leader was interestingly different compared to other

*The Futuristic Leader*

British designs for the period, the cycle parts were even more so. Not only was there the previously mentioned scooter-like enclosure and weather protection, but just about everything else was unorthodox to say the least.

Eight main steel pressings comprised the bodywork, the tail section being hinge-mounted – and could thus be raised for rear wheel removal. The other seven were: the main frontal fairing; the two lower fairing panels; the two extended side covers; the dummy tank and seat base; and the cover that enclosed the headlamp. The actual fuel tank was housed within the beam frame, the latter being a truly massive-looking assembly, which, in fact, carried out several tasks – beside fuel container and main frame. These also included acting as a central mounting point. Certainly the 'frame' was not as generations of motorcyclists would have known it to be.

Unfortunately, whilst theoretically the various panels were quickly detachable, in practice this was not quite so. This was not helped by the use of normal slot-headed screws rather than pukka Dzus fasteners.

*Low Weight*
Although the Leader looked a somewhat heavy bike, this was not in fact the case. For starters, the weight of the Leader power unit – complete with carburettor and generator, clutch and gearbox internals was only 84lb (38kg). In 'as delivered' guise, the bike weighed in at 300lb (136kg) and 330lb (150kg) with every available option – pannier cases and bags, luggage carrier (made of aluminium), prop and front stands (in addition to the standard fit centre stand), trafficators, parking light, Smiths 8-day clock, neutral indicator and inspection lamp – but without fuel.

*The Beam-Type Frame*
There is no doubt that besides the low weight of the engine assembly, the light but torsionally rigid beam-type frame (often referred to as a 'large-section box member') was a major reason for the bike's lack of weight. This assembly comprised two 20 gauge-steel pressings welded together down the machine's centre line; the cross section being rectangular with radiused corners and slightly bowed sides to resist drumming. At the front the beam was upswept and tapered to embrace the steering head tube, and at the rear it widened and was forked to form the anchorages of the upper ends of the Armstrong (non-adjustable) rear suspension units.

*A Baffled Fuel Tank*
Within this beam was the fuel tank (maybe we should refer to it simply as a container). This was baffled to minimize surge (often found in racing machinery); it had a capacity of 2.5gal (11.4ltr), including ½gal (2.3ltr) reserve. In practice, this 'tank' was merely a rectangular steel box with a three-point bottom mounting on rubber buffers. The fuel tank was inserted through the open rear end of the beam and behind it was bolted-in a perforated and ribbed bulkhead. The tank filler cap, a circular nylon moulding, was accessed by raising the hinged dual seat. Incidentally, this seat featured a plywood base which was termite-proofed to comply with export regulations!

*Amal Monobloc Carburettor*
A single ⅞in (22mm) Amal Monobloc 375/33 carburettor was specified when the first batches of Leader models went on sale. Not only was only one carb fitted, but the way it was fitted was to preclude the easy fitting of two assemblies, although this was eventually overcome.

The problem which the design team gave later tuners was that at the rear of the crankcase casting was one of the engine-mounting supports which also doubled up as an inlet tract for the aforementioned carburettor. The rear face was machined to take the carb and the lug was bored out, leaving a hollow inlet passage for the two cylinder barrels. This tract split and ran to the rear of the barrel spigot holes where the ports were formed. It was the presence of this lug and its dual role which was to make the fitting of twin carburettors so difficult for would-be racers later on. It also shows that at the time of its inception the design team viewed the Leader as a touring machine with no sporting intentions.

In retrospect, this was a serious error – just as giving the machine full enclosure was to be. But again this is with the benefit of hindsight, something that its creators were not allowed. The simple fact was that in the Britain of the mid-1950s motorcycling was largely touring/commuter based. The era of the small affordable car had not yet arrived when the initial design process began toward the end of 1955.

*Front Suspension*

The front suspension on the Leader was of the trailing-link fork type, and upon the machine's launch was described by *The Motor Cycle* as 'unique'. Heat-treated aluminium alloy was employed for the links which were die-cast and of I-section, pivoting on nylon bushes. In side-elevation each fork link was of near L-shape, having a short downward projecting arm just ahead of the wheel spindle eye. This eye of the arm was also nylon bushed, forming a pivot mounting for an inverted U-stirrup member welded to the base of the Armstrong-made shock absorber. The wheel spindle passed through the oval holes in the stirrup members.

Geometry of the links was such that the wheelbase remained almost constant (the links being horizontal at the mid-travel position), 'providing improved tyre wear', claimed Ariel. In addition, because the arc achieved was virtually axial to the units, their angularity barely altered.

*The streamlined look of the Leader's enclosed trailing-link front forks. Note original white-walled tyre exchanged for an Avon Speedmaster Mk II.*

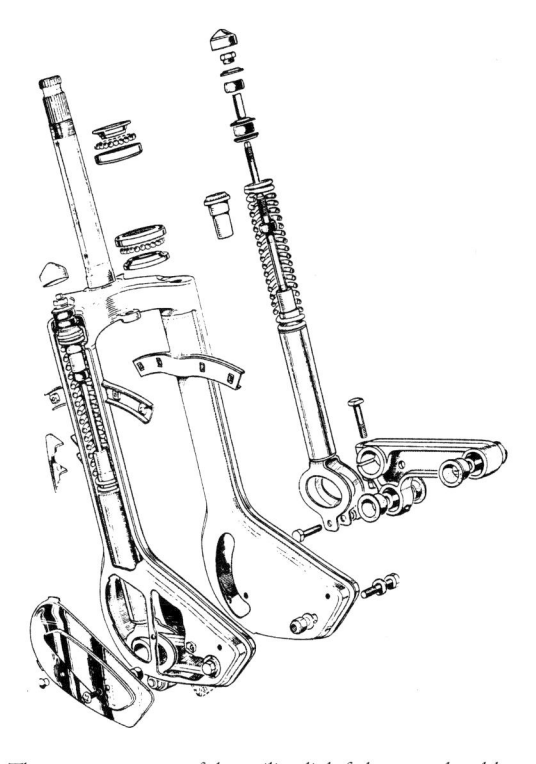

*The component parts of the trailing-link forks as employed by the Leader, plus Arrow series models. Steering head bearings consisted of cups, cones and steel balls. There was no conventional top yoke.*

## The Futuristic Leader

### The Damper Units
The damper units of the shock absorbers had extended rods and were anchored to the fork yoke in a similar way to the rear suspension units. The fork yoke was a malleable casting to the top of which was brazed a massive taper-tube steering head column. Also brazed onto this yoke were the two stanchion members, each of which was formed of two 16-gauge steel pressings joined by what Ariel called a 'hook stem', in which a flange on one pressing was folded over a shallower flange on the other.

The lower ends of these stanchions were extended forward to conceal the links and also housed the link pivot bolts in welded-in tubes. Each inner pressing featured an arcuate slot – to provide wheel spindle clearance, whilst the outer pressing had a hole for spindle access in the event of wheel removal. This hole was normally concealed by a chromium-plated cover. Slots in the underside of these pressings permitted assembly and gave clearance for the links on full rebound.

### A Near-Parallelogram Linkage
A near-parallelogram linkage was another Leader feature, being used to isolate the front suspension from brake reaction – anchorage of the front brake shoe plate being of the floating pattern. The torque stay itself was built up from two pressings spot-welded together and featuring part-spherical formation of the ends. In the resultant spaces between them were inserted spherical nylon bushes for the anchorage bolts. This arrangement accommodated any minor misalignment between the bolts.

### Aluminium Brake Hubs
A feature of the original Leader was the use of full-width aluminium brake hubs. They were 6in (153mm) and 1⅛in (29mm) wide (braking area), with cast-iron liners. Wheel diameter was 16in front and rear, with 3.25 section tyres with white walls; the front tyre was of the ribbed pattern, the rear a block section.

The rear hub carried a trio of studs which passed through holes in the final drive sprocket and were clamped together by securing nuts. A stop light operated off both brakes.

### A Two-Piece Front Mudguard
The front mudguard was manufactured in two halves with an overlap joint at the fork stanchions to which the halves were sealed by rubber trim. Each mudguard half was secured by a pair of bolts each side (from the inside) and one upward into the fork yoke, thus there was no external evidence of the mudguard being a two-piece affair.

### A Perspex Screen Moulding
The comprehensive panelling was augmented by an equally comprehensive clear perspex moulding, bulged to provide the rider with enough hand clearance even on full lock. This 'windscreen' sat in a rubber-lined channel at the top of the frontal fairing. Six through-bolts with tubular distance pieces were used to retain the screen – four of them also doubling up to retain the pressed-steel installment console. To enable a screen to be removed without taking the bolts out, its base featured U-shaped grooves rather than circular holes. In addition, the screen was supported by a pair of tapered tubular pillars attached to the perspex at the top by nylon mountings. At their base, the pillars had self-aligning ball-and-socket mountings in the instrument board.

### The Instrumentation
On the instrument console were the centrally mounted speedometer, the ammeter, ignition and lighting switches, sockets for the inspection lamp (an optional extra) and a lever to enable the rider to alter the headlamp beam setting. As *The Motor Cycle* commented in July 1958: 'This is a most commendable feature in view of the appreciable variation in machine attitude: one up and two up.' On the offside (right) of the console, balancing the ammeter, was an Ariel badge, replaceable at additional cost by the eight-day clock.

## The Futuristic Leader

*The rider's eye view of the handlebars, controls and instrument console. The circular Ariel badge could be replaced by an eight-day clock.*

### Lucas Headlamp

A 6in (153mm) sealed glass-reflector Lucas headlamp unit had a 6-volt 30/24 watt bulb and was mounted in a shallow body bolted from the inside into captive nuts within the headlamp cowl. Spring washers located between the headlamp body and the mounting brackets provided sufficient grip to retain the lamp in the correct position, whilst the adjusting lever was attached directly to the body. A single 6-volt circular horn was stowed in the nose of the mid-section behind the frontal fairing.

### Hidden Control Cables

The control cables were largely hidden from view under a steel pressing, this component being retained by a trio of screws. Besides the traditional rear brake light switch, a second switch was operated by the front brake lever – and again was hidden from view by the previously mentioned cowl.

### Flashing Direction Indicators

Today, at the beginning of the twenty-first century, most motorcycle pundits think that it was the Japanese who introduced flashing direction indicators to mainstream motorcycling, but actually it was Ariel and the Leader, even though they were an optional extra, rather than standard equipment. These were mounted on the frontal fairing and the panniers at the rear; there was a warning light on the instrument panel. The panniers themselves were not fibreglass, as many may have thought, but of pressed steel with inner plastic-cloth bags. The steering lock and the lock for the dual seat (which hinged sideways) were only accessible from within the compartment secured by the hinged flap on the top of the dummy tank.

When the Leader went on sale during the summer of 1958. It cost £168, plus £41 11s 7d purchase tax, making a total of £209 11s 7d (in Great Britain only). However, those wishing to kit out their machine with all the additional equipment such as panniers, carrier, eight-day clock and so on could be looking at a price which would have bought a five-hundred or even, in some cases, a six-fifty twin-cylinder model.

## Testing the Leader

When *The Motor Cycle* tested an example of the Leader in its 9 October 1958 issue, the headline read: 'Sprightly Two-stroke Twin with Excellent Roadholding and Steering:

## The Futuristic Leader

*This Leader has all the extras – plus original fitment white-walled tyres.*

*Another Ariel brochure illustration of the Leader, this time in a glamorous race setting, with what looks like a D-type Jaguar.*

*Seat lifted to expose fuel tank and 'cubby hole'; the latter was for tools, plugs and the like.*

Built-in Weather Protection: Many Practical Features'. The tester went on to say:

> In laying out the Leader, Ariel aimed at a roadster providing a new level of refinement in motorcycling. The sprightly performance and superlative handling of the thoroughbred solo were considered essential features, but were to be married to cultured manners and the sort of conveniences demanded ever more insistently, such as built-in weather shielding, accommodation for luggage, enclosure of mechanism, sleek lines and cleanliness in use.

The tester continued:

> The makers have achieved their aim and more. A pressed steel, beam-type frame of great torsional rigidity, in conjunction with a very ingenious trailing-link fork and a conventional pivoted rear fork, contributes to a magnificent blend of steering and comfort.
>
> The potentialities of the parallel-twin two-stroke engine have been thoroughly exploited to combine pep with sweetness. Not only are the conveniences mentioned inherent in the basic layout, they are supplemented by a host of other highly practical features – such as extensive thief-proofing and a lever for trimming the headlamp

## Leader 1958

| | | | |
|---|---|---|---|
| Engine | Air-cooled parallel twin; piston port induction; alloy heads; cast-iron cylinders, inclined forward at 45 degrees; one-piece aluminium crankcase casting | Rear suspension | Swinging arm, twin Armstrong shock absorbers |
| | | Front brake | 6in full-width alloy with cast-iron liner, SLS |
| | | Rear brakes | 6in full-width alloy with cast-iron liner, SLS |
| Bore | 54mm | | |
| Stroke | 54mm | Tyres | 3.25 × 16 front and rear |
| Displacement | 247cc | | |
| Compression ratio | 8.25:1[1] | **General Specifications** | |
| Lubrication | Petroil mixture | Wheelbase | 51in (82mm) |
| Ignition | Twin coils, twin contact breaker points, 6-volt battery | Ground clearance | 5in (127mm) |
| | | Seat height | 30in (762mm) |
| Carburettor | Single Amal 375 Monobloc ⅞in | Fuel tank capacity | 2.5gal (11.4ltr)[2] |
| Primary drive | Chain | Dry weight | 300lb (136kg) |
| Final drive | Chain | Maximum power | 16bhp @ 6,400[3] |
| Gearbox | Four-speed, Burman, foot-change | Top speed | 70mph (113km/h) |
| Frame | Beam type of welded-steel construction | [1] 1961, 10:1. | |
| | | [2] 1961, 2.5gal (11.4ltr). | |
| Front suspension | Trailing-link, Armstrong shock absorbers | [3] 1961, 17.5bhp. | |

beam – and an extraordinary range of items available at extra cost.

### Almost a PR Job

When reading *The Motor Cycle* tester's views, one could be forgiven for thinking that he was actually employed by Ariel's PR company. So, was the Leader really that good?

Well, as the test report went on to say, most of the Leader's features had, at some time or other, been incorporated in earlier designs or offered as accessories. However, this was the first time that a motorcycle had 'provided' such a complete and coherent answer to what *The Motor Cycle* called 'a plea for progression along civilized lines'.

There is no doubt that, good as the basic idea was, the Leader was not perfect. To start with, Val Page and his development team were not given an open cheque book. In other words, even though freedom of design was there, they had to come up with something that could be economically produced' – another word for cost-cutting. To fully realize this statement one has only to stand an Ariel (either a Leader or its 'naked' brother the Arrow) against the previously mentioned German Adler M/MB250 to appreciate the matter. This is not to say that the Ariel was poor; it was not, but there were faults and there were clear signs of economy in materials and design.

On the credit side – the low centre of gravity, torsional rigidity of the frame and excellent handling and roadholding (which are further proved when one studies the Arrow's racing successes – *see* Chapter 10), the conveniences of the scooter-like weather protection, the leading-link fork action which worked well with little nose-diving under heavy braking, unified threads throughout the machine and the comprehensive extras list (if one could afford the additional cost).

Against these pluses, came the Leader's failings. For one thing, its scooter advantages played against it within the dyed-in-the-wool motorcycle fraternity – to say nothing of traditional Ariel (four-stroke!) buyers. Then there

## The Futuristic Leader

were the colours – bright they may have been, but the two-tone finish (combining Admiralty Grey with Oriental Blue or Cherokee Red) was seen as 'vulgar' (Steve Wilson), to say nothing of the standard fitment of white-walled tyres!

The bodywork was not as quickly detachable as it could have been, particularly the right (offside) panel, which needed removal of both the kick-start and gear levers. The 16in wheels made for a limited choice of tyres, while the original full-width aluminium brake hubs were prone to cracking. The rear wheel had to be taken out before the engine could be removed from the frame.

Another problem – but not really of Ariel's making – centred around the engine's ability to smoke, mainly due to the inferior two-stroke oil available in the 1950s. As oil technology improved so the problem tended to lessen; Ariel had actually switched from a recommended 25:1 ratio to 32:1 by the time the company finally shut its doors. But it should be noted that poor starting and heavy smoking tend to point to worn bearings and/or crank seals. And in service the crankshaft/mains/seals proved the weakest link in the Leader's power unit. In contrast, the gearbox was its most robust feature.

*Owner's Guide for Leader and Arrow models. Having fifty-three pages, it covered all the essentials for basic maintenance. A comprehensive workshop manual was also available. Both were official factory publications.*

*Performance*

In its original form when tested by *The Motor Cycle* in 1958, the Leader achieved a maximum speed of 69mph (111km/h) (conditions: negligible wind; rider normally seated). The tester found that 'except when revved to the limit the engine was delightfully smooth and revelled in hard work' and that 'under average conditions a cruising speed of a genuine 60mph could be maintained as long as desired'. The Leader test bike lapped the Motor Industry Research Association's high-speed test track near Nuneaton at an average speed of over 64mph (103km/h).

*The Motor Cycle* test ended by saying:

> The torque peak of the engine occurs fairly high up the rpm scale and this tends to give the Ariel Leader a dual personality. If upward gear changes are made early to keep engine speed low, it is a model of docility, but if the engine is allowed to spin fast by suitable use of the gearbox, then acceleration and climb are quite sprightly. Indeed, it was commonplace to cover 140 to 145 miles in three hours, inclusive of normal traffic delays and fuel stops.

The minimum non-snatch speed in top (fourth) gear was 13mph (21km/h).

## Development and Gear Changes

As with most other Ariel models, the Leader was the subject of yearly updates. Where this also involved the Arrow series these are catalogued in Chapter 14. The Leader changes are listed below:

- the main jet size was reduced from 170 to 140
- the Leader received cast-iron wheel hubs as on the Arrow series and brake shoes were fabricated, manufactured from a pair of heavy gauge steel pressings rather than previous light alloy, with serrated operating lever pressings without fulcrum adjusters

# The Futuristic Leader

- a trip meter was fitted to the speedometer
- the flashing direction indicators could now be fitted to the rear mudguard, as well as the panniers
- the original Leader silencers featured flange perforated discs with a detachable baffle unit; these were replaced by a guide vane shaped to provide a spiral effect on the exhaust gases
- an optional holder for inspection lamp material changed from brass to plastic.

## Stunted Sales

At the time of its launch in the summer of 1958, the Leader's future seemed assured. The press gave it generally good reviews whilst its modern cleanliness promised buyers a new era of ownership with excellent weather protection and a host of practical features. However, as with the Aermacchi Chimera, the Leader did not prove as popular as was expected and, like the Italian design, the Ariel was 'undressed' in an attempt to increase flagging sales.

The record sales of British motorcycles during the immediate post-war period (1945–59) were about to take a prolonged and ultimately fatal nose dive as the 1960s progressed. The scooter-like styling did not help and in any case scooter sales themselves were on the slide. Finally, as if all this was not enough, the mortal blow for Ariel and its Leader was the advent of the Austin Mini. Designed by Alec Issigonis, this was a landmark in small car design, which, together with

*Rear end of Leader, showing silencer braces, rear carrier, panniers – note 'Leader' badge at the base of the number plate.*

### ARIEL OPTIONAL EXTRAS

**Leader** — PRICE including P.T.

|  |  | £ | s. | d. |
|---|---|---|---|---|
| Parking Lamp and Switch |  |  | 19 | 0 |
| Inspection Lamp |  |  | 15 | 1 |
| Carrier with Two Straps |  | 1 | 19 | 10 |
| Prop Stand |  | 1 | 8 | 0 |
| Front Stand |  |  | 12 | 8 |
| Pannier Cases | per pair | 9 | 7 | 0 |
| Pannier Bags | per pair | 2 | 10 | 0 |
| Neutral Gear Indicator |  | 1 | 4 | 2 |
| Flasher Set (for use with Panniers) |  | 7 | 9 | 7 |
| Flasher Set (where Panniers are not fitted) |  | 7 | 19 | 3 |
| Eight-day Clock |  | 5 | 8 | 7 |
| Dualseat Waterproof Cover |  |  | 9 | 4 |
| Mirrors | per pair | 1 | 6 | 3 |
| Windscreen Extension |  | 1 | 5 | 0 |
| Rear Fender with Reflectors |  | 1 | 17 | 5 |
| Tins of Enamel (for retouching) | each |  | 3 | 6 |

**The Ariel Arrow**

|  |  | £ | s. | d. |
|---|---|---|---|---|
| Carrier complete with Straps |  | 1 | 11 | 1 |
| Prop Stand complete with Plate |  | 1 | 12 | 7 |
| Front Stand (detachable) |  |  | 12 | 8 |
| White Wall Tyres |  | 1 | 11 | 0 |
| Waterproof Cover for Dualseat |  |  | 9 | 4 |
| Dualseat Strap |  |  | 6 | 3 |
| Petrol Tap with Reserve |  |  | 4 | 0 |
| Tins of Enamel (for retouching) | each |  | 3 | 6 |

*The optional extras list for the Leader and Arrow, from 1961.*

## The Futuristic Leader

other small cars that came on stream shortly after the Mini had gone on sale in 1959, effectively conspired to kill many aspects of motorcycling – including family sidecar outfits and touring bikes such as the Leader.

In all, a total of some 17,000 Leaders were built over a seven-year production life, which spanned mid-1958 until mid-1965. Officially, the reason production finally came to an end (together with that of the Arrow) was due to Burman ceasing production of the gearbox. But in truth sales, particularly of the revolutionary Leader, never met expectations. Amongst potential customers the Leader was simply *too* different for its own good. And motorcyclists were not ready to embrace the qualities and styling it offered.

It was not until the advent of BMW's R100RS and Moto Guzzi's SP1000 Spada during the late 1970s that motorcycles with serious rider protection were to be offered again. Even then, such comprehensive enclosure as found on the Ariel did not arrive for another decade and bikes such as the Honda Pan European and BMW K100LT finally won riders over, but of course these were all large capacity, top-of-the-range modern 'Superbikes'.

As is recorded in Chapter 12, Ariel and Val Page had designed just such a motorcycle which could have entered production during the 1960s, but never did. Essentially, this futuristic design embodied the protection of the Leader with a four-cylinder engine – it was a K series BMW, more than a quarter of a century before the German company got there. The Leader and the existence of the four-cylinder prototype are proof that innovation in the British motorcycle industry of the 1950s and 1960s was not dead; instead, as in Ariel's case, it was simply suppressed (by BSA in this case).

*Actually all the Leader needed, in the author's opinion, was a larger (preferably four-stroke) engine, a less garish paint job and, as here, the deletion of the white-walled tyres – plus time for the rest of motorcycling to catch up on the concept. Remember, luxury touring bikes from the likes of BMW, Honda and Triumph are all the rage at the start of the twenty-first century.*

# 12 Prototypes

Down through the years, many of the potentially most interesting, innovative and exciting Ariels were the largely little-known prototypes, which never reached production. In the early days this was largely on cost grounds; later in the post-Second World War era it was because often the BSA board poured cold water over most of Ariel's best ideas.

## Some Brilliant Designers

There is no doubt that Ariel, over its long history, had several brilliant designers, including men such as Val Page, Edward Turner, Frank Anstey and Bert Hopwood. Because of this, the company often created some great motorcycles, as is documented elsewhere in this book. They were also responsible for having a particularly wide range of engine types: singles; twins; fours; side valves; overhead valves; overhead camshaft; two-strokes – Ariel produced them all.

## The Forgotten Prototypes

Probably the most interesting story of all are the designs that never made it into the showrooms – the forgotten prototypes. To catalogue every Ariel prototype would need a book in itself, so only the most interesting ones will be related here. As with the more well-known models that went on to reach series production, the now-forgotten prototypes used one, two and four cylinders.

## The Square Four

The design and development of the famous Square Four is recorded in Chapter 5, but actually there was the earlier, original prototype which preceded the first production series and made its bow at the Olympia Motor Cycle Show in London during late 1930. The Four had, in fact, been around at least eighteen months prior to that date. Journalist Denis May had even tested this first prototype on Christmas Eve 1929, giving it in the process its legendary nickname 'Squariel' – derived from the configuration of its cylinders.

Displacing 500cc (as did the first production series coded Model 4F31), the original prototype engine was extremely compact and, unlike the production version, was of unit construction design. It took its primary drive from the coupling gear in the middle of the rear crankshaft to a three-speed gearbox built 'en bloc' with the vertically split aluminium crankcases. Essentially, the engine was two parallel twins geared together with bore and stroke dimensions of 51 × 61mm and running on a compression ratio of 6.5:1. The engine ran on the bench at over 9,000rpm – a phenomenal figure for 1930.

The design of the Square Four engine came from Edward Turner (his first major assignment for Ariel); he was assisted by Bert Hopwood (then a young draughtsman in Val Page's department) and Ernie Smith.

Turner, who had been recruited by Charles Sangster, was allowed a virtually free hand. As the late Bert Hopwood said in his book, *Whatever Happened to the British Motorcycle Industry?*, it seems that Turner was given very scanty terms of reference and no commercial guidelines whatever. This author's feelings are that if this had originated from a board composed mainly of financiers with an ex-racing cyclist and a gentleman farmer thrown in, they would have been hopelessly short-sighted. As a result, Turner seemed to be given a free hand, with no restrictions, so that he started with a clean sheet of paper and designed a completely new motorcycle.

Hopwood went on to say:

> His brilliance as an inventive designer was never better and this classic new design had an engine of 500cc capacity with the cylinders arranged in a square four formation, a gearbox built-in unit and wet sump lubrication. The chassis and wheels were brilliant in conception and the whole machine weighed no more than motorcycles of half the engine capacity that were then being made. This design, which the public never saw, was undoubtedly much more outstanding and commercially worthwhile than the type that later was to go into production.

*Tester's Delight*
The Ariel test riders were full of praise for the new four – in fact, there were two prototype machines, these racking up a considerable mileage during the road test programme. Because of the compact nature of the design, the two bikes were, as one tester put it 'so easy to handle, so easy to ride and so smooth'. Bert Hopwood described the original prototype thus: 'Exciting to ride with its revolutionary power-to-weight ratio and its zestful exhaust note.'

As far as development problems were concerned, the major one was gear knock from the coupling that joined the two crankshafts, but as Hopwood admitted 'was not nearly so pronounced as its later production relatives'. Otherwise very little went wrong, with the exception of crashes through the over exuberance of one tester in particular.

On tickover, the prototype five-hundred Square Four had what Bert Hopwood described as a 'sewing machine' noise, 'a ticking rather than a rattle characteristic, which was not unpleasant to the ear and indeed infinitely more acceptable than the noises emanating from normal motorcycles of the day, with the exception, perhaps, of the Scott'.

*The Mystery Four*
'Ixion' of *The Motor Cycle* also tested one of the prototype machines, his report appearing in the 18 September 1930 issue. The sub-heading for the test ran: 'No Vibration: Super Silence: 5mph "On Top": amazing Acceleration'. Ixion's lips were 'largely sealed by solemn promises to the designer'. So there were no detailed specifications, illustrations or, for that matter, a real sense of exactly what the machine he had been riding was really about. However, what limited information was published, did at least hint of the advanced nature of the machine.

Surprising perhaps were his comments regarding the 'Orthodox Appearance' section. This read as follows:

> I have been riding it over crowded roads and among keen motor cyclists for a week past; yet hardly a soul has spotted anything unusual about the bus. There is nothing of the dachshund about it – it is not eight feet long, or anything of that sort, its wheelbase, on the contrary, is approximately 53in, which would be a quite normal dimension for a single cylinder. It does not look in the least like four to the casual observer; and when I am sitting on it in road garb there is much excuse to be made for a pump attendant who mistakes it for something entirely different.

The prototype, as tested, with 'tanks full' tipped the scales at 376lb (171kg). Two of the exceptional features of the design were its total lack of vibration and the equal lack of noise. First the vibes:

> There is no vibration. I contrived to balance a tumbler of water on it with the engine ticking over and the gear in neutral, and a brimming tumbler did not spill, though there was a faint ripple on the surface of the water. If a hand was placed on the tank, frame or headlamp, with the engine running, it is barely possible to detect by

*Tests were also carried out with the trailing-link front forks as fitted to the Leader/Arrow series.*

*This view of the Leader-forked Square Four prototype shows its relatively narrow frontal area thanks to its cylinder layout.*

the feel whether the engine is running or not. In other words, it has the smoothest motorcycle engine I have ever encountered.

Ixion described the silence as 'phenomenal', going on to say: 'It is only possible to create any exhaust uproar by racing the engine in one of the lower gears; and thus raced, the engine emits a smooth, subdued roar entirely devoid of the staccato racket usually associated with motorcycle power units.'

Ixion also commented about the torquey nature of the Ariel's engine, saying:

> The power unit is extremely flexible. It will fire evenly and pull smoothly down to about 5mph in top gear, on which I rode it up a kerb, through a gate, and round a sharp corner into my garage. In heavy traffic it is almost too silent, as pedestrians are often unaware of its approach, and additional horn-blowing is required.

As recorded in Chapter 5, eventually it was decided to authorize the Square Four for production, but in a much modified form. Bert Hopwood went as far as saying: 'so watered down that as a money spinner it was doomed from the start'. Not only were the engine and transmission made much more bulky and heavy due to the production model having separate engine, gearbox and clutch assemblies, but as Hopwood revealed: 'We were instructed to make use of the largest frame and wheels which were then in production.'

Of course, one has to realize also that by now the effects of the Wall Street crash of October 1929 had begun to take their effect – resulting in a major worldwide downturn in economic fortunes, but as Bert Hopwood ended by saying: 'This should have been the incentive to press on with a world beater, rather than an also-ran.'

*Prototypes*

*The project employed swinging arm rear suspension and the trailing-link forks – but once again top brass vetoed its production status.*

## The Earles Fork Project

Another interesting prototype-only project that was killed off was the Earles front fork of 1953. Ariel had designed its own telescopic front fork, which had made its debut on the Square Four and the new five-hundred twin-cylinder models in 1946 and was adopted as standard for the 1947 model year.

So, why was the Birmingham company thinking of switching yet again? Well, at the beginning of the 1950s, another new type of front fork appeared that was set to challenge the by-now widely used telescopic type. This was the Earles type. Essentially, it was a bottom link design, embodying a pivoted fork in place of separate links, and was the work of Birmingham-based engineer Ernie Earles of Elms Metals Ltd (an aluminium-alloy welding specialist).

The Earles-type fork first appeared in public during 1951, with a couple of privately entered racing machines using the design in the Isle of Man TT races that year. Then in 1952 MV star Les Graham used this type of fork on his four-cylinder five-hundred racer and nearly won the premier race event of the era, the Senior TT. Eventually he was narrowly beaten by Norton-mounted Reg Armstrong.

*Earles and the Ariel Experimental Department*
Actually, Ernie Earles and the Ariel Experimental Department were already known to each other. For example, Earles had been involved earlier in manufacturing aluminium petrol tanks for the Selly Oak firm's VCH Competition bike. The first signs of the Ariel-Earles cooperation with a fork assembly came in February 1953, when Clive Bennett, who worked as an assistant to Ernie Smith in the Ariel Experimental Department, rode a VCH equipped with suitably modified Earles forks in the Midland area Colmore Cup Trial. A couple of weeks later, another Ariel, this time a 1000G Mark II Square Four, with a similar set of forks (and also an experimental twin leading shoe front brake), made an appearance in the local Birmingham Club's Victory Trial.

*The Public Announcement*
Then on 9 April 1953 the British press, in the shape of *The Motor Cycle* and *Motor Cycling*, jointly carried the story that Ariel was to fit Earles-type front forks to three of its models: the Square Four (to be known as the Red Hunter), the twin-cylinder all-alloy five-hundred KHA twin (Hunt Master) and the VHA single (Hunt Marshal).

Ariel and Ernie Earles claimed several technical advantages for the new fork, which had been specially adapted for its use in the Ariel production models. Most important, it was claimed, was the fact that the wheelbase and steering geometry remained 'virtually unaltered throughout the movement of the wheel, and that worthwhile reduction should be possible in the weight of the unsprung mass'.

A further advantage, and not readily appreciated, was that the wheel spindle was required to lift only the height of whatever obstruction the wheel surmounted, whilst in the case of the telescopic fork the spindle moved along the hypotenuse of a triangle. With a fork angle of 65 degrees, the additional travel of a telescopic fork on a 3in bump was approximately ¼in.

*Sidecar Use*
As BMW found on its range built from 1955 through to 1969, by making provision in the Earles fork of alternative spindle holes at the lower ends of the main stanchions, a simple alteration could be quickly made to the trail when a sidecar was fitted to the machine. Spring and damper units were easily dismantled for servicing and a replacement unit could be fitted in a matter of minutes.

*Vertical Loads*
All vertical loads were carried by the top spring unit lugs, close to the head stem, and horizontal forces imposed by motion and braking were resisted by the main stanchions. This meant that the spring units were relieved entirely of side thrust and had two functions only, that of damping wheel movement and of carrying the suspension springs.

*Materials Used*
All tubes employed in the construction of the Ariel-Earles fork were tapered and the main curved tubes tapered from 1⅜in 10 gauge to ¾in 16 gauge. At the rear of thee curved tubes were compression struts joining the lowest point of the stanchions to the lower of the two head stem forgings. Plates were disposed at the base of the main fork members to carry the ½in diameter, 60-ton steel spindle of the suspension arm. All the tube joints and the spindle plates were welded together.

A trio of tubes formed the suspension arm. One of these, a short 1¼in, 10-gauge parallel tube, carried rubber bushes and formed the pivot housing to which the tapered tubes were welded. Both the wheel spindle clamps and the attachment ears for the lower ends of the hydraulic dampers were also welded into position. Coil springs encircled the damper bodies and were held between an abutment on the damper tube and a cap at the top that was retained by circlips. The dust covers were of steel. A pressing welded to the main fork stanchion formed the attachment point for the upper eye of each damper.

A neat Triumph nacelle-type shroud, fabricated from two sheet-steel pressings, encased the upper section of the fork assembly and housed the headlamp, a circular, much smaller secondary light (directly below the headlamp), an ammeter, speedometer and light switch. This shroud was secured by the two top fork cap bolts and by small screws, where the pressing was moulded round the fork tubes. Adjustment of the headlamp beam was carried out by slackening the two top hexagonal cap bolts and sliding the headlamp assembly forwards or backwards in the slots provided.

*A Smoother Ride*
Testers found that although there was not the same apparent movement at the front of the machine as there was with the conventional Ariel telescopic fork, there was no doubt that at touring speeds, the Earles fork gave a smoother ride. As one tester of the day said:

> Normal irregularities were absorbed with virtually no up and down motion of the steering head, and it was not until a sizeable road bump was encountered that the machine moved vertically in a noticeable fashion. When it did lift, the lift was

*Prototypes*

quickly controlled with an absence of pitching that indicated the speed with which the movement was subdued by the dampers.

When an Earles-fork equipped KHA five-hundred twin was tested by *Motor Cycling*, the publication reported: 'Handling proved light and sensitive, with a pleasant balance between extremes. Directional change was noticeably positive and bends could be taken in a clean sweep. In spite of the undoubted weight of the machine as a whole, manoeuvrability at walking speeds was light and untiring.'

A noticeable characteristic of the Ariel equipped with the Earles fork came with the application of the front brake. At low speeds, the brake reaction tended to overcome the weight transfer and lifted the front of the bike. At high speeds, the two forces seemed to cancel out and there was no movement, either up or down; this was in marked contrast to the sudden dipping experienced when one applies the front brake on a motorcycle with conventional telescopic forks.

*Problems*

But just as everyone confidently expected these new Earles-fork equipped Ariels to enter series production, came the problems.

First, according to one of the test riders employed by Ariel, Clive Bennett, a number of development glitches appeared. The main ones were: rapid wear of the steering head races; a tendency to weave at maximum speeds; and a braking performance inferior to machines equipped with telescopic forks. However, all these problems could probably have been resolved with time.

What could not be changed was the fact of two totally unconnected deaths. First, at the end of April 1953, Ted Crabtree, Ariel's Director and General Manager – and the chief backer of the Earles-equipped models – was fatally injured in a car accident. However, as Peter Hartley describes in his book *The Ariel Story*: 'The final nail in the coffin of the Earles-type fork came in the Isle of Man Senior TT race in June, with the death of Les Graham on his MV Agusta machine.' There was much speculation as to the cause of Graham's fatal crash (at the bottom of the Bray Hill section), but most informed observers concluded that the Earles fork had been a contributing factor.

So, events conspired to kill off the Earles-fork Ariel range – the new models never reaching production.

**A New General Manager**

Following the unfortunate death of Ted Crabtree, Ariel appointed Ken Whistance to replace him, and it was under Whistance's guidance that Ariel was to move forwards. Or perhaps that should read sideways, as increas-

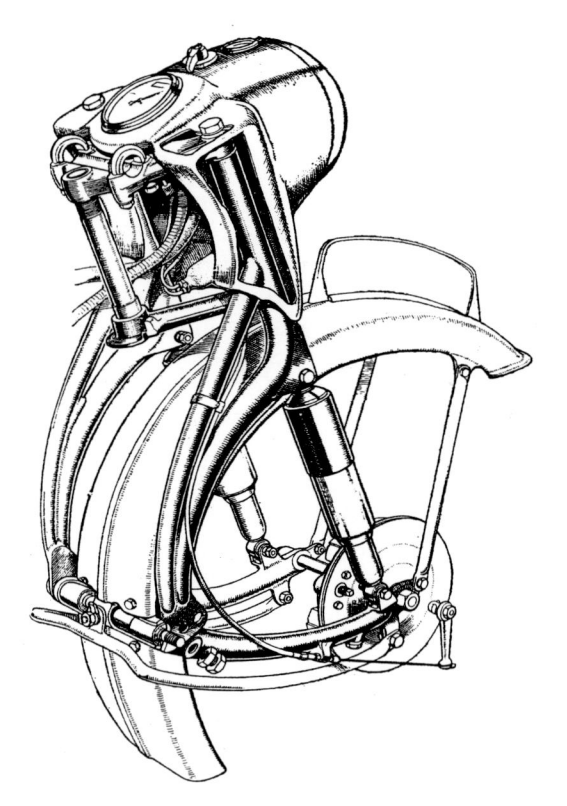

*Revealed to the public in the spring of 1953, the Earles fork very nearly became part of the Ariel range. But Les Graham's fatal crash on a four-cylinder MV Agusta with a similar type of fork in the Senior TT that year literally killed this off.*

ingly over the years the shadow of Ariel's parent company BSA was to loom ever larger. Even so, there was considerable progress during the Whistance reign, including swinging arm frames for the big singles and ohv twins, the revolutionary Leader, the Arrow series and finally the 50cc Pixie. There were also several interesting prototype-only machines.

## Arrow Derivatives

Many of these prototypes centred around the Leader. When Ariel dropped its entire four-stroke range at the end of the 1950s, it meant that potential buyers were severely restricted in what they could purchase from the company. This led Val Page and his development team in the Ariel Experimental Department to consider an array of fresh designs. Many, such as a 250cc four, a 350cc triple two-stroke and a 350cc parallel twin with a belt-driven overhead camshaft never left the paper stage.

*A 350cc OHV Twin*
During the early 1960s an interesting three-fifty overhead valve twin was constructed using Arrow cycle parts, Page taking the view that having a four-stroke would widen the range, and also give the company a model with a larger displacement engine. Using existing running gear with, in effect, only a new engine, would keep costs down.

The result was a 349cc (63 × 56mm) twin with an alloy cylinder head and cast-iron barrel, these being inclined 45 degrees, similar to the Leader/Arrow series. The camshaft ran crossways behind the cylinders, with the contact breaker points positioned within the timing cover. A single Amal Monobloc carburettor fed both cylinders, whilst there were two separate exhaust pipes, with Leader/Arrow-type silencers. The lubrication system used a wet sump, with plain bearing big-ends. The four-stroke twin was married to an Arrow gearbox. The engine unit looked neat from the left (nearside), but untidy – ugly even – from the right (offside). With a maximum speed of 75mph (121km/h) it was very much a tourer, rather than a sportster. Surely, with the newly introduced (1961) British learner laws limiting new riders to 250cc or under its success would have been debatable to say the least. A more practical way, at least with the benefit of hindsight, would have been to have built a 350cc or 400cc Arrow triple. In fact, just such engines were constructed privately, for both the road and racing. Why didn't Ariel do it?

*Tubular Frame*
A tubular-framed Arrow was also built. Using a standard 247cc Arrow twin cylinder two-stroke engine this was built in 1963 and coded TS5. It used a full duplex frame, swinging arm rear suspension, telescopic front forks and an entirely new style – which is best described as Japanese. Once again, the BSA board said no.

## 50cc OHC of Advanced Design

Another model that reached an advanced stage of development only to be axed by orders from above, was a 50cc ohc single. This employed toothed bolts for both the camshaft and primary drive. The frame at least, albeit in modified form, was to be utilized in the later Pixie model of 1963.

## A Swinging Arm Square Four

Another stillborn project was the 4G (Square Four) Mark IV. Essentially, this was a swinging arm version of the long-running 'Squariel'. Housing one of the all-alloy engines, four pipe engines in a modern-type swinging arm chassis with hydraulic damping, instead of the plunger-framed model, this was the logical step for the famous bike. But as the author's friend Roger Barlow (an ex-Ariel factory man) said: 'It was a step too far for Edward Turner, and it got the chop.' Yet another case of the BSA Group interfering with Ariel's affairs. In typical Turner fashion he did not want anyone 'messing around' with his design. That design, penned some thirty years before had, of course, been considerably changed down the years, something Turner seemed to forget! At least today's enthusiasts have a chance to view what without doubt is the ultimate development of a legendary lineage, as an example is on display in the National Motorcycle Museum, just off the M42 near Birmingham.

## The Flat-Four Project

Also now residing in the National Motorcycle Museum is the prototype of potentially the greatest of all Ariels not to see a showroom: the Leader 4. Like so many Ariels, this came from the pen of Val Page and was intended as a long-distance de luxe touring machine that would combine the weather protection of the Leader two-fifty twin with the power, flexibility and long life of a lightly stressed large capacity engine. In today's terminology it would have been referred to as a 'Superbike'.

Page opted for a displacement of 700cc, effectively four 175cc cylinders. Like the K-series BMW of the 1980s, the Leader was an in-line four with the crankshaft axis running longitudinally on the offside of the bike, with the cylinders, heads and valve gear on the nearside. But unlike the BMW it was air-cooled (using a duct fan) and had pushrod-operated valves rather than double overhead camshafts.

The engine featured square bore and stroke dimensions, and was all aluminium to ensure a relatively light weight. With mild cam lifts giving 15 degrees of overlap, the prototype engine gave only 27bhp. However, with development Page envisaged this rising to some 40bhp for production versions. Plain (split shell) big-ends, steel connecting rods, three-ring pistons, a single carburettor, a car-type clutch, parallel valves, a distributor and battery/coil ignition were some of its technical specifications. The lubrication system comprised a wet sump with a high-pressure output to the trio of plain main bearings and big-ends.

### A Single Exhaust

A single exhaust (from a four-branch header pipe) ran alongside the left (nearside) of the bike, whilst the alternator was mounted at the front of the crankshaft. Final drive was by a cardan shaft – again very similar to the later BMW K series; however, on the Ariel the shaft drive was left exposed, rather than enclosed within the fork leg.

*The 1000 4G Mark II Square Four with swinging arm rear suspension was built during the late 1950s. However, it was not authorized for production. Note single downtube (twins and singles had a duplex frame).*

*A Leader-Based Chassis*
The chassis was essentially a modified Leader, strengthened in places to accept the additional power and weight of the 700cc four-cylinder engine unit. The front forks were the normal Leader trailing-link type, whilst the rear swinging arm was redesigned to take into account the shaft final drive. The wheel hubs remained standard, although the tyre and rim sizes were altered to 3.25 × 17 front and 4.00 × 16 rear. As for the bodywork, this was little changed with the exception of a new twin headlamp fairing at the front.

*Development Problems*
Although a major priority in the development of the flat four was, as Peter Hartley said, 'to market a machine that would be able to cover some 100,000 miles without major overhaul', in practice a number of problems surfaced early in the machine's life. Many in fewer than 1,000 miles. The following are some of the problems:

- Originally, the oil level in the crankcase was above that of the pushrod tubes. In practice, this meant that although the engine would start and run on all four cylinders, it proved impossible for long. However, this glitch was soon cured
- There was the problem of the rear suspension bottoming when the throttle was fully opened up
- There were porous head casting problems.

There is no doubt that other problems would have needed addressing, to do with the differences between the Leader engine and its larger four-cylinder brother, and as regards the suitability or otherwise of the frame, suspension and braking components. For example, in the author's opinion a larger brake at least would have been needed.

It was still basically a forward-looking design with considerable development potential. It was also relatively light, the engine was easily accessible for maintenance and it had the advantages of shaft final drive, a narrow front area and comprehensive weather protection. But once again, another Ariel creative design was killed off for largely political reasons.

There is also little doubt, as recorded elsewhere, that its designer Val Page became ever more 'cheesed off' with the various cancellations, and decided to retire earlier than he had planned to, in January 1959, at the age of sixty-seven. He was replaced as Chief Designer at Ariel by his former deputy Bernard Knight.

*Two 'great white hopes' for Ariel: left the Page-designed 700cc flat four, with Leader-like style; right the swinging arm 1000 4G Mark II (or should that really have been Mark III?). Luckily, both prototypes escaped BSA's subsequent crash, to reside today in the National Motorcycle Museum, Birmingham.*

*Prototypes*

## Final Developments

During the 1960s, besides the Arrow, the only Ariels to reach production status were the Pixie ohv ultra-lightweight and the Ariel 3 trike powered by an imported Dutch Anker two-stroke engine. However, there were still more designs that did not make it for various reasons – mainly either economic or BSA interference.

The last of these that could be referred to as an Ariel motorcycle was an abortive attempt to place in production a 160cc two-stroke as a possible Bantam replacement. This used mainly Italian-sourced components, including the Minerelli unit construction engine that featured an alloy head and cast-iron cylinder. Only one example was built before the project was abandoned in 1968. All in all, a sad end to a once great marque, if one discounts the Ariel 3 debacle that followed in 1970.

*The 160cc Minerelli engine was of modern design, with an aluminium cylinder head and full unit construction of the engine and gearbox. Note the typical Italian heel and toe gear lever and Dell'Orto carburettor.*

*This 160cc Ariel prototype dating from 1966 used an Italian Minerelli engine. The bike was intended as a replacement for the BSA Bantam. Maybe too much for BSA to swallow?*

# 13 Arrow and Golden Arrow

Based around the Leader (*see* Chapter 12), the Arrow series was born of a need to reach sales targets that the Leader had trouble meeting. However, when the first of the Arrow series was launched in a blaze of publicity at the very end of 1959 the story put over by the press of the day was somewhat different, as the following extract from *The Motor Cycle* dated 10 December 1959 shows:

> Previously one of the most conservative manufacturers, Ariels virtually dropped a two-stroke bomb on the motorcycle world when, just 18 months ago, they swept aside the Selly Oak curtains to reveal the incomparable 249cc Leader twin. It was, and is, a machine crammed with novelty from stem to stern. And that the public took it to their hearts is amply proved by the numbers now on the road. Well, Ariels have done it again! This week the all-enclosed Leader has a stimulating stablemate. Arrow is the newcomer's name, a sporting lightweight which embodies many of the proved Leader features, but which is demonstrably a model in its own right.

*The Motor Cycle* launch story continued in a similar vein: 'Offered fully equipped at a highly competitive price, it is an arrow aimed at the ride-to-work man and at the shallow-purse enthusiast with a yen for the satisfying, zestful performance of a two-fifty two-stroke twin.'

## Price Considerations

Amongst all this blatant PR, one point stands out: price. When the Leader had gone on sale back in the summer of 1958, the price (including UK purchase tax) was £209 11s 7d – and even this price did not include any of the additional cost-option extra equipment, such as panniers, direction indicators, clock, carrier and so on. With the launch of the Arrow not only was this new model something of a bargain at £167 13s 5d (including purchase tax), but the Leader was reduced in price to £197 16s 6d.

There is no doubt that by introducing the Arrow, Ariel gave itself something of a fillip. One also has to take into account that with the Leader not reaching its sales targets *and* that the entire four-stroke range had been discontinued, the marque's entire fortunes rested on the success of the two-fifty twin cylinder two-stroke duo.

## The Arrow's Details

### The Engineering

By utilizing the engine unit, transmission, the frame and trailing-link front fork on the incoming Arrow, development and production costs had been kept to the bare minimum. Moreover, experience had shown that these components were generally reliable.

In appearance, the Arrow gave the impression, at least, of being different from its older brother. The engine-gear unit was exposed and the exhaust pipes as well as the silencers were chromium-plated. At the rear, a conventional valanced mudguard, supported cantilever style, had been grafted on to the rear of the frame beam. The upper shell pressing, which occupied the position of a fuel tank on

183

Arrow and Golden Arrow

*1961 advertisement showing the Arrow Leader and Arrow Super Sports (Golden Arrow). Sorry it's too late to post off for the free folders!*

a more orthodox motorcycle, extended forwards of the steering head to form brackets that supported the 6in (153mm) diameter Lucas headlamp.

*A Shared Engine*
The 249cc (54 × 54mm) parallel twin two-stroke with its integral foot-controlled four-speed gearbox was taken directly from the Leader. This meant a one-piece die-cast aluminium crankcase, also comprising the inner half of the primary chaincase and the gearbox shell. Supported on a trio of ball race bearings, the two-piece crankshaft had a key and taper coupling in the middle. On the right (offside) end of the shaft was a Lucas 50-watt RM13/15 alternator which supplied lighting and ignition current; at the left (offside) end,

*The Golden Arrow had an excellent reputation both for speed and roadholding.*

outboard of the engine sprocket, was the twin contact breaker points assembly.

As with the Leader, there were light-alloy cylinder heads, with the separate cast-iron barrels inclined forwards. The cylinder barrel finning was angled so as to assume a plane that was not quite horizontal. This meant that air passing across the finning surfaces had a scrubbing action that improved the cooling process.

The same Amal ⅞in 375 Monobloc carburettor and a butterfly-type choke were operated by a rod supported by a bracket on the left of the motorcycle. The butterfly incorporated a suction-type clack valve that was drawn open when the engine fired, thus (in theory at least) reducing the risk of stalling through over-richness.

### New Features

New features in connection with the carburettor saw the choke-operating rod now being 'notched' to provide for a half-open position and the carburettor jet spray nozzle having its top slanted towards the engine to improve atomization (and hence fuel economy) and reduce the risk of a possible harmful blowback through the carburettor.

Intake of the carburettor was, as before, coupled to the rearmost of the fabricated mounting brackets that suspend the engine assembly from the frame beam. And this bracket's interior acted as an air-silencing chamber to which a cylindrical air filter was attached at the right (offside).

### The Torsional Rigid Box Frame

One of the Leader's strongest features was due to the torsional rigidity of its box frame, formed by welding together along the machine's centre line two 20-gauge steel pressings. The frame was unaltered for the Arrow, and, as before, the beam embraced the steering head at the front and the upper mountings for the rear shock absorbers.

As with the Leader, within the beam was located a rectangular, 2.5gal (11.4ltr) fuel tank. Positioned beneath the dual seat, the plastic filler cap was, however, of a new design and incorporated a clever oil measure: to prevent oil escaping through the air vent when the cap was inverted, a captive steel ball moved downwards to form an effective seal.

### Twin Ignition Seals

The twin ignition seals were housed underneath the front of the frame beam ahead of the fuel tank. Rearward of the tank was a recess in the beam which accommodated the

13-amp hour, 6-volt Lucas-made battery. As with the Leader, the dual seat hinged at its right (offside) and the seat had a plywood base. A quartet of rubber buffers set in the seat base engaged with metal cups on the top frame beam when the seat was lowered, whilst spring clips at the front and rear ensured a form of fastening. The seat height at 28.5in (724mm) was considerably lower than that of the Leader, due to the latter bike's top metal pressing.

## The Dummy Fuel Tank

The upper shell pressing of the Arrow had what *The Motor Cycle* referred to as 'the semblance of an orthodox fuel tank' (but still a dummy), an effect heightened by the circular Ariel marque badges which 'decorated' each side. In truth, these badges were mounted through the 'dummy' shell in pvc grommets, and the left (nearside) badge, when removed, gave access to the electrical rectifier that was located in the cavity between the shell and frame beam. The dummy tank shell was attached by two screws at either side, engaging with angular brackets and by two further bolts/nuts inside the pressing and rearward of the steering head. Again, in the author's view, as with the panelling of the Leader, Ariel should have plumped for the much more convenient method of quickly detachable Dzus fasteners for these tasks.

Retained by a single screw, a lid (similar to the one found on the Leader) in the upper face of the pressing covered the tool tray. After the releasing of a cross-strap, the said tray could be removed to reveal a 7½ × 5¼in (191 × 133mm) aperture that gave access to additional space within the shell; the standard issue-tyre pump was clipped in position within this cavity.

## The Suspension

The suspension, as mentioned at the beginning of this chapter, followed that of the Leader. In other words, at the front was the by now well-known trailing-link front fork, which provided an almost constant wheelbase irrespective of wheel deflection. Pivoted on nylon bushes, the trailing links incorporated downward-projecting lugs, which were attached to the lower ends of the spring, and damper Armstrong-manufactured shock absorbers concealed within the fork leg pressings. Two-way damping was provided. The damper rods projected upwards through the fork yoke to provide anchorage at the top. Conical moulded polythene caps snapped into place over the damper rod extensions. The link inspection covers were pointed, instead of chrome-plated as on the Leader.

## 16in Wheels

The Arrow's development team retained the 16in diameter wheel rims and 3.25 section tyres from the Leader, but the full-width 6in × 1⅛in brake hubs were now of cast iron rather than aluminium with an iron liner. This was done mainly on cost lines, but it also solved a problem as a few of the aluminium hubs had suffered cracking in service. The new iron hubs had three shallow external ribs to improve rigidity. As with the Leader, both wheel spindles were of the quickly detachable type, with integral tommy bars, whilst the final drive sprocket was retained by a trio of studs and nuts – the rear wheel being easily removable without disturbing the chain.

## Rear Mudguard

The rear mudgard was pre-drilled to accept a special carrier; this latter item, as with the Leader, was available at extra cost. The drillings were plugged with rubber when a carrier was not fitted. Attached to the base of the separate number-plate assembly were chromium-plated brackets which supported the silencers. The silencers were essentially those found on the Leader. This meant that the long, tapered silencers had solid disc baffle plates bent to provide a gas passage between the disc edge and silencer wall. These baffle assemblies were easily removed for cleaning purposes.

# Arrow and Golden Arrow

*Handlebar Arrangement*

The handlebar arrangement of the Arrow was considerably different from the Leader. This was chromium-plated and held in position by a clamping device that permitted rotary adjustment. The clamp was spline-mounted to the steering column. Control layout was orthodox and comprised, on the right (offside), a Doherty combined twistgrip and front brake lever, inboard of which was a hornbutton mounted directly in the handlebar. On the left (nearside) was the clutch lever assembly and dip switch. The ignition/lighting switch, Smiths-made 100mph speedometer, ammeter and ignition warning light were loc-ated in the top face of the headlamp shell.

As with the Leader, the footrests and centre were fixed to the base of the crankcase casting, as also was the optional side stand (a cost option). The footrest hanger was a ¼in (6.4mm) thick steel pressing. Val Page and his development team showed considerable interest in providing sensible details to the design. Typical was the centre-stand operation. Not only were there extension pieces incorporated into the tubular, roll-on centre stand, but also lifting handles at each side, positioned below the rear of the dual seat.

*Standard Equipment*

Standard equipment included a rear chaincase (as on the Leader). A smoothly finished right-hand (offside) steel pressing enclosed the alternator and gearbox end cover; a convenient aperture, normally sealed by a rubber plug, provided access to the gearbox oil-level check plug. All in all, a pretty neat, effective and economical conversion from the fully enclosed Leader to the more conventional-looking Arrow had been achieved.

*Finish*

Finish of the frame beam, mudguards, front forks, swinging arm, rear shocks, headlamp shell and rear chaincase was in Light Grey. The dummy tank (outer shell), alternator/gearbox cover pressing, rear number plate/rear light support and front forks inspection covers were in Dark Seal Grey. Without the Leader's white-walled tyres, the Arrow was a much more conservative-looking motorcycle.

## An Improvement in Sales

There is no doubt that the introduction of the Arrow helped Ariel to increase its sales greatly. For example, in one month alone in 1960, a

*The Arrow first appeared for the 1960 season, basically a naked Leader. It was partly created because the Leader's sales never reached target and partly to widen the model range now the four-strokes had gone.*

total of 1,600 of the Ariel Leader and Arrow two-stroke twins were produced. In addition, the roaring success of the Hermann Meier-tuned Arrow in that year's Lightweight (250cc) TT (*see* Chapter 10) upped the model's profile considerably. This success in both the showroom and race circuit also led to a new sports version and a significant number of improvements for the existing Leader and Arrow models.

## More Zip in 1961

When the 1961 Ariel model range was announced at the beginning of October 1960, there were soon to be three main changes for both the Arrow and the Leader:

- high-compression cylinder heads
- repositioning of the anchorage for the floating front brake plate on the right (offside) stanchion of the trailing-link fork
- an increase in fuel tank capacity from 2.5 to 3gal (11.4 to 13.6ltr).

### Revised Cylinder Heads

Probably the most notable was the change from part-spherical combustion areas in the cylinder head giving a compression ratio of 8.25:1 and spark plugs inclined forwards 25 degrees from the cylinder axes. Development in the racing Arrow prepared by the German Hermann Meier had shown this set-up could be improved upon. So the latest heads now featured squish-type combustion chambers, boosting the compression ratio to 10:1, and a central plug location. The squish effect was obtained by a $^3/_8$in-wide (9.5mm) annular shoulder that conformed closely to the outer part of the slightly domed piston crown at tdc (top dead centre), so concentrating the combustion space around the spark plug.

Repositioning the plug also involved a small attention to the layout of the cooling fans. In terms of power output the new heads gave an increase of 1.5bhp, the maximum power output rising to 17.5bhp at 6,400rpm. Ariel sources also claimed slight gains in cooling and fuel economy.

### Front Brake Anchorage

The purpose in modifying the front brake anchorage was to achieve smoother braking whilst retaining the pivoted linkage that isolated wheel suspension from brake reaction. Previously the linkage lay below wheel spindle height level and was anchored near the front of the 16-gauge pressed steel stanchion, but

*Former World Champion Cecil Sandford with an Arrow during the 1960 Thruxton 500-mile race. Partnered by Sammy Miller, the bike came home second in its class. Another Arrow ridden by Robin Good/B Fortescue came third.*

now the anchorage was at the top of the stanchion, close to the steering column yoke into which it was brazed, and so flexing of the fork under brake torque was virtually eliminated.

In the new arrangement the original brake shoe plate and torque link were retained, though the link was now cranked slightly to clear the inside of the fork stanchion. However, the link was no longer attached directly to the plate but to a triangular torque arm bolted to it; since the link now operated at a greater radius from the wheel spindle, the loading in the link was reduced.

The brake shoe plate, in effect, had been rotated backwards rather less than half a turn. Flanged all round the outer edge, the pressed steel torque arm was clamped to the plate at two points – the original link attachment and an extended shoe pivot. As before, the link pivoted on a spherical nylon bush at either end. The anchor bracket welded to the stanchion was concealed by a clip-on plastic moulding.

*Increased Fuel Capacity*
The increased capacity of the petrol tank had been achieved by extending it forwards; at the bottom the extension followed the upward curvature of the frame beam. Space for the extension was provided long before by raising the two ignition coils; originally they were positioned just in front of the tank, but their relocation made them more accessible than before. Another tank alteration, incorporated into production at an earlier date, was the elimination of the baffles.

*More Minor Changes*
Other changes for the 1961 model year were of a more minor nature and concerned equipment and finish. Some, as explained in Chapter 11, only concerned the Leader; the Arrow was not available in the same three two-tone colour schemes as the Leader: Admiralty grey with either Cherokee red, Oriental blue or Dark Seal grey.

Amongst the components uprated over the previous couple of years were:

- connecting rods
- silencers
- clutch
- carburation
- contact breaker cover.

The con-rod modification saw a move from I-section to oval section with a maximum thickness of $3/16$in (1.6mm), and since the

*Another Arrow in production racing, this time Michael Burton, during the 1962 Thruxton marathon.*

original detachable baffle assemblies in the silencers tended to stick in the silencer body through carbon build-up, the flanged perforated discs were replaced as explained earlier in this chapter. Used in the Arrow from the start, the modified unit was much easier to remove, though, since only the rearmost baffle was perforated, cleaning could be effected after merely detaching the silencer and cap without withdrawing the baffle. Ariel sources commented: 'If a specialized two-stroke lubricant is used, cleaning should not be required more frequently than at 10,000-mile intervals, especially as the carburettor main jet size was reduced from 170 to 140.'

To provide a lighter clutch operation, clutch spring pressure was reduced by fitting spaces on the retaining screws. Access to the contact breaker points originally involved threading the cover along the electrical leads, but these were now led in through a groove formed in the cover flange, and the cover could be lifted away on removal of the three retaining screws.

*An Arrow seat lifted to reveal beam frame; unlike the Leader, only the fuel fill cap and battery are visible; the four circular cone devices are seat supports.*

*Nearside view of Arrow/Golden Arrow engine. Note the centrally mounted spark plugs; the early Leader engine had offset ones.*

## The Golden Arrow

The next development in the story of the Ariel twin-cylinder two-stroke came with the launch in January 1961 of the Arrow Super Sports – affectionately known unofficially as the 'Golden Arrow'.

A press report of the day said:

> Ariels, that factory with the happy knack of producing sure-fire winners at will, have done it again. There are now *three* 249cc two-stroke twins in the Selly Oak line-up, and the latest creation – officially the Sports Arrow, but almost certainly destined for fame as the Golden Arrow – is as eye-popping a model as ever brought a crowd flocking round a showroom window.

*Real Improvement*
Unlike many so-called 'sports' models of the era, the newcomer brought real improvement, not just in looks, but also performance. The compression ratio had been raised to 10:1, a larger Amal Monobloc fitted – a Type 376 replacing a 375 and with the size increased to $1\frac{1}{16}$in (27mm) from $\frac{7}{8}$in (22mm)). In addition, the main jet size had risen to 230. There was also attention to the inlet passages in the crankcase casting. However, as explained earlier, due to the design of the crankcase, fitting twin carburettors was ruled out, at least as far as series production was concerned. Even so, the power output was now up to a claimed 20.2bhp at 6,650rpm.

*A Glamorous Finish*
The Ariel publicity machine heralded the new Arrow Super Sports as 'The Most Glamorous Sport 250cc Twin ever Designed'. If nothing else this was probably true, at least as regards its colourful finish. Compared to the standard Arrow this comprised:

- gold tank and rear plate surround, with Admiralty Grey frame and mudguards
- chromium-plated ball-end control levers
- white-wall tyres
- red handlebar grips
- chromium-plated toolbox cover
- chromium-plated fork inspection covers and offside (right) engine outer cover
- folding kick-start lever
- chromium-plated lifting handles
- lowered handlebars
- side (prop) stand
- polished primary chaincase
- two-way petrol tap
- racing-type perspex screen.

And, if all this was not enough, the price, at £187 11s 5d upon its January 1961 launch, was only £16 less than the Leader. As *The Motor Cycle* commented 'no mere black-and-white photograph' could illustrate just how much more exciting and colourful the Golden Arrow looked in comparison to the standard version.

The late Bob Currie, then *The Motor Cycle*'s Midland correspondent became the first pressman to sample the latest Ariel, in a report published on 19 January 1961. In typical Currie prose he described his ride thus:

> Stark against the setting sun, the black bulk of the Malvern Hills made an irresistible goal, with a chance to try out the hill-climbing ability of this little golden beauty. And know what? There's nothing top-end-only about the Arrow sportster. Midlanders, anyway, will know that long drag up from Malvern to the Wyche Cutting, a saddle through the crest of the hills. Third gear and half-throttle all the way is a most respectable climb for a two-fifty, any day of the week. Looking westwards from the hillside road, the red-tinted hills of Herefordshire made a scene only an artist's brush could have captured. But already the valleys were in darkness and it was time to turn for home.

During his initial ride, Bob Currie found much to his liking (drop handlebars apart!):

> First-prod starting, no vibration anywhere in the rev range, outstanding roadholding (with that Ariel trailing-link fork you don't steer – you just

## Arrow and Golden Arrow

think at the model), and a finish that is truly glamorous. . . . The average sports model sings its song a mile too loudly for comfort; but not the Ariel. This one has a soothing lullaby of an exhaust note, deeper, quieter even than that of the Arrow. Why that should be so I wouldn't know, for the silencers are similar.

### A Full Road Test

Later in the 12 April 1962 issue of *The Motor Cycle* Bob Currie carried out a full and comprehensive test of the Golden Arrow. He began by saying: 'As tested in its 1962 guise, the machine appears even more glamorous, for now the gilded tank shell is allied to an ivory finish for the frame, forks and mudguards, so producing almost a Regency effect.'

What of the overall impression of the machine? His answer was:

Favourable, most favourable. Speed, the test machine produced, and then some, but the charm lay in the manner in which the model produced

*Brightly chromed offside engine cover denotes an Arrow Super Sport (Golden Arrow); the standard cover is simply painted.*

*A special show model. A Golden Arrow was cut away to show internals such as engine, exhaust, forks, tanks and frame.*

## Arrow Super Sport 1961

| | | | |
|---|---|---|---|
| Engine | Air-cooled parallel twin, piston port induction; alloy heads; cast-iron cylinders, inclined forwards at 45 degrees; one-piece aluminium crankcase casting | Front suspension | Trailing-link, Armstrong shock absorbers |
| | | Rear suspension | Swinging arm, twin Armstrong shock absorbers |
| | | Front brake | 6-inch full-width cast-iron hub, SLS |
| Bore | 54mm | | |
| Stroke | 54mm | Rear brakes | 6-inch full-width cast-iron hub, SLS |
| Displacement | 247cc | | |
| Compression ratio | 10:1 | Tyres | 3.25 × 16 front and rear |
| Lubrication | Petroil mixture | | |
| Ignition | Twin coils, twin contact breaker points, 6-volt battery | **General Specifications** | |
| | | Wheelbase | 51in (1,295mm) |
| Carburettor | Single Amal 376 Monobloc 1 1/16in | Ground clearance | 5in (127mm) |
| | | Seat height | 28.5in (724mm) |
| Primary drive | Chain | Fuel tank capacity | 3gal (13.6ltr) |
| Final drive | Chain | Dry weight | 278lb (126kg) |
| Gearbox | Four-speed, Burman, foot-change | Maximum power | 20.2bhp @ 6,600 |
| Frame | Beam type, of welded steel construction | Top speed | 81mph (130km/h) |

its performance. Its range-mates, the Leader and Arrow, had already achieved a reputation for rock-steady steering and this attribute is, of course, equally applicable to the sports version. Normally, a tuned two-stroke can be a thirsty little beast but the Ariel turned out to be surprisingly light on fuel and, in give-and-take going throughout the test, produced an average figure of about 70mpg.

In both acceleration (the standard quarter-mile in 17.6sec) and maximum speed (81mph (130km/h)) the Golden Arrow received top marks. And, as in his all-too-brief a run on one of the first bikes produced in January 1961, tester Currie found that unlike many other sports two-strokes, the 'power build-up is more evenly spread and as a rule there is less need to lower gear ratios.'

As an illustration of the machine's flexibility he found it was: 'quite possible to allow the machine to accelerate steadily from speeds as low as 25mph in top, though, of course, a drop into third produced a much zippier getaway'. Furthermore: 'where time was not pressing, long main-road hills could be climbed with top gear still engaged'.

Other positive features that Bob Currie praised in his test included steering, braking, gear change, lack of exhaust noise, hot starting and a 'commendably low level' of mechanical noise from the engine and transmission.

*The Debit Side of the Ledger*
However, as Bob Currie was to note 'there were also one or two points to be noted on the debit side of the ledger'.

The first of these was starting from cold which 'usually called for a dozen or so prods of the pedal'. Then there was the riding position. Currie described it in the following words: 'A down-turned handlebar is certainly not to everyone's taste though, admittedly, it is traditionally a part of the sports machine specification; but here the footrests are in a normal, forward position and, if full use is to be made of the dropped bar, the resulting crouch is not the most comfortable.' As for the flyscreen, while this may have its advantages when the driver is well tucked down, for

*A factory publicity shot of the Super Sport/Golden Arrow. This shows standard fitment flyscreen, chromed outer engine cover and fork inspection covers and white-walled tyres.*

normal riding it is little more than ornamental and indeed, tends to obscure part of the speedometer dial. Another 'source of annoyance' concerned the toolbox. Inset in the upper face of the dummy tank shell 'access to the box itself was simple enough, but to extract the tyre pump the tool tray, which was held in place by a spring crossbar, had first to be removed – and replacement of the bar was something of a fiddle'.

But overall there was still much to applaud and, as the performance gained in production racing during the early 1960s was to prove, to say nothing of machines converted into pukka racers, the Ariel twin-cylinder two-stroke was one of the very best handling bikes of its era.

## The 1962 Model Range

When the 1962 Ariel model range had been announced in early September 1961 the Leader, Arrow and Arrow Super Sports were still the only models offered by the Selly Oak factory.

The most noticeable change was actually a cosmetic one with an ivory (white) finish being adopted for the main frame, front fork and mudguards in place of Admiralty Grey. Whilst the Arrow was offered in black and ivory only, for the Leader there was now the choice of four colours – the additional one being black (like the other three, now with ivory). The Arrow Super Sports was to be offered in what *The Motor Cycle* said was 'a lush – almost Regency – finish with ivory lower parts and the tank and rear number plate in gold'. An added touch of luxury for the standard Arrow was the provision of polished aluminium knee-grip surrounds, as already specified for the Leader and Super Sports.

*Electrical Update*
Technically, the major change was to the electrical specification, all three bikes now being fitted with the Lucas RM18 alternator, which superseded the original RM13/15 assembly; though there was the advantage of slightly higher (55-watt) electrical output at higher speeds, the principal advantage was a more substantial output at lower engine revolutions.

A modified wiring harness incorporated a plug-and-socket connection to the lighting and ignition switches, whilst the ignition switch was of a new type, fitted with a detachable key. To prevent the emergency start position being engaged inadvertently, it was now obtained by pressing down the key against spring pressure before turning. Applicable to the two Arrow models only was a more powerful Lucas horn.

*Brake Improvements*

The other notable technical improvement was to the brakes. For several months, a water-excluding flange (pioneered by Sammy Miller, whose trials bike featured Leader-type wheel hubs) had been fitted to Ariel front shoe plates, and was now to be fitted to the rear brake also. Internal ribs resulted in a very much stiffer front brake shoe plate, but it was discovered during experimental testing that the stiffer plate created brake squeal as the result of flexing of the shoes. Because of this problem, transverse 'anti-squeal' springs were fitted to the shoes at the point of maximum frequency; these damped out vibration and thus noise when the brake was applied.

From September 1961 the prices had risen as follows:

- Leader            £203 7s 1d
- Arrow             £179 2s 6d
- Arrow Super Sports   £190 15s 7d.

## Competition for Sales

From around the time when Ariel introduced the Arrow Super Sports (Golden Arrow), the two-fifty market suddenly became more competitive. Besides British-built machines such as the AJS/Matchless Model 14/G2 respectively; and the BSA C15, Norton Jubilee, and Royal Enfield Crusader Sport, there were also the first Japanese machines (including Honda's C72/CB72), plus Italians such as the Aermacchi Ala Verde and Ducati Daytona (Diana outside UK). All in all, it had suddenly become a hugely competitive market – and more important as new British learner laws introduced in 1961 meant that new riders were to be restricted to a maximum engine size of 250cc. However, any benefit that Ariel boss Ken Whistance might have thought was coming his way with the trio of twin-cylinder two-stroke models was effectively negated by a combination of intense competition *and* declining sales – the latter brought on by ever cheaper and better cars.

## No Changes

When the 1964 model range came around towards the end of 1963, it was 'no changes'. This probably had more to do with the company's move from its old home at Selly Oak to the giant BSA works in Small Heath than anything else. Everyone could see then that Ariel's days as a separate entity had come to an end.

## The 200

The next – and as it turned out final – development in the Ariel twins came at the beginning of May 1964, when a '200' Arrow was launched. This, the company said, came as an all-out bid to beat increases in insurance premiums that were hitting 250cc sales. With a typical comprehensive premium that was half that of the 250 Arrow, a 200 version seemed to make commercial sense. Ariel also claimed that this saving was boosted by the better fuel consumption of the smaller-engined Arrow without sacrificing more than some 5mph (8km/h) in top speed.

*Technical Details*

Technical details of the new power unit largely conformed to the existing two-fifty, but with the bore size reduced to 48.5mm, giving a swept volume of 199.4cc. Left at 54mm, the stroke thus became longer. This, if anything, provided slightly superior pulling power at lower engine revolutions. External cylinder barrel and head dimensions were unchanged, with the advantage of slightly increased metal mass around the bores, thus helping to reduce mechanical noises such as piston slap.

A fraction down on that of the larger Arrow, the 200's compression ratio was 9.5:1. Ariel sources claimed the power output to be 14bhp at 6,250rpm. The gear ratios were slightly lower, top now being 6.2:1 against the 250 Arrow's 5.9:1, and a smaller 13/16in 375 Monobloc carburettor was fitted, with a main jet size of 120.

## Arrow and Golden Arrow

*Robin Good (2) with the Golden Arrow he shared with . . .*

*. . . co-rider Peter Inchley during the 1962 Thruxton 500-miler.*

---

### Ken Whistance

Born in the West Midlands (known to the locals as the Black Country), K J (Kenneth John) Whistance was the son of a local motorcycle dealer and served his apprenticeship in his father's dealership. Ken Whistance got his driving licence the day he reached fourteen years of age (which was possible in those far-off days), and, as a member of the West Bromwich Motor Cycle Club he entered the world of trials, and the branch of motorcycle sport at which he was something of a star turn — moto-ball (essentially a form of football with the players mounted on motorcycles).

Ken was also a road racer of some note and in 1933 he was signed up by the Birmingham factory New Imperial to ride for the works team in the Junior TT. But it was to prove a disastrous year for New Imperial, with its whole trio of riders being forced to retire. In fact, Ken Whistance's bike was the last to pack in — with big-end problems on the third lap.

After serving his apprenticeship Ken had moved into the industry proper. In those days, during the interwar period of the 1930s, Birmingham was the centre of the motorcycle trade, with countless factories, large and small, scattered all over the area. One of his first major tasks came with the development of the wartime Wellbike — a small motorcycle that could be folded up for easy transport by troops in the field. After the war it was developed into the civilian Corgi, built and distributed by Brockhouse Engineering of Southport, Lancashire. Then came a spell with BSA at that company's Small Heath works in Birmingham. Finally, in 1953, he moved to nearby Selly Oak and Ariel.

As a Director and General Manager, Ken Whistance fought to keep Ariel independent of BSA (which had purchased the company from Jack Y Sangster in 1944). He and Chief Designer Val Page were largely instrumental in the birth of the new two-stroke range which began in 1958 with the launch of the revolutionary Leader. But, ultimately, Ariel suffered a drop in sales like virtually everyone else in the British motorcycle industry, and Ken Whistance's battle to keep Ariel a separate body ended when the BSA directors axed the Selly Oak works — the result being that Ariel was moved lock, stock and barrel into a small corner of the BSA works in Small Heath.

*Visual Changes*

Besides the '200' badges on each side of the outer 'dummy' tank shell, the newcomer sported a different colour scheme from its larger, older brother. The dummy tank-top tool and oddment compartment and also the rear chaincase were finished in Aircraft Blue or, alternatively, British Racing Green, with the remainder of the body area, front and rear mudguards, headlamp shell and rear suspension units in standard Ariel Ivory. The dual seat (as on the 250 Arrow) was black and the offside (right) engine cover was grey.

Ariel also claimed that the £187 10s 4d purchase price (including UK taxes) was due to 'improved production methods rather than a cheapened specification'. Proof of this, they said, was the retention of qd full-width hubs, the comprehensive toolkit, tyre pump, pillion footrests and even a licence holder.

It is worth noting the prices of the Leader, Arrow and Arrow Super Sports on the day of the 200's arrival:

- Leader            £255 0s 0d
- Arrow             £196 15s 6d
- Arrow Super Sports £211 14s 1d.

## End of the Line

In truth, the end of the line for the Ariel marque and its range of twin-cylinder two-strokes was fast approaching. The first to go, at the end of 1964, was the standard 250cc Arrow. The Leader, 200 Arrow and Arrow Super Sports lived on until mid-1965 before being axed. As Roy Bacon was later to recall: 'The tragedy was that the formula was so right and could so easily have been developed on for the 1970s.' What was really needed was an increased power output, twin carburettors, five or six speeds, an oil pump, electric starting and 12-volt electrics. Quite a 'wish list', but by no means impossible – had the will and the money been there.

Ariel, along with the rest of the British industry, was not around when sales picked up in the 1970s. Instead, it was left to the Japanese, particularly Suzuki and Yamaha, to bring out modern versions of the twin-cylinder two-fifty theme.

*A 200 Arrow (199.4cc – by reducing the bore size to 48.5mm) came at the beginning of May 1964. It was largely introduced to combat rising insurance costs.*

### Arrow 200 1964

| | | | |
|---|---|---|---|
| Engine | Air-cooled parallel twin, piston port induction; alloy heads; cast-iron cylinders, inclined forward at 45 degrees; one-piece aluminium crankcase casting | Front suspension | Trailing-link, Armstrong shock absorbers |
| | | Rear suspension | Swinging arm, twin Armstrong shock absorbers |
| | | Front brake | 6in full-width cast-iron hub, SLS |
| Bore | 48.5mm | | |
| Stroke | 54mm | Rear brakes | 6in full-width cast-iron hub, SLS |
| Displacement | 199.4cc | | |
| Compression ratio | 9.5:1 | Tyres | 3.25 × 16 front and rear |
| Lubrication | Petroil mixture | **General Specifications** | |
| Ignition | Twin coils, twin contact breaker points, 6-volt battery | Wheelbase | 51in (1,295mm) |
| | | Ground clearance | 5in (127mm) |
| Carburettor | Single Amal 375 Monobloc $1^3/_{16}$in | Seat height | 28.5in (724mm) |
| | | Fuel tank capacity | 3gal (13.6ltr) |
| Primary drive | Chain | Dry weight | 278lb (126kg) |
| Final drive | Chain | Maximum power | 14bhp @ 6,250 |
| Gearbox | Four speed, Burman, foot-change | Top speed | 71mph (114km/h) |
| Frame | Beam type of welded steel construction | | |

Of course, the Ariel twins were not without faults, but with continued development, these could have been eliminated. Instead, the House of the Horse was allowed to die, effectively starved to death by largely uncaring and incompetent BSA management.

And to add insult to injury, as is recounted in Chapter 14, the name was used for that financial disaster, the infamous Ariel 3, a cross between a trike and a moped, which must rate as one of the worst motorcycle-industry products ever.

*A surprisingly large number of Ariel's 250 twin-cylinder two-stroke series have survived and are to be seen at modern-day classic events, like this Gloden Arrow.*

# 14 End of an Era

By mid-1962, the initial successes gained by the Leader and Arrow series had begun to wane. This then placed Ariel as a separate manufacturing unit with its own site at risk. The result was that the parent BSA Group decided to integrate Ariel's manufacturing facilities with its own motorcycle division.

## The Press Report the Beginning of the End

In its 13 September 1962 issue *The Motor Cycle* carried the following report:

> Bang goes a link with the early days of motorcycling, for Ariels are packing their goods and chattels, saying farewell to Selly Oak and making the short trek across to Small Heath. It was such a long link, too, stretching way back to 1894. Not that the Components empire, of which Ariels were initially a part, was at that time involved in our game – the first connection came in 1898, with the Ariel tricycle. But it was an empire indeed, whose products at one time included tyres and rims. Componentsville included the present factory (except for the assembly shop, which began life as a cinema) and much more besides; it was the home not only of Ariel motorcycles, but also the one-time Ariel car and Fleet commercial three-wheeler. In the financial reconstruction of 1930 much of the original property had to go, leaving the Ariel flame of life to flicker fitfully in a somewhat cramped corner of the erstwhile Componentsville. That had its problems in more recent years, when Ariels came back to popularity but found themselves with little enough room in which to breathe. Therein lies the real reason for the present break – which has, in fact, been on the cards for the last eight years. It had to come, sometime. But all the same, Selly Oak seemed such a romantic address; so much less bleak than Small Heath.

Of course, in hindsight we can see that *The Motor Cycle*'s reasoning behind the move was wrong – BSA was in fact moving Ariel because it was cutting back rather than expanding. Another press report of the time also tried to paint a similar story:

> Production of Ariel machines is being transferred to part of the BSA works of Small Heath, Birmingham. The move will be completed next December, BSA announced last weekend. No change in Ariel policy or management is involved. The object is to provide the subsidiary company with improved facilities and make economic use of the Small Heath premises.

Actually, this last press report sounds almost to have been taken straight from the BSA Group press release! All in all, it appeared, at least to the general public, to have been an upward move for the Ariel marque, when, in fact, it really signalled the beginning of the end.

## Badge Engineering

As proof of how the BSA Group saw its future during the very same week that it announced the Ariel relocation was another news story. This concerned the none-too-successful Triumph Tina. This lightweight auto-transmission scooter was from henceforth

*End of an Era*

to 'drop its association with any particular marque. As just simply the Tina, it is now to be supplied by any Triumph, BSA or Ariel dealer'.

Assembled by Triumph at Meriden, the Tina employed an engine built by BSA in the one-time Sunbeam works at Redditch, pressings came from Carbodies of Coventry and other parts (such as the plastic front mudguard) were supplied by Motoplas, Birmingham. As Carbodies and Motoplas were BSA Group companies it is easy for readers to see how the BSA Group operated at that time.

The Tina story also shows the muddled approach by the parent BSA, as Triumph, the most successful component in BSA's two-wheel empire, should have been left alone to produce its best-selling range of motorcycles, rather than fiddling around with assembling a poor-selling scooter.

## The 1963 Range

When the 1963 Ariel model range was announced at the beginning of September 1962 it had appeared that not only would the Leader/Arrow series continue unchanged into the following year, but everyone presumed Ariel would still be in its Selly Oak home. But, of course, this was an illusion.

Another surprise was just around the corner. On the eve of the London Earls Court Show in early November, *The Motor Cycle* dated 8 November 1962 said: 'Biggest news for years in the little-machine field is the entry of the BSA Group into the featherweight battle.' The machines in question were the BSA Beagle 75cc and Ariel Pixie 50cc. Except in cylinder bore, the engines were identical, with ohv, cast-iron cylinder barrel and aluminium-alloy head.

BSA's Edward Turner, in introducing the models at the show, commented:

> A two-stroke would certainly be cheaper to make, but the four-stroke has a much better fuel consumption and is an altogether more sporty proposition. We have incorporated a four-speed gearbox, the better to take advantage of the high rpm which the new unit has been designed to withstand. Our object is to provide a pair of machines – exciting little things to ride – which will appeal to those interested in motor cycling as such, rather than as a mere means of transport.

At the time of their launch, it was stated that 'both the Pixie and the Beagle are expected to be in production by April or May, 1963'. But these forecasts were to prove overoptimistic.

*A Box-Section Frame*
In designing the chassis for the new Pixie, Bernard Knight, Val Page's successor as Chief Designer of Ariel, and one of the brains behind the Leader and Arrow range, again decided to employ a stressed box-section frame in place of the conventional tubular type.

As with the Leader/Arrow, two pressings were welded along the centre line into an integral structure. In the Pixie's case this meant a totally integral structure, with the rear section of the pressings forming a mudguard and number plate, whilst the forward part housed a 1⅛gal (5ltr) fuel tank.

Centrally, the body carried an oval pan-type seat beneath which was carried the toolkit and tyre pump. A reinforcing panel under the seat provided a cross-bracing effect and doubled as an anti-splash plate.

Bolted into the centre structure was a welded-up sub-frame carrying the engine and the pivot for the rear swinging arm, which was mounted in nylon bushes and grease-loaded on assembly. Welded steel pressings were also employed in rear fork construction. A bonded rubber spring unit operated in tension and compression to control movement of the swinging arm assembly.

*The Sub-Frame*
The sub-frame of the Pixie was removable from the main body, complete with engine assembly, footrests, centre stand and swinging arm, by the withdrawal of three studs and nuts.

Leader design technique was to be seen plainly in the front fork assembly. Each leg carried an enclosed trailing-link unit, controlled by a pair of rubber buffers in each leg. These worked in compression only, with stops to arrest rebound. Nylon-bushed pivots carried the leading links. The brake pedal was also nylon-bushed and grease-packed when fitted. This, it was claimed, obviated the need for further lubrication.

The fork crown and headstock consisted of an ingenious pressing – being simple but effective. The stem was carried in a tubular lug welded into the neck of the main body, which terminated at the front of a nacelle, with a chromium-plated rim, housing a 6-volt 18/18watt headlamp.

*Wheels and Brakes*
The wheel size was 15in, incorporating 4in brakes, the latter being quickly detachable. The chrome-plated steel rims carried 2.50in-section tyres. Other details of the running gear included a fully-enclosed chain, comprehensive (Leader type) front mudguard, folding kick-start lever. The handlebar assembly was fabricated with tubular end-pieces, the handlebar being adjustable for height, bicycle fashion – with a long bolt with expander nut passing inside the steering stem. In the middle of the handlebar was provision for the (optional) speedometer.

*Nylon Bearings*
Nylon (plastic) bearing use was at the centre of the Pixie design. Ariel's General Manager Ken Whistance commented: 'The need for maintenance has been cut to a minimum. Nylon-bush bearings are everywhere – the cross-shaft, rear-fork pivots, front fork link pivots, even the front brake anchor arm, which is slotted so that it rises and falls with the wheel and so maintains true braking geometry, is sandwiched between a pair of nylon blocks.'

*The Engine Design*
The engine design of the Pixie was essentially shared with the BSA Beagle. In each version the stroke remained the same at 42mm, but whilst the small-displacement Ariel had a bore of 38.9mm, that of its BSA cousin was 47.6mm, exact capacities being 49.94cc and 74.77cc respectively.

Cast iron was employed for the cylinder barrel, light alloy for the head. Widely splayed, the pushrods on the offside (right) operated rocker arms disposed transversely and housed in rocker boxes integral with the cylinder head. The three-ring piston gave a compression ratio of 8.8:1, whilst the crankshaft was supported by three ball bearings: two on the nearside.

*The chassis of the new 50cc Pixie was the work of Val Page's successor, Bernard Knight, but the engine owed much to the 75cc BSA Beagle. Both ohv unit construction designs had shared technology and both, ultimately, were to prove unsuccessful.*

A novel feature of the Pixie/Beagle engine was the built-on sump – a pressing attached by two studs and nuts, with distance pieces, to the crankcase base. The single plunger oil pump fed the plain bearing big-end via a sump filter and drilling in the timing-side shaft. A second system utilized crankcase oil mist, drawn up by the depression caused by piston movement, to lubricate the rocker gear. There was a drain-back to the crankcase sump with a system of bleeds, one oiling the chain.

Also unusual was the 3.3:1 gear priming drive, employing a straight-cut engine shaft pinion with twin clutch wheel gears. These gears had sufficient float to act as 'plain' clutch surfaces, sandwiched between Neolangite-bonded friction plates.

*Flywheel Magneto Ignition*
A flywheel magneto with direct lighting coils was mounted on the engine nearside (left) mainshaft, outboard of the primary drive pinion. Since gear primary transmission was adopted, engine rotation was the reverse of normal practice. Based on that of the Triumph Tiger Cub, the integral four-speed gearbox featured an 'up-for-up, down-for-down' operation. This gearbox had a foot-change operation and provided final drive ratios of 11.2, 14.8, 23.0 and 30.3:1.

Ariel claimed a peak power of 3.8bhp at 9,000rpm, which gave the Pixie a maximum road speed of around 40mph (64km/h).

The previously mentioned speedometer (not then a legal requirement on a machine of under 50cc in the UK) was available at an additional £3 3s on top of the Pixie's £81 18s price (including British purchase tax). A windscreen, leg shields, panniers, rear carrier and front shopping basket were other cost options.

Ivory was the main colour of the Pixie, used for the frame, front forks and mudguards; the secondary colour – red or blue – was used for the handlebar shield, seat, swinging arm and chainguard.

## A Premature Launch

The launch of the Pixie (and the Beagle) in November 1962 proved premature to say the least, and it was not until twelve months later, in early November 1963, that *Motor Cycling* was able to repeat 'Ariel's Pixie is coming off the line'. This showed, yet again, the poor management in charge of the BSA Group at the time. After all the launch publicity, the public and press alike had almost forgotten that the Pixie existed by the time anyone could actually buy one. As it (and the Beagle) were intended as British challengers to the supremacy of the invading Japanese, this was a disaster in more ways than one. The result was that, although the Pixie continued to be available throughout 1964 and into 1965, few were sold and no-one, including BSA, seemed to care when the plug was pulled. The whole exercise cost the BSA Group dearly.

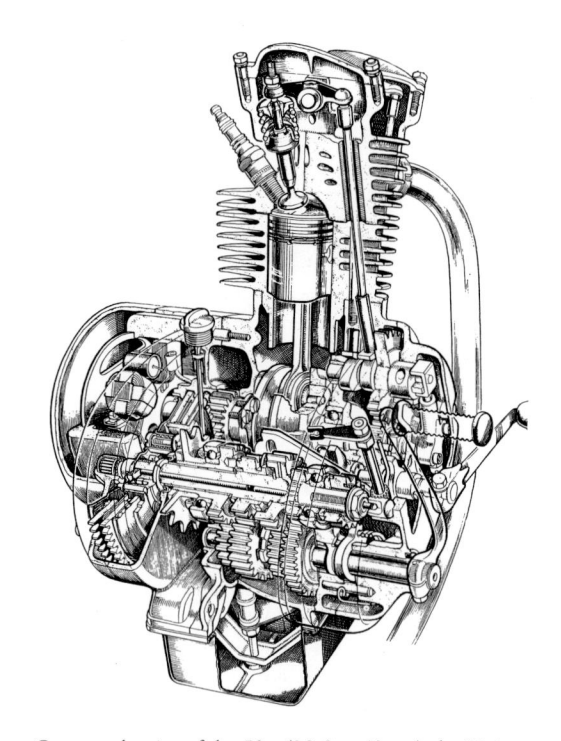

*Cutaway drawing of the 50cc (38.9 × 42mm) ohv Pixie engine, showing valve gear, piston, crankshaft and transmission.*

| | Pixie 50 1963 | | |
|---|---|---|---|
| Engine | Air-cooled overhead valve single unit construction with inclined cast-iron cylinder barrel and alloy head; plain bearing big-end | Frame | Steel pressings, welded construction |
| | | Front suspension | Trailing-link fork |
| | | Rear suspension | Rubber suspension medium |
| Bore | 38.9mm | Front brake | 4in full-width drum, SLS |
| Stroke | 42mm | Rear brakes | 7in full-width drum, SLS |
| Displacement | 49.94cc | Tyres | 2.50 × 15 front and rear |
| Compression ratio | 8.8:1 | | |
| Lubrication | Wet sump, single plunger pump | **General Specifications** | |
| | | Wheelbase | 42in (1,067mm) |
| Ignition | Flywheel magneto, 6-volt | Ground clearance | 4in (102mm) |
| Carburettor | Amal type 15½in | Seat height | 26.5in (673mm) |
| Primary drive | Gear teeth cut on clutch friction plates; no clutch drum | Fuel tank capacity | 1.12gal (5ltr) |
| | | Dry weight | 120lb (54kg) |
| Final drive | Chain | Maximum power | 3.8bhp @ 9,000rpm |
| Gearbox | Four-speed foot-change | Top speed | 40mph (64km/h) |

## The Ariel 3

The Ariel 3, which arrived on the market in 1970, was an even bigger disaster than the Pixie/Beagle saga. Why? Well, read on to see just how bad things really were and, sadly, how the famous old and highly respected Ariel brand name was once more dragged through the mud by the total mismanagement of what remained of a once great company by BSA. The best one could say about the Ariel 3 was that even BSA did not know what it really was, with their infamous advertisement headed 'Here it is. Whatever it is'.

As Roy Bacon described the debacle that led up to the introduction of the Ariel 3:

> This was part of a larger picture and the Ariel company was subject to the whims of the overall group board. They had been forced out of their traditional home and to drop their traditional line-up of models. Their fresh ideas for the future were either blocked or distorted and in the end the Ariel company was just put down with a humane killer. To many observers the horse was nobbled, kept short of rations until ill, and then given the coup de grâce.

When the Ariel 3 arrived in the middle of 1970, one could truthfully say that the marque which bore its name was dead and buried. In reality it was a product of BSA – not Ariel – but still, the Ariel name was used, so an Ariel it has to be. Although BSA claimed the Ariel 3 project to have been the 'result of a massive market research exercise', the result was one of the motorcycle world's most bizarre creations of all time.

*A Moped, But Only Just*
The concept of the Ariel 3 was to offer the customer the convenience and ease of use that a moped offered, but with the stability of three wheels to provide potential owners with safety, economy and the chance to own something different from the competition. The latter, at the time, meant in practice designs such as the best-selling Austrian Puch Maxi, various Italian designs from the likes of Garelli, Demm and the Vespa Ciao, the French Velosolex and Motobecane (sold in UK under the Mobylette brand name) and Honda's legendary C50 step-thru.

The layout of the newcomer exploited a loophole in British vehicle regulations allowing a pair of wheels to be counted as one if set close enough. BSA's engineering team, by restricting the rear track of the 'Ariel', made sure that it could be classed as a moped, as then defined – the engine displacement was limited to 50cc and the machine was fitted with pedalling gear.

*The Banked Trike*
Legally, it might have been a moped, but in reality the Ariel 3 was a trike, in which the front section could be banked over to negotiate a corner whilst the rear half stayed upright. To achieve this, the front wheel, forks, pedals, front frame and seat were treated as one assembly, the two rear wheels, engine unit and transmission as another. The two assemblies were joined by a pivot on the machine's axis and twin torsion bars on this same axis lifted the front end up when the corner was passed and held the machine upright when parked.

*A Dutch Engine*
The motive power for the Ariel 3 was provided by an imported Dutch-made Anker single-cylinder two-stroke engine mounted above the rear axle. It operated courtesy of an automatic clutch and toothed belt to a countershaft that contained a dog clutch to allow the engine to be disengaged if the trike had to be pedalled (for example, if the user ran out of petrol). At the end of the crankshaft outboard of the drive belt was a cooling fan, whilst the drive pinion incorporated a spring clutch – enabling the pedals to turn the engine over to start.

*A One-Sided Affair*
In what is best described as a one-sided affair, only the nearside (left) rear wheel was driven or braked – with a chain connecting it to the countershaft. A second chain ran forwards to the pedals with various pulleys and guides to tension it and prevent it jumping off the sprockets when the front end of the machine was leaned over. The offside (right) wheel was fixed to a dummy live axle and was without a brake; however, all three wheels were fixed to the hubs on the three studs, car-like, and were interchangeable.

*A Large Alloy Fork*
The rear section featured a large aluminium fork that pivoted on a cross-rod carried in a trunnion with torsion springs acting as the suspension medium as well as holding the front end upright. These could be adjusted with screws to suit the pre-load to the rider's weight. The front frame was constructed from pressings and carried a trailing-link fork with rubber suspension. The front brake unit was the same size as the rear, whilst the tyres were 2.00 × 12 (of Dunlop manufacture) mounted on pressed-steel wheels.

*Built-In Leg Shields*
Leg shields were built-in to the front section and a windscreen offered as a cost option, whilst at the rear the panelling could be hinged up to provide access to the engine unit. When down, this cover also encased the fuel tank, but the filler cap for the latter protruded through the top so was accessible on the forecourt. A shopping basket with cover was another extra, which could be fitted on the top of the cover.

## The Designer

So who actually designed the Ariel 3? Well, at least in concept it was the creation of Yorkshire-born inventor George Wallace. He, however, was none too happy with the BSA Group's 'messing around' with his (patented) idea, saying that in the Group's attempt to save money, most of his original ideas had been ditched. Although BSA had convinced itself that the Ariel 3 was a winner, and that no fewer than 2,000 could be produced and sold every week, things did not go quite as planned.

## The Expensive Launch

There was a lavish and costly press launch, but the press was not sure, and the buying public

| Ariel 3 1970 | | | |
|---|---|---|---|
| Engine | Air-cooled Anker two-stroke single, with alloy head and cast-iron barrel; cooling fan | Front suspension | Trailing-link fork with rubber suspension |
| | | Rear suspension | Torsion springs |
| Bore | 40mm | Front brake | 4in drum |
| Stroke | 38mm | Rear brakes | 4in drum |
| Displacement | 48cc | Tyres | 2.00 × 12 front and rear |
| Compression ratio | 7:1 | | |
| Lubrication | Petroil | **General Specifications** | |
| Ignition | Flywheel magneto | Wheelbase | 49in (1,247mm) |
| Carburettor | N/A | Ground clearance | 3.5in (89mm) |
| Primary drive | Belt/chain | Seat height | 28.5in (724mm)[1] |
| Final drive | Chain | Fuel tank capacity | 0.75gal (3.4ltr) |
| Gearbox | Automatic, single-speed; sprag clutch | Dry weight | 98lb (45kg) |
| | | Maximum power | 1.7bhp @ 5,500rpm |
| Frame | Combination of steel pressings joined by a pivot on the machine's axis, providing a hinged effect | Top speed | 30mph (48km/h) |

[1] Lowest position.

was even less convinced, with very few actually purchasing the strange-looking device. Nonetheless, BSA pushed ahead with its big production schedules. Then came the first sales figures, which were truly disappointing, the number going out of the dealers' doors being a mere trickle. But worse was to come when reports filtered back to Birmingham of a host of problems. These included poor stability, bad starting, poor engine reliability and quality control problems. Not only this, but performance, at 30mph (48km/h) was hardly impressive, and fuel consumption figures of around 120mpg (2.36/100km) were not up to those of the opposition.

The Ariel 3 rapidly descended into a huge financial flop. Only a few hundred were actually sold to dealers – and even fewer to customers. The tooling costs were never recouped, whilst the BSA computer continued to buy in components, including the Dutch Anker engines, in the many thousands. The author, visiting accessory specialist Ken Cobbing in 1972 remembers vividly seeing thousands of Anker engines from BSA occupying an entire section of Cobbing's Hertfordshire warehouse. The whole exercise was estimated to have cost BSA a minimum of £2million and was certainly a factor in the group's ultimate collapse.

As an example of why the Ariel 3 did not sell, the author can relate his own experiences when one came into his Wisbech, Cambridgeshire dealership for repair during the early 1970s. Owned by a lady customer, it was suffering from an almost total lack of performance. This was found to be caused by a blocked exhaust system. On being replaced with a new component the engine started and ran sweetly. However, not one of the dealership's mechanical staff would actually test ride the machine.

So as the dealership owner, the author himself gave the Ariel trike its required test. Not only did this provide an insight into what it was actually like to ride – and it was not as bad as feared – but also provided a unique experience. Never before had I been the subject of quite so many comments – usually 'What is it?' The Ariel 3 did not look like anything else out on the street, but although it wasn't perfect I could appreciate why George Wallace had dreamed up the idea, even if BSA

*End of an Era*

had not followed through his idea of how it should have been constructed. This, he says, would have greatly improved the stability, comfort and handling of the tiny machine.

## Wallace Gets a Successful Outcome

George Wallace did not give up on his ideas, and in fact went on to make quite a big fortune when the Japanese firm Mitsubishi used the principle in the design of a small three-wheeled truck for use in Third World countries. Later still, in the early 1980s Honda paid George Wallace another considerable amount of money when it built the beautifully executed Stream during the early 1980s. However, even though the Japanese company did the engineering and styling correctly, it still was not a commercial success, due to an ultra-high purchase price. But at least Honda proved that the concept, properly executed, worked. This showed that George Wallace was right in levelling the blame at BSA for putting cost-cutting above engineering requirements.

With the demise of the '3', Ariel's great history was finally at an end, even though, in truth, the real Ariel marque had been extinct for several years.

With the coming of the classic scene at the end of the 1970s, the genuine Ariel motorcycles of the past were once more in demand from enthusiasts and collectors alike. Machines such as the overhead-valve singles, the Leader and Arrow two-stroke twins, the five-hundred and six-fifty ohv twins and of course the legendary and long-running Square Four in all its guises were again in demand. Since then, thousands have been restored all over the world and in the process have become popular for both touring and sport.

*A BSA Group publicity shot from the official launch of the Ariel 3.*

# Index

Abingdon 14
ACU 22, 46, 64, 87
Adler 158–160, 163
  M200 160
  M250 160, 169
  MB250 160, 169
Aermacchi
  Ala d'Oro 141
  Ala Verde 195
  Chimera 141, 171
AJS 84, 87, 148
  Model 14 195
Alec Ross Trial 92
Alves, P H (Phil) 84
AMC 38, 87, 122
Anker 182, 204, 205
Anstey, Frank 17, 29, 49, 55–57, 72, 82, 84, 107, 109, 121, 132, 173
Ariel cars
  Model Nine 17
  Model Ten 17
Ariel motorcycles
  1000 4F ohv 35, 50, 60
  4G Mk I 61–68, 71, 127, 132
  4G Mk II 67, 69–80, 176
  500 4F ohc 42–46
  600 4F ohc 39–49, 173
  600 4F ohv 34, 50–52
  Ariel 3 182, 203–206
  Arrow 95, 141–147, 154, 165, 175, 179, 183–198, 200, 206
  Arrow 200cc 195, 197, 198
  Arrow Super Sports (Golden Arrow) 183–198
  Colt (post-war) 74, 138, 148–154
  Colt (pre-war) 21, 96, 98, 148
  HS Scrambler 87–90
  HT Trials 87–92, 120
  HT3 90, 91, 118
  HT5 90, 91, 118
  KG 126–129, 132
  KH 122–140
  KH Huntmaster 76, 132–136, 139, 140
  KHA 86, 129–131, 134, 176, 178
  LB31 18, 22, 25
  LB32 21, 22, 25
  Leader 76, 92, 95, 141, 147, 154–172, 175, 179–189, 191, 200, 201, 206
  LF 96, 101
  LF131 18, 22
  LF231 18
  LG 96, 98, 105, 106
  LH 74, 101, 105, 148, 151–154
  MB32 21, 22, 24
  MF31 21
  MF32 21
  Model A 25, 93, 96
  Model B 25, 93, 96, 98
  Model C 93–96
  Model D 93, 96
  Model E 95, 96
  Model F 96, 98
  Model G 96, 98
  Model O 148
  NF3 100
  NF4 100
  NG 35, 36, 59, 60, 105, 109, 110, 115–117, 120, 134
  NH 100, 105, 106, 109, 110, 115–117, 120, 134
  OG 107
  OH 107
  Pixie 179, 182, 200–203
  Red Hunter series 27, 29, 53, 59, 81–120, 126, 128, 134, 176
  SB32 25
  SE32 98
  SF31 18, 19
  SG31 18, 20
  SG32 21, 23
  Sloper series 18–24, 40, 41, 43, 46, 98
  Square Four series 29, 34, 35, 39–80, 98, 99, 108, 109, 115, 127, 132, 133, 138, 140, 154, 173, 206
  Tricycle 9, 10, 199
  VA 26, 27, 29, 35
  VA3 34
  VA500 31
  VB 26–35, 76
  VB31 25, 98
  VB32 25
  VB600 25, 30–35, 60, 114, 115, 117
  VCH 82–89, 109
  VF3 100
  VF31 98
  VF4 100
  VG de Luxe 111, 112
  VG31 98, 99, 105
  VG32 21, 98, 99
  VH 59, 60, 81, 99–110, 113–115, 117, 134
  VH32 22, 29, 99
  VHA 113, 115, 176
  W/NG 35–38, 87, 109
  W/VA 38
Ariel prototypes
  1929–30 500cc ohc Square Four 173–175
  160cc Minerelli project 182
  250cc Twin (half Square Four engine) 121
  350cc ohv twin 179
  50cc ohc single 179
  700cc Flat Four 180, 181
  Earles Front Fork experiments 176–178
  Hunt Marshall ohv twin 176
  Swinging Arm Square Four models 176, 179, 181
  Tubular Frame Arrow 179
Armstrong, Reg 176

Bacon, Roy 76, 203
Barlow, Roger 141, 179
Barrow, Louis 8
Bennett, Clive 158, 176, 178
Bentley 44
Bianchi 143
Blackburne 15
BMW 177, 180
  K100LT 172
  R100RS 172
Boddice, Bill 145
Boughey, Ray 147
Bourne, Arthur 53, 59
Boyd, John 8
Brands Hatch 121, 146
Brockhouse Engineering 196
Brooklands Circuit 46, 53, 82
Brough Superior 81
Brown, Antony 147
Brown, George 147
BSA 17, 32, 38, 76, 84, 118, 120, 121, 139, 141, 147, 148, 154, 158–163, 172, 173, 179, 182, 195–206
  A10 Golden Flash 132, 135
  A10 Road Rocket 132
  A10 Super Rocket 132
  Bantam 151, 158, 163, 182
  Beagle 200–202
  C10L 150
  C11 148, 149
  C11G 148
  C12 154
  Gold Star 87
  M20 38
Buck, George 90
Burman gearboxes 20, 37, 40, 51–55, 81, 84, 87, 95, 96, 106, 131, 132, 134, 141, 146, 150, 153, 163
Burton, Michael 189

Clarke, F W S (Freddie) 53
Cobbing, Ken 205
Colmore Cup Trial 176
Components Company 8–10, 17, 96, 99, 199
Corgi 196
Cotton
  Telstar 147
Crabtree, Ted 178
Crystal Palace 8–11, 17
Currie, Bob 191–193
CZ 91

Dacis, Tom 17, 27, 121
Daniell, Harold 141
Daytona circuit 82, 108
De Dion 9, 10, 17
De Dion-Bouton 9, 10
Demm 203
DKW
  RT125 158
DMW
  Hornet 147
Donington Park Circuit 143
Dragonfly Motorcycles 120
Ducati
  Daytona 195
  Desmo Twin 250cc
  Diana 195
du Cros, Harvey 8, 13
du Cros, Harvey Jnr 8, 10
Dürkopp 40

# Index

Earls Court Show 131, 148, 151, 200
Earles, Ernie 144, 145, 176–178
Edge, Selwyn F 9, 10
Egli 78
Excelsior 152

FB Mondial 91
Ferbrache, Peter 82
Fleet 9, 24, 199
FN 40
Fortescue, B 92
Francis Barnett 90, 152
Frazer, Peter 92
Friedrich, Hermann 160

Garelli 203
Good 141, 144, 188, 196
Graham, Les 176, 178
Greeves
   Silverstone 147
Guest, Charles Henry 8

Hartley, Laurence 17, 82
Hailwood, Mike 142
Hall, Robert 8
Hansen, Bob 82
Hardy, Fred 142
Hartley, Peter 22, 26, 46, 93, 121, 178, 181
Healey 78–80
Heath, Len 102
Helkama 88
Hildebrand & Wolfmüller 40
Hill Terry 91
Hillman, William 7
Hitler, Adolf 108
Holden, Major Henry Capel Lofft 40
Holmes, N S 86
Honda 18, 143
   C50 203
   C72 195
   CB72 195
   Pan European 172
   Stream 206
Hopping, C E 108
Hopwood, Bert 132, 173, 174, 176
Hose, Mike 147
Hughes, Herbert 27

Inchley, Peter 141, 144, 196
Indian 18
International Six Days' Trial 53, 81, 84–86, 102, 116, 129
Isle of Man TT 143, 176, 178, 188, 196
Issigonis, Alec 171
Ivy, Bill 145

Jaguar
   D-type 168
James 90, 152
JAP 12, 17, 25, 93, 95, 156, 158
Jarrot, Charles 10
Johnson, Bill 108
Johnson, J T 7

Kawasaki 82
Kleyer, Heinrich 160
Knight, Bernard 158, 161, 181, 200, 201
Kralichek-Soboleff, I S (Ivan) 24

Lambretta
   TV175 162
Langstron, Ron 90

Lauren & Klement 40
Laverda 78
Le Vack, Bert 17
Lucas A S 27

MacQueen, W 81
MAG 15, 16
Mallory Park Circuit 144
Matchless 87, 148
   Model G2 195
Maudes Trophy 22
May, Denis 173
McKeever, Bob Jnr 108
McPherson, Peter 104
Meier, Hermann 17, 141–145, 188
Mellors, Phil 85
MGP Special 145, 146
Miller, Sammy 17, 90–92, 12o, 141, 143, 144, 188, 195
Minerelli 182
Minerva 10–12
Mini 80, 171
Mitsubishi 206
Mole, Vic 17, 41, 93, 95, 97, 98, 148
Moore, Frank 10
Morris, Eddie 22
Moss, Len 121
Motobecane 203
Moto Guzzi 94
   SP1000 Spada 172
MV Agusta 143, 178

National Motorcycle Museum, Birmingham
Nelson, H 81
New Imperial 196
Norman 152
Norton 38, 85, 122, 145, 146, 176
   16H 38
   Jubilee 195
   Manx 108
NSU 143
   Sportmax 91

Olympia Show 22, 41, 44, 93, 95, 98, 173
O'Rourke, Michael 141, 142, 144, 145
Oulton Park 144

Page, Val 17, 24–27, 41, 58–61, 82, 84, 93, 95, 99, 121–123, 129, 132, 141, 148, 155, 159–165, 169, 173, 179–181, 187, 200, 201
Parsons, W S G 86
Patterson, G 81
Pearson, Les 22
Perry, Harry 23
Piper Gerald, 145
Piper, Michael 145
Povey, Fred 35
Price, Harry 146
Puch
   Maxi 203

Ray, C M (Bob) 84, 86, 129, 131
Read, Phil 145
Rein, Matti 88
Rein, Raino 88
Renouf, Paul 9
Rist, F M (Fred) 84
Rover 14, 38
Royal Air Force 14, 38
Royal Enfield 84, 122, 138

Royal Flying Corps 14
Rudge 18, 81, 82, 107
Rudge, Dan 8

Salt, George 144
Sandford, Cecil 141, 143, 188
Sangster, Charles 8–10, 12–14, 16–18, 24, 26, 41, 99
Sangster, Jack Y 17, 24, 26, 99, 107, 109, 121, 196
Science Museum, London 40
Scott, Alfred 41
Scottish Six Days' Trial 35, 84, 88, 89, 91
Sevens Test 23, 46
Shorey, Dan 142
Silverstone Circuit 141, 143, 146
Slater, Roger 78
Slater, Sid 22, 46
Smith, Ernie 46, 173, 176
Snetterton Circuit 87
Stanford Hall 65
Starley, James 80
Steel, H 81
Stocker, W J (Bill) 84
Stocks, Jack 10
Sun 152
Sunbeam 81, 200
Swift 24

Tamaguchi, Naomi 143
Tandon 152
Thacker, Ted 46
Triumph 82, 84, 107, 108, 138, 172, 173, 177
   Speed Twin 122
   Terrier 152
   Tiger Cub 202
   Tina 199, 200
Thruxton Circuit 143, 188, 189, 196
Turner, Edward 17, 27, 40–42, 48–52, 99, 107, 121–127, 173–175, 179, 180, 200

Velosolex 203
Vespa
   Ciao 203
   Victory Trial 176
Villiers 90, 108
Vincent 147
Viney, R H M (Hugh) 84
VMCC Founders Day 65

Wallace, George 204–206
Watsonian 30, 83
Wellbike 196
West Bromwich Motorcycle Club 196
West, Jock 82
Wheeler, W R ('Big Bill') 98
Whistance, Ken 178–180, 195, 196, 201
White & Poppe 13–16, 34, 94
White, Alfred James 13
Whitton, H 10
Wilkins, Frank 85, 87
Wilkins, Kay 85, 87
Wilson, Steve 156, 159, 170
Woolley, Brian 40
Woolley, Nick 90
Wraith, Peter 87

Yamaha 145, 159, 160
   TZ four cylinder 120